1951

PAUL VI

PAUL VI

by

J. L. GONZALEZ - T. PEREZ

ENGLISH VERSION
BY

EDWARD L. HESTON, C.S.C.

*English-language Press Officer
of the Second Ecumenical Vatican Council*

ST. PAUL EDITIONS

IMPRIMATUR:

✠ Richard Cardinal Cushing
Archbishop of Boston

July 22, 1964

Library of Congress Catalog Card Number: 64-7923

Contents

9

11

13

INTRODUCTION

The Conclave of June, 1963, opened in unprecedented circumstances. Never before in the history of the Church had there been such a large Sacred College—eighty-two members, eighty of them present. The majority required for election, fixed by most recent decisions at two-thirds plus one, was fifty-four.

There could have been reasons for fearing some indecisiveness in the balloting, even more so than in all the preceding elections, in the majority of which the electors had felt their way for days before making their choice. But there was one special fact which would prove most helpful this time: the Cardinals knew one another better than ever before. Sixty of their number had taken part in the sessions of the Central Preparatory Commission prior to the Council and had had opportunities to express themselves on each one of the schemas prepared by the special Commissions. From October to December, 1962, all had been able to assist at the General Congregations of the First Session of the Council. Many of them had participated in the various discussions with authority and competence deriving from their positions as heads of Curia offices or as pastors of important dioceses.

Although the preliminary soundings of the first two ballots on the first morning might direct attention to certain names, there was one name which, more than any other, as everyone knew, would be at the head of the list. It was the name of the Cardinal Archbishop of Milan, Giovanni Battista Montini.

After the death of Puis XII, several members of the Conclave which later elected John XXIII did not refrain from expressing their regrets over the fact that the former Under-Secretary and Pro-Secretary of Pius XII had not yet been elevated to the dignity of the Cardinalate.

15

His eight years spent as head of the archdiocese of Saint Ambrose had undoubtedly added new qualifications to his prominence. Hence it is not surprising that, on the evening of the first day of the Conclave, the Romans declared they could not understand why the election had not yet taken place. It is not certain that everyone wanted Cardinal Montini, but the majority understood that things could not be otherwise.

No other Sovereign Pontiff was ever better prepared for this sublime office, whose responsibilities have been constantly on the increase, especially in the last half-century, because of the growth in world population and the multiplication of new sovereign States.

In these first ten months of his Pontificate, Paul VI has proven in fact, after proclaiming it in words, that in all sectors he is ready to walk in the path traced out by his predecessor John XXIII. The Council and the Ecumencial Movement are no less close to his heart than they were to that of Pope John.

In irresponsible quarters some criticism has been voiced, as though Paul VI were too slow in implementing the reforms which he himself had declared necessary. Paul VI knows how to judge things and he also knows how to wait for the right moment.

We should have confidence in him and, each one in his own field, make ready to help him through prayer and action, when the right moment comes.

EUGENE CARDINAL TISSERANT
Dean of the Sacred College
Librarian and Archivist of
the Holy Roman Church

ROME, May 16, 1964
Vigil of Pentecost

TRANSLATOR'S PREFACE

This volume on Pope Paul VI is less a biography in the conventional sense than the study of a man. The book might be called a study of the man and of the dominant ideas now guiding him in his gigantic task as Visible Head of the Roman Catholic Church.

This explains the rather unusual order of the volume. The chapters do not follow strict chronological order. Historical facts are considered more as forerunners of the future than as isolated incidents marking off the career of a prominent churchman. After a brief chronological sketch of the life of Paul VI, our volume starts with Paul VI at the center of the world's attention, first in the opening of the Second Session of the II Ecumenical Vatican Council and, secondly, as a humble pilgrim on the Via Dolorosa and the other paths walked centuries earlier by the Man God.

The account then works back, so to speak, demonstrating how the ideas and the ideals reflected by Paul VI in these two historic moments did not just appear on the spur of the moment, but were only the logical sequel of that mysterious process of spiritual and intellectual formation which God's Providence had secretly but effectively been guiding for decades. The text thus makes it abundantly clear that Paul VI did not just happen on the world scene on the morning of June 21, 1963, but that his election marked the peak of a divine plan long in the unfolding.

The pressing invitation to present this volume to the English-speaking world was accepted by the translator as an apostolate. Too many know of Monsignor, later Cardinal, Montini only as the right-hand man of Pope Pius XII, remaining in the background with discreet effacement. Too few are aware of his hidden qualities as a man and as a churchman, as he matured unto the measure of the age of the fullness of a Vicar of Christ. The opportunity to put this important message into English thus outweighed an initial reluctance to undertake the task because of other urgent commitments. The translator has learned much from his work. It is his modest hope that his readers will be equally enlightened.

The English version of the work reproduces substantially the Italian original. Some changes and adaptations have been introduced, because of stylistic differences and methods of approach characterizing the two languages. But there are no radical departures from the original. Translations of discourses of the Pope were made directly from texts printed in L'Osservatore Romano.

A more than special word of thanks is due to Brother Jerome Matthews, C.S.C., of the United States Eastern Priests' Province of the Congregation of Holy Cross. His devoted and efficient collaboration has really made this translation possible. It was no small task to transcribe the initial rough text of dictated translation and then to re-copy a manuscript which had been revised almost to the point of illegibility. The readers owe him appreciation and a prayer of thanks.

EDWARD L. HESTON
English-language Press Officer of the II Ecumenical Vatican Council

Rome, Italy
June 30, 1964

First Anniversary of the Coronation of
Pope Paul VI

THE CHRONOLOGY OF THE LIFE OF GIOVANNI BATTISTA MONTINI

1897

Giovanni Battista Montini, second son of Giorgio Montini, lawyer, and of Giuditta Alghisi, was born at Concesio, Province of Brescia on September 26th. On the 30th of the same month he was baptized in the local parish church by the Archpriest Don Giovanni Fiorini. His godfather was Enrico Manzoni, also a lawyer.

1907

Young Montini received his First Communion on June 6th in the chapel of the Sisters of the Child Mary. On June 21st Bishop Giacomo Pellegrini, Bishop of Brescia, confirmed him in the chapel of the "Cesare Arici" college in Brescia.

1920

Bishop Giacinto Gaggia, Bishop of Brescia, ordained him priest on May 29th. The following day he celebrated his first Mass in the Sanctuary of Our Lady of Grace.

In November of that same year his Bishop sent him to Rome to reside in the Lombard College and to pursue advanced theological studies at the Gregorian University.

1924

In October, Don Montini began his regular duties in the Secretariate of State. The following year he received his first promotion through his appointment as *minutante*.

In that same year he was appointed National Counselor for the FUCI (Federation of Italian Catholic University Students), an assignment which brought him into contact with one of his dearest friends, Igino Righetti. Along with Righetti, after the National Congress of the FUCI at Cagliari, Don Montini founded the Association of Catholic Graduate Students, as a complement to the Catholic University Movement. The next year he resigned his office as Counselor of the FUCI in order to have more time for the duties entailed by his position in the Secretariate of State.

1925

In May Don Montini received his first diplomatic assignment, to the Apostolic Nunciature in Warsaw, where he came into contact with Monsignors Lauro and Chiarlo, both future Cardinals. In October of that same year he returned to Rome to continue his studies at the Ecclesiastical Academy.

1939

Pius XII, who succeeded Pius XI on March 2nd, appointed Cardinal Maglione as his Secretary of State, and Monsignor Montini was named Under-Secretary.

1944

On the death of Cardinal Maglione, the Secretariate of State, for all practical purposes, was taken over by Monsignors Montini and Tardini, who were subsequently appointed Pro-Secretaries respectively for Ordinary and Extraordinary Affairs.

1953

In the Secret Consistory held in January, the second of his pontificate, Pope Pius XII revealed that Monsignors Montini and Tardini had voluntarily declined the Cardinalate... "thus giving outstanding proof of virtue."

1954

On November 3rd Monsignor Montini was appointed Archbishop of Milan, succeeding the late Cardinal Schuster.

On December 12th, he was consecrated in Saint Peter's Basilica by Cardinal Tisserant, substituting for Pope Pius XII who at the time was gravely ill.

1955

On January 6th, a cold and rainy day, Archbishop Montini took solemn possession of his Archdiocese. The weather did not stop him from leaving his automobile and kissing the ground as he arrived on the territory now entrusted to his pastoral care.

1958

Archbishop Montini's name headed the list of new Cardinals appointed by John XXIII on December 15th in his first Consistory.

1963

Cardinal Montini was elected Pope at 11:22 A.M. on June 21st taking the name of Paul VI.

On June 30th he was solemnly crowned in Saint Peter's Piazza in the presence of ninety-three Extraordinary Government Missions and approximately 200,000 persons. The entire ceremony was seen throughout Europe via Eurovision and, some hours later, was televised to the United States and Canada via Telstar.

On September 29th as he opened the Second Session of the Vatican Council II, Paul VI pronounced one of his most outstanding discourses.

1964

Pope Paul VI made an unprecedented journey to the Holy Land, returning over the route followed by the first Pope, Saint Peter, as he brought the Faith to the capital of the Empire and established the seat of the Church in the city of the Caesars. The Pope's intention was to go on pilgrimage to the Holy Places which had beheld the birth, death, and resurrection of the Divine Savior, in order to pray for the Council and for unity.

POPE PAUL TAKES THE REINS
OF THE CHURCH

The arrangement of this book could have followed a strictly more chronological order. Nevertheless, it seemed possible, logically speaking, to take up immediately the Second Session of the Ecumenical Council, the session which is "all Montini," and which represents the most recent great chapter of the life of Paul VI. It seemed advisable to do this before undertaking the direct chronology of a life which is both extraordinary in its simplicity and at the same time most simple even though extraordinary.

We called the Second Session of the Council the most recent chapter of the life of Paul VI. This chapter was closed on December 4, 1963. The ink of the signatures of the Council Fathers on the documents already promulgated was still wet as these lines were being written.

The Second Session of the II Vatican Council had first been scheduled for May 12, 1963. But in the 28th General Congregation of the First Session, held on November 27, 1962, it was publicly announced that the date had been changed by the Holy Father, who had decided that the session would open rather on September 8, 1963. With the death of John XXIII all these plans were automatically suspended. Even the convocation, or rather the resumption, of the Council depended entirely on what the new Pope would decide.

As they filed by to pay their respects for the last time to the mortal remains of John XXIII, laid out on the very spot in Saint Peter's Basilica where, just a few months earlier, he had delivered the now famous opening Allocution of the Council, many persons were wondering if things would remain exactly where they were and if the Council Hall, now so mournful and empty, would be put to further use or would remain vacant indefinitely.

From the very first day of his pontificate, Paul VI dissipated all misgivings. When it was announced that Cardinal Montini had been elected Pope, anyone who knew the Cardinal of Milan and his enthusiasm for everything connected with the Council was certain that Vatican II would soon follow its normal course or even be speeded up. This certainly was expressed by the Holy Father himself in his address to the Cardinals on the morning after his election: "The pre-eminent part of Our pontificate," he declared, "will be devoted to the continuation of the Second Vatican Council." The "Council climate" would remain unchanged.

On June 27th, just six days after his election, in a decree granted "in audience," Paul VI announced September 29th as the date for the reconvocation of the Council. This meant a delay of only some twenty days in relation to the original date of September 8th. This delay corresponded exactly to the length of time the Holy See had been vacant.

Thus, for all practical purposes, it can truly be said that the work of the Council was not even interrupted. The Commissions continued their meetings at their normal pace, with only some minor changes in dates. The Co-ordinating Commission, the principal organism of the Council—in his letter to the Bishops on January 3, 1963, Pope John XXIII had called it the "main commission"—and which had been organized at the end of the Second Session to meet an evident need, had held meetings from January 1st to January 27th and again from March 25th to March 29th. Its third session, originally set for June 4th, had to be postponed because of the death of the Pope on June 3rd. But Paul VI convoked it for July 3rd to July 5th, just two weeks after his election. The Commission met for the fourth time on August 31st, and again just before the Council re-opened. Since this Commission had to study all the schemas, which had been apportioned to its ten Cardinal members, one can see in its regular sessions in the interim period, how the general work of the Council had really gone on without a let-up.

In the same way the National Conferences of Bishops, which had played such a decisive role in the First Session of the Council, continued to hold meetings and were particularly active throughout the whole of August. In early August there were meetings of the Bishops of the United States of America, Africa, and Argentina. From August 26th to August 29th the Bishops of Western Germany held their now famous meeting at Fulda, along with representatives of the hierarchies of Austria, Switzerland, Scandinavia, France, Belgium, and Holland. The Italian Bishops also convoked an extraordinary meeting. The Spaniards in turn assembled at Los Negrales, in Madrid, on September 16th, under the presidency of the Cardinal Primate Enrico Pla y Daniel. There were also special gatherings of Bishops from different nations, for joint study of points suggested by the Council's agenda, with the valued collaboration of Council theologians and other experts.

Paul VI Takes Over the Council

The last week of September saw numerous groups of Council Fathers arriving in Rome by all the means of transportation afforded by the progress of the jet age. The special Reception Room in the Fiumicino airport which had been set up exclusively for the Council Fathers, resumed its activities on a full scale. Trains pulling into the Stazione Termini likewise brought illustrious Council Fathers. Chief among these was Cardinal Wyszynsky, whose presence in the Second Session of the Council had been doubtful until the last minute, because of conflicts with the Polish government which had refused passports to some twenty-five Bishops. Cardinal Wyszynsky's activities in Rome are watched very closely and his every arrival in the Eternal City arouses warm enthusiasm.

Rome then took on again the cosmopolitan character which comes from the presence of close to three thousand Council Fathers from every corner of the world. In Saint Peter's Basilica, where special technical improvements had been made in the interim period, everything was ready for the Second Session to get under way.

It had been widely claimed that this Session would be the turning-point of Vatican II, because of the importance of the topics up for discussion. Thus, on the day set, September 29th, dedicated in a special way to Saint Michael the Archangel, Protector of the Church, Paul VI presided over the re-opening of the Council. He had decided not to repeat the very solemn ceremony which had inaugurated the First Session. The Fathers went directly to their places in the Council Hall, without the previous imposing procession across the piazza. Thus, this celebration was more of a family feast but one which turned out to be most solemn just the same. In fact, no ceremony can fail to be solemn in the awe-inspiring framework of the world's largest basilica, with the tribunes packed with white copes, mitres and pectoral crosses whose sparkling was like living eyes reflecting the panorama of all the nations of the world, with the emotion experienced by the Fathers as they found themselves assembled in a new Cenacle.

From a distance came the first echo of the *Ave Maris Stella*. This meant that the papal cortege was on its way from the Sistine Chapel down the Scala Regia. As in the previous year, the work of the Council was inaugurated with the confident invocation of the Blessed Virgin. The Pope entered the Basilica on the traditional portable throne, but he immediately had it set down and continued towards the altar on foot, out of respect for the Council Fathers assembled on either side. John XXIII had been the first to make this significant gesture, which was intended as a homage to the Pope's lofty concept of the sublime mission of Bishops, a theme which the Council was to study more profoundly and set off in bolder relief.

The Council Fathers fixed their eyes on the face of the new Pope as he greeted them affectionately. Some began to applaud, while others followed suit immediately, thus giving public expression to their emotion and their devotion to the new Pontiff.

Then followed the invocation of the Holy Spirit, the Chief Figure of the Council, whereupon Cardinal Tisserant began Solemn Pontifical Mass. "Bless the Lord, O all you angels," sang the Sistine Choir. This was the introit of the Mass of Saint Michael. "Bless the Lord, O you his angels, who are great in power, always ready to carry out his orders and to heed the whisperings of his words. . . ."

The entire basilica seemed filled with festive wings. It is easy to see how the words of the day's liturgy were easily applicable to these messengers of peace—"angel" means "messenger"—to the Council Fathers, assembled from all over the world, to obey the orders of God, to listen to His words and carry out His will.

The gospel of the Mass proclaimed to all these venerable pastors and to all men of good will that, unless they accept to become as little children, they cannot enter into the kingdom of heaven. Is not this the melting point, the exact point where authority received and the exercise of this authority blend together, an exercise which must be fatherly, unpretentious, devoid of all arrogance or violence? Such exercise of authority is not domination, but service; there are no heads, masters, or generals, but only fathers and shepherds. This was the main theme, pursued and elevated to the dignity of an ideal in all the work of the Second Vatican Council.

The *Gloria,* the *Credo,* and the *Sanctus,* were sung by all the Council Fathers in a majestic chorus, already heard in the First Session when the assembled Fathers had joined in the well-known Gregorian Mass *De Angelis.* The harmony of their voices was symbolic of the concord uniting them on all the essentials and fundamentals of the doctrinal or disciplinary questions coming up for discussion. With the *Kyrie* and the *Agnus Dei* from the "Mass of Pope Marcellus" for six mixed voices, the Sistine Choir reminded all those present of their vast differences of language, civilization, customs, and color. That was probably why at the end of the First Session, Pope John XXIII had remarked that "In Vatican Council II there was more polyphony than Gregorian chant!" At times there would be a different beat, but there would be only a question of blending parts or of irregular pauses and different tones. But, basically, there is perfect agreement, just as there was substantial harmony in the Gregorian Mass sung by the Fathers all together.

After the Holy Father's Blessing the Council work strictly so called got under way: the enthronement of the Gospel Book by Archbishop Pericle Felici, Secretary General of the Council, the solemn Profession of Faith read by Paul VI according to the lengthy traditional formula, the obedience to the Holy Father by all the Cardinals and Patriarchs, as well as by representatives of the Archbishops, Bishops, Abbots, and Superiors General of religious orders. Among the representatives of the Archbishops was Archbishop Carinci, who had reached the venerable age of 101. He was the only Council Father who could boast of having known two Councils, since he was eight years old when the First Vatican Council was suspended and he still remembered this event very clearly. At the end of this inaugural function of the Second Session, the Fathers coming into the Council for the first time made their Profession of Faith according to the formula read by Archbishop Felici in the name of all.

A Spoken Encyclical

The most anxiously awaited moment of this whole function was undoubtedly the Allocution of the Holy Father. Until that time, anyone speaking of the "Pope of the Council" was alluding exclusively to Pope John XXIII, who had decided on the Council, convoked it, opened it, and directed it. But from now on Paul VI would likewise have the right to be called the "Pope of the Council," since he had decreed its continuation and had pointed out its general policy lines. Even juridically, this Second Session belongs with full right to the Pauline phase of Vatican II. Hence there was lively interest as to what directives the new Pope would give for "his" Council, just as in the preceding year everyone had waited expectantly for the eloquent Allocution of Pope John.

Pope Paul's viewpoints on the Council were already known in general outline because, aside from the very noteworthy role he had played in the First Session as Archbishop of Milan, he had already spoken his mind on various occasions during the first three months of his pontificate. Among these were his first address to the Cardinals and to the entire world in the Sistine Chapel, the discourse pro-

nounced on the day of his coronation, and his remarks in
various meetings with groups of faithful or with representatives of the episcopate during his summer stay at Castel
Gandolfo. Nevertheless, this was now the official moment
when he was to set down the main directives he wanted
set before this imposing assembly of Council Fathers.

"Greetings to you, most beloved brothers in Christ,"
the Pope began, "whom We have summoned from all over
the world, from wherever the Holy Catholic Church has
set up its hierarchy. Greetings to you, who have accepted
Our invitation and hastened here to hold with Us the Second
Session of the Second Ecumenical Vatican Council, which
it is Our joy to inaugurate today under the protection of
Saint Michael the Archangel, the heavenly Protector of
the People of God. . . .

"Greetings, brothers! Thus are you welcomed by the
least among you, the Servant of the Servants of God, even
though he bears the keys of supreme office given to Peter
by Christ our Lord. Thus he shows you concretely that he
wishes to pray with you, speak with you, work with you.
The Lord is Our witness when, at this first moment of the
Second Session of the Great Synod, We declare to you that
in Our mind We are not motivated by human domination or
jealous guarding of exclusive power, but only by the desire
and the will to carry out the divine mandate which, among
you and as one of you, makes us brothers, makes Us the
Supreme Shepherd and which requires of you what will
be to his joy and his glory, namely, the Communion of
Saints, your fidelity, your loyalty, your collaboration. This
same mandate also offers you what this Shepherd is most
happy to give, namely, his veneration, his esteem, his trust,
his charity."

Paul VI then described the consoling reality of the
Church in language which was richly biblical, charismatic
and mysterious. The reason for this is that the Church is
above all a great and comforting mystery which has the
Pope as its Head. "It is not futile," continued the Pope, "to

realize at the very outset the human and the divine phenomenon which we are bringing about. Here once more, as if in a new Cenacle, made small not by its vast dimensions but by the multitude of those assembled within it, . . . here we shall rejoice in the unfailing grace of the Holy Spirit, present, vivifying, teaching, strengthening. Here all tongues will be but one voice and one single voice will speak its message to all the world. Here the pilgrim Church has arrived with rapid strides after almost twenty centuries of journeying. Here, all together, the ranks of its apostles, spread throughout the world, find refreshment at that fountain which quenches every old thirst and stimulates every new thirst, and as they depart from here they will confidently resume their journey in the world and in time towards that goal which is beyond the world and beyond ages."

The Holy Father then recalled the custom of the Popes to address to the world an Encyclical in the first months of their reign, to map out the general program of their pontificate. But this time, because of the happy circumstances of the Council, the Pope declared that he had been able to change this custom, or rather had been able to delay for some time the preparation of this important policy pronouncement, since he would here proclaim by word of mouth his intentions, ideas, and plans. Thus this discourse was, "a spoken Encyclical," which echoed through the Council Hall with the happy festiveness of everything which is new and young, and flashes marvelous new ideals on the horizon. The future Encyclical which the Pope is now preparing and whose title is rumored to be "Non nobis," in full harmony with Cardinal Montini's motto "In Nomine Domini," will doubtless develop the key ideas which Paul VI set forth in his historic discourse on September 29, 1963. This Allocution reveals a synthesis of a completely dedicated life and of an outstanding personality. For anyone who wants to understand Paul VI, a careful study of this Allocution is absolutely essential, because it alone can provide a complete picture of the man who has taken in hand for the world of today the reins of the Church.

Four Cardinal Points

After an affectionate tribute to Pope John XXIII, the Pope faced up to the difficult task of guiding the Council— a task which, in the picturesque language of Pope John XXIII, was more like an ocean voyage than just a simple crossing of the Lake of Galilee. He had to determine precisely where it was starting from, the route to be followed and the destination to be reached.

"From what point, my brothers, do we set out? Bearing in mind that we should pay more attention to divine directives than to the practical question just mentioned, what route do we intend to follow? What will be our destination? We have a goal which belongs to the realm of earthly history, insofar as concerns the time and mode of our present life, but this goal must be orientated towards the destination which we know must be the term of our pilgrimage.

"These three very simple and at the same time very important questions have, as we well know, only one answer, namely the one which here, at this very hour, we must proclaim to ourselves and to the world around us: Christ, Christ our beginning, Christ our life and our guide, Christ our hope and our end."

Thus Christ is the hinge holding all things together and the foundation which can never be replaced by any other. Saint John says simply that "the world was made through Him," through Christ. Supposing this first basic truth, the world can never rest on any other foundation than this one which sustains all things. Only when this foundation has been assured, will it be possible to build with confidence, certain that the rains and the winds will not shake this structure. If we place before our minds, venerable brothers, this supreme ideal that Christ is our Founder and our head, invisible but nonetheless real, and that we receive everything from Him so as to form together with Him that "complete Christ" of whom Saint Augustine speaks and who

pervades the entire theology of the Church, then we can
the better understand the main objectives of this Council.
For reasons of brevity and clarity We shall sum them up
in four points: the knowledge, or if you like the consciousness of the Church, its reform, the re-union of all Christians,
the dialogue of the Church with the contemporary world."

Church of Christ, What Say You of Yourself?

As will be related more in detail elsewhere, the then
Cardinal Montini, at the end of the First Session of the
Council had emphasized before this august assembly the
necessity of seeking out, among the various topics to be
discussed in Vatican II, a focal point which would co-ordinate the vast material, comprising many volumes, found
in the suggestions sent in by Bishops and other competent
persons. As this central theme the Archbishop of Milan
proposed that of the Church. Just the day before this speech
to the Council, on December 4, 1962, Cardinal Suenens
had delivered a noble discourse in which he had affirmed
that "just as the I Vatican Council rightly deserved to be
called the Council of the primacy of the Sovereign Pontiff, so also the II Vatican Council would seem to have
been given its most appropriate title when, two months
before it opened, the Vicar of Christ, the Visible Head of
the Church, hailed the coming ecumenical assembly as
"Ecclesia Christi, lumen gentium," "The Church of Christ,
Light of the Nations."

The next day Cardinal Montini gave his unqualified
support to the proposal advanced by the Primate of Belgium, along with its deeply pastoral and biblical program.
Re-reading Cardinal Suenen's discourse today, and recalling his close friendship with Paul VI, one is tempted to see

in this discourse something like a joint project, one which provided the Pope with a canvas on which he could outline for the Fathers a precise program of work as the Second Session of the Council was launched.

Cardinal Montini has always had a deep love of the Church. On this topic he has written masterful pages, and has spoken of it on many occasions. Consequently, no one will be surprised that he wanted to place the theme of the Church at the very center of the Council's agenda and that the first schema to be taken up in the Second Session was precisely the one dealing with the Church.

The Pope continued: "There can be no doubt whatever that it is the Church's desire, need, and duty to give a more thorough definition of herself. We are all familiar with the magnificent images which Holy Scripture uses to describe the nature of the Church: the building raised up by Christ, the house of God, the temple and tabernacle of God, His people, His flock, His vine, His field, His city, the pillar of truth, and, finally, the bride of Christ, His Mystical Body. The very richness of these images has guided the Church so as to see herself as a historic, visible and hierarchically organized society, yes, but one animated by a mysterious principle of life. The celebrated Encyclical of Pope Pius XII, *Mystici Corporis,* has in part answered the Church's longing to express her nature in a full doctrinal form, and has been a factor in spurring her on to evermore complete self-definition. The I Vatican Council had decided to discuss this point and a host of extrinsic circumstances made of it a timely topic for study, both inside and outside the Church. Among these influences were the increased social sense of temporal society, the development of the media of communications, the need to judge the various Christian denominations in the light of the authentic and universal concept contained in Divine Revelation.

"Consequently, it should come as no surprise that after twenty centuries of Christianity and of the vast historical and geographical expansion of the Catholic Church as well as of other religious confessions which claim the name of Christ and are honored with that of churches, the truly profound and complete concept of the Church, as Christ founded it and the Apostles began to build it, should need to be formulated with greater precision. The Church is a mystery, that is, a reality permeated by the divine presence and therefore ever open to new and deeper investigation. . . .

"The time has now come, We believe, when the truth on the Church of Christ should be examined, co-ordinated and formulated, not perhaps in those solemn pronouncements which are called dogmatic definitions, but rather through those declarations which proclaim to the Church with more explicit and authoritative teaching, exactly what she thinks of herself. It is this consciousness of the Church which is clarified by faithful acceptance of the words and the thought of Christ, by respectful attention to the authoritative teaching of ecclesiastical tradition, and by docility to the interior light of the Holy Spirit who seems precisely to be wanting the Church to do everything she can, so as to be recognized for what she really is. . . .

"For this reason, the principal theme of this Session of the Council will be one which looks into the intimate nature of the Church, aims to probe its inner essence and then, as far as possible in human language, to provide that definition which will best instruct us on its real and genuine constitution and unfold to us its manifold mission of salvation."

The Role of the Episcopate

Through a very complex historical process, whose roots must be traced back to the general trend of medieval culture, the Church, although called to unceasing expansion in area and numbers, had, so to speak, become dwarfed and shrunken. In other words, the concept of the Church had come to be identified more or less explicitly with the concept of hierarchy or clergy. Even within the bounds of this restricted circle, after the necessary interruption of the I Vatican Council, the position of Bishops in the Church was not entirely clear. There was a feeling that, with the definition of the primacy of the Sovereign Pontiff, Bishops had lost some of their importance. So widespread was this thinking that not a few persons were surprised when the present Council was convoked. Why convoke a Council, they asked, if the Pope can do and teach on his own authority whatever is necessary?

It is the Pope himself who now wants the importance of Bishops in the Church to be clarified and brought into clearer focus. Already in the First Session of the Council, one of the comments of the Archbishop of Milan on the schema on the Church, which was up for discussion in the last General Congregation, was precisely that it was not sufficiently clear in its teaching on the episcopate. This point was to have a prominent place in the Second Session:

"First among the various questions raised by this consideration, venerable brothers, is one which affects all of you as Bishops of the Church of God. We do not hesitate to say that We look forward expectantly and with sincere confidence to this discussion which, without prejudice to the dogmatic declarations of the I Vatican Council regarding the Roman Pontiff, will go on to investigate the doctrine on the episcopate, its function, and its relationship with Peter. For Us personally it will provide doctrinal and practical criteria by which Our apostolic office, endowed though it is by Christ with the fullness and sufficiency of power, as you recognize, may be better assisted and strengthened, in ways to be determined, by more effective and responsible collaboration with Our beloved and venerable brothers in the episcopate."

This first clarification was followed by others dealing with priests, religious, and all the faithful, in a combined effort to enhance the position of all the members of the Mystical Body of Christ. In an organism, there can be no divisions. All the members composing it must be perfectly united and above all must be clearly alive. The aim of the Council is to complete this work of rejuvenation:

"We have said that the Church wants to see herself reflected in Christ and should there be seen on the face of the Church, on her wedding garment, any shadow, defect, or stain, what should be her instinctive and courageous re-action? The answer is clear: to renew and correct herself, to endeavor to make herself once more like her Divine Model—this is her basic duty.

"Only after this process of internal sanctification will the Church be able to show herself to the entire world and say: 'Who sees me sees Christ,' just as Christ had said of Himself: 'Who sees me, sees the Father also' (John 14:9) . . . Consequently, the reform at which the Council aims is not an upheaval of the Church's present way of life or a break with the essential or venerable elements of her tradition. Rather is it an honoring of tradition in the very act of stripping it of what is unworthy or defective, in order to make it genuine and fruitful."

In a discourse to a youth group in the last year of his pontificate, Pius XII declared that he saw breaking on the horizon of the Church's life a smiling spring. John XXIII had harsh words—the only harsh words ever uttered by the Pope of kindness—for the prophets of doom who see and sense nothing but calamity and ruin. In complete harmony with his predecessors, Paul VI sees in the Council an authentic flowering of the spring which had been foretold. And just as, with the coming of spring, we feel new vital energies pulsating within us and pack away our winter clothing, so the Church intends in this Council to re-awaken its hidden spiritual and moral energies and to shake off rules and canonical structures which are clearly out-moded.

In a word, the Church wants to work only with what is
essential, without dragging along useless weights and historical hobbles which perhaps had some meaning and value
in earlier times but which today are as useless as ropes in
a guided missile.

A House With Open Doors

The spirit of ecumenism has penetrated deeply into
the minds and hearts of the Council Fathers, principally as
a result of the breadth of view and the exquisitely fraternal
and evangelical efforts of Pope John XXIII. In this connection there comes to mind the first announcement of the
Council made to the world by Pope John on January 25,
1959, the last day of the Octave for Church Unity. After
praying in the Basilica of St. Paul with a recollection and
fervor which deeply impressed all those present, the Pope,
visibly conscious of his crushing responsibilities, spoke of
the Council as of the perfect means of realizing the highest
ideal of his pontificate: *That they may be one.* It might be
added here that the Pope then announced the interior renewal of the Catholic Church as the first task of the coming Council, not as an end in itself, but as a necessary condition for making it more attractive and enhancing its
prestige before other Christian confessions.

All of us are aware of the genuinely miraculous
progress which has marked the Ecumenical Movement
from that day on, as it gave impetus and strength to the
enormous stores of good will existing within all Christian
churches. From the very beginning of his pontificate,
Paul VI brought to this Movement the contribution of his
enthusiastic and intuitive interest. Already as Archbishop
of Milan, he had been, so to speak, the second party in
the dialogue with those of our separated brethren who had

begun to draw closer to Rome. Later he clearly favored the frank and open policy of Vatican II towards non-Catholic Christian confessions.

From the first day of his pontificate he gave assurance that the direction taken by the dialogue under way with all those who glory in the Christian name would not be reversed: "We open our arms to all those who glory in the name of Christ. We greet them with the loving name of brothers and We know that they will find in Us unfailing comprehension and kindness. They will find in Rome their father's house, which ennobles and enriches with new splendor the treasures of their history, their cultural patrimony, their spiritual inheritance."

Taking advantage of the atmosphere of extraordinary communion of thought and sentiment which had been created in the last months of the life of Pope John XXIII and which culminated in the world-wide wave of sympathy and admiration on the death of the Pope in all religious and political circles, Paul VI was in a position to unveil immediately and more confidently the vastness of the ideals and the sincerity of the feelings of the Church for all Christians. The Church should never have been fearful before endless horizons or ideals reaching to the ends of the earth, because her divine Founder had sent her to preach the good news to the entire world. Perhaps there were periods in which the Church at least appeared to adopt an excessively rigid stand. But today her doors are thrown open wide once more. Today she wants once more to breathe the pure air of universal co-operation in the service of the gospel.

In the Episcopalian church of St. Paul in Rome there will soon be inaugurated a bronze door in iron and glass, whose bas-reliefs will record the meetings of John XXIII with Doctor Fisher, Archbishop of Canterbury and Primate of the Anglican Church, meetings which ended four hundred years of unyielding separation from Rome. The door will also show the Pope's meetings with Doctor Litchtenberger, the Presiding Bishop of the Episcopalian Church of the United States. "This door," declared Reverend Wood-hams, Rector of the church, "will be a symbol of those which John XXIII opened to Protestants, and will demonstrate to all passers-by that, like Catholics, we too agree with Pope John and are grateful to him."

Not only doors but the entire heart of the Church has been thrown open in an attempt at mutual understanding which, without compromising in the least any dogmatic truths, gives grounds for hope that in a future which is perhaps not too remote, we may reach a perfect understanding in the formulation of the doctrine of Christ, venerated and accepted by all. These same ideas were repeated by Paul VI in his opening discourse to the Second Session:

"A third purpose also interests this Council, one which in a certain sense constitutes its spiritual drama, one which was fixed for us by John XXIII and which concerns 'other Christians,' that is to say, those who believe in Christ but whom we have not the happiness of counting with ourselves in the perfect unity of Christ which only the Catholic Church can offer them, but to which through Baptism they are really entitled and which they do desire.

"Recent movements, at present in full swing in Christian communities separated from Us, clearly demonstrate two things: that the Church of Christ is only one and therefore must be the only one and, secondly, that this mysterious and visible union cannot be achieved except in identity of faith, participation in the same Sacraments, and the organic harmony of only one ecclesiastical guidance, even though this may be attained with respect for a great variety of linguistic expressions, ritualistic forms, historical traditions, local prerogatives, spiritual trends, legitimate institutions, and favorite activities.

"What will be the attitude of the Council towards the immense ranks of separated brethren and towards this pluralism in the manifestations of unity? The convocation of the Council has a special characteristic under this aspect also. The Council aims at complete and universal ecumeni-

city at least in its desires, its prayers, and its plans. Today
it does so in hope, in order that tomorrow it may do so in
reality. In other words, this Council, while calling and counting and leading into the sheepfold of Christ those sheep
who make it up and belong to it in the fullest and truest
sense, opens the door, calls out, and anxiously awaits the
many sheep of Christ who are not at present in the one fold.
Hence this is a Council of invitation, expectation, and confidence, looking forward towards a wider and more fraternal participation in its authentic ecumenicity."

After this first breaking of the ice, meetings between
representatives of all the Christian confessions became more
numerous and distances between them shrank considerably.
It was not so many years ago that Catholics were exhorted,
even in high places, to avoid all doctrinal contact with
non-Catholic Christian confessions. But today we are wit-
nessing a rapid succession of international meetings on all
levels, aiming to eliminate or at least to blunt centuries-old
bones of contention. All these are very serious efforts on the
part of all Christians to achieve this desired unity, which
is the fond dream of all sincere followers of Christ.

Ecumenical Break-throughs

It is related that during the Conclave, two Anglicans
were voicing conjectures on the possible successor of
Pope John, and were anxiously asking each other: "Who
will be *our* next Pope?" In the plans of God, this Pope was
Paul VI. When they heard his name announced, both of
them understood that his pontificate would be characterized by a universality without limitations.

In the few months between his election and the re-
opening of the Council, the new Pope was seeking out
rapprochements with separated Christians through a series

of thoughtful kindnesses and profoundly fatherly attitudes which went far beyond the predictions even of those who had known him at close range as Bishop and Cardinal. For the first time in history there were present at his coronation official representatives of non-Catholic churches, the Patriarchate of Moscow, the monks of Taizé, and the Anglican and Episcopalian churches. Paul VI sent Bishop Francois Charrière, Bishop of Lausanne, Geneva and Fribourg, along with Father Charles Dumont, O.P., Director of the Istina Center in Paris, as official representatives of the Catholic Church to the celebrations in honor of Patriarch Alexius of Moscow on the Golden Jubilee of his elevation to the episcopate. The journey of these two representatives of Rome, was "highly significant," as it was the first of its kind after several centuries of complete and total separation.

For the first time Paul VI received in audience the Metropolitan of Minsk, Nicodemo. For the first time also he sent five Catholic Observers to the fourth Conference of the World Council of Churches, held in Montreal from July 12th to July 16th. Cardinal Léger this also was something unprecedented—addressed that assembly, calling it "a family reunion." "Is not this ecumenical meeting," said the Cardinal, "a symbol of our common hopes? We recognize gratefully the sincere desire and the firm will of all here present to establish unity among those who glory in a share in the faith of Our Lord Jesus."

At this same conference, a representative of the Russian Orthodox Church, the Exarch Johann, voiced cautious optimism on the possibility of closer relations between the Catholic Church and the world behind the Iron Curtain: "The proverb says that one swallow does not make a spring. But," said the Exarch, "there are two swallows who have flown from the East to the West and from the West to the East. Consequently, we may hope that they will be the harbingers of a real spring."

With further reference to Canada, we might recall another dialogue between Catholics and Protestants, promoted by Bishop Coleman of the Anglican Church, and the Catholic Bishop Doyle. Taking part in this dialogue were fifty-seven clergymen of the two confessions and some Observers from the United and Baptist Churches. Bishop Coleman said of the assembly: "At the beginning, a certain diffidence was evident. Nevertheless, as the discussions continued—the general theme was "The Word of God and the Sacraments"—we began to sense a greater spirit of mutual understanding and we noted that, notwithstanding differences in terminology, the questions on which we agreed on matters of faith were numerous. None of us is so naïve as to believe that complete unity can be realized tomorrow. But the movement towards unity and mutual respect has already made remarkable progress. Discussions of this kind teach us to take a new look at our differences, and this attitude can lead to unity and complete reconciliation. It is evident that meetings of this kind, organized on a regional basis and within restricted groups, will enable us to know each other better. Still, it will be necessary to discuss more at length the more difficult and more delicate problems which are at the basis of our divisions." On that same occasion, Bishop Coleman affirmed that the Second Vatican Council is the most grandiose ecumenical event of our century.

Great interest was aroused also by the simultaneous theological discussion in Rome, London, and Princeton, which was arranged for October 15, 1963, via Telstar. Participating in this discussion were Cardinal Rugambwa, the first Negro Cardinal, and Professor Hans Küng, President of the Theological Faculty of Tübingen, on the Catholic side, while England was represented by the Reverend Cestie Newbigin, Secretary of the World Council of Churches, and the United States by the Reverend Franklin Clark Fry of the Lutheran Church of America, President of the Central Committee of the World Council of Churches.

In Cameroun, at the Lyceum Manengoba in Nkonsgamba, a missionary pastor of the Dutch Reformed Church and a Catholic priest, with the explicit permission of their respective superiors, agreed to collaborate in their courses of religious instruction. For three months, Father F. Kangue and Professor J. Schipper taught side by side in a mixed school composed of Catholics and Protestants. "Why," as many students asked, "cannot we Africans carry on in this way while efforts are being made towards unity, instead of having to wait for the end of divisions created in Europe centuries ago and which really have no meaning for us at all?"

The month of August, 1963, saw two Anglican pilgrimages to the sanctuary of Lourdes. The first was composed of fifty-six persons, among whom were nine priests and three sick children whose expenses had been paid by the Catholic Committee. The second pilgrimage was directed by Dr. Westall, Bishop of Crediton, who declared that he had gone to Lourdes "to pray, in union with Catholics and through the intercession of the Holy Mother of God, for the union of the Church throughout the world."

Three Churches in India, namely the Orthodox Church of Malabar, the Church of Mar Thoma, and that of South India, in a meeting of the Ecumenical Center of which Cardinal Gracias and representatives of five other Churches are members, expressed of their own accord a desire to be invited to send Observers to the Second Session of the Council.

In Madrid, on Pentecost Sunday, 1963, the Church of the Dormition of Our Lady was the scene of an inter-confessional vigil under the auspices of the Information Office of the Center of Oriental Studies in that city. Father Francesco Herrero, stated in his homily: "Just as the Apostles spoke on the first Pentecost and all the peoples of the earth heard them in their own languages, so should we know one another, and think and live in union with prayer and charity, with love and mutual understanding."

In conclusion, we may recall the various phases of the discussions within the Greek Orthodox Church until it reached also unanimous agreement to open a theological dialogue with the Catholic Church. Patriarch Athenagoras made no secret of his liking for John XXIII, the Second Vatican Council and lastly, for Paul VI. "We have great hopes," he said one day to a correspondent of the Second Vatican Council. "We have emerged from our isolation and have opened the doors which held us prisoners. Catholics and Greek Orthodox have many things in common: traditions, dogmas, the Sacraments, the catacombs and the common traces of the blood of martyrs. This blood cries out to us: Why are you separated? We laid down our lives for one cause! John XXIII," continued the Patriarch, "was a very great Pope, and the present Pope will be no less great. I regret particularly that I was unable to visit John XXIII because of his illness. I wanted to very badly, in order to become personally acquainted with him. This will be possible with the present Pope.... We have decided to open a dialogue between the Orthodox Church and the Roman Church. Isolation is a misfortune, and all monologue is isolation. We need dialogue. How beautiful it is to see how dialogue opens up hearts one to the other and lets people look each other straight in the eye. We are ready to recognize the Pope as 'the first among equals,' as was the case for a thousand years in the history of both the East and the West.... All of us, Catholics and Orthodox, have the same theology, but the difficulties blocking the way to mutual understanding are many." Paul VI reacted favorably to this attitude of Patriarch Athenagoras, writing to him personally and thanking him for his congratulations on the occasion of his elevation to the Chair of Peter.

A discordant note came from Patriarch Chrysostomos of Constantinople, who showed himself openly hostile to the invitation to send Observers to the Council. His stand was criticized by many members of his clergy and his faithful, especially by those in university circles. For this reason, perhaps, the Patriarch declared at the Conference of Rhodes, held from September 26-29, 1963, that his policy had been dictated by political pressure, and showed that he inclined

towards a less intransigent attitude. The fifty-three Metropolitans of the hierarchy decided to support this new
orientation of their Patriarch. Consequently, their dialogue
with the Catholic Church may begin with the appointment
of Observers to Vatican II.

The Mind of Paul VI

This rapid bird's-eye view of the world-wide ecumenical movement provides the proper setting for the core of the
discourse of Paul VI, on relations with all Christians. Never
before had any Pope recognized in such flattering terms
all the good elements found in the separated Churches.
Although ecumenism is not something suddenly new in the
Church—there had been noteworthy ecumenical activity
from the very beginning of the present century—nevertheless in these latter years the ecumenical movement has
entered upon a phase which may be called decisive, or at
least new.

"Our discourse," said the Pope, "is addressed to the
representatives of Christian denominations separated from
the Catholic Church, which have nevertheless been invited
to take part as Observers in this solemn assembly.

"We salute them from Our heart.

"We thank them for being here.

"Through them We transmit Our message as father
and brother to the venerable Christian communities which
they represent here.

"Our voice trembles and Our heart beats faster both
because of the ineffable consolation and fond hopes which
their presence stirs up within Us, and because of the deep
sadness We feel over their prolonged separation. If We are
in any way to blame for that separation, We humbly beg
God's forgiveness and ask pardon too of Our brethren who

may feel they have been wronged by us. For Our part, We are ready to forgive the injuries which the Catholic Church has suffered and to forget the grief caused to her during the long history of heresy and schism. May our Heavenly Father deign to hear our prayers and restore to us true brotherly peace."

No one has ever seen Paul VI show such deep emotion, emphasize his words with such force, accompany them with such deliberate gestures, or give his voice such a vigorous ring. If John XXIII regarded the presence of the Observers as something significantly important for the Council and watched over it as "the pupil of his eye," the same can be said of Paul VI, if the presence of the Observers could inspire within him such a moving passage on mutual pardon.

The figure of John XXIII was attractive even from a physical viewpoint, and he had a natural gift of communication which swept away all obstacles and likewise dissipated any preconceived distrust. "A few minutes after we had met," recounted Dr. Fisher, "we were already conversing with the ease and cordiality of two old friends talking about our spiritual experiences as Christians. And our conversation, which did not stop for a moment and was never tiresome, lasted for an hour."

Paul VI is different. He appears somewhat cold, but he is on the contrary most cordial with all those fortunate enough to have to treat with him. In their audience last October, the Council Observers were amazed at his affability, which they had not expected to find so marked. The Pope repeated to them pretty much the points just mentioned but did so "more familiarly, in more friendly fashion, in simpler language, which, better than the solemn Latin—he was addressing them in French—could reveal the depths of his soul." He thanked them once again for accepting the invitation, for coming and being present at the sessions of the Council "because the reality, the great reality, is that you are here, honored sirs and beloved brethren in Christ." Through their spokesman, Professor

Skidsgaard, the Observers expressed their satisfaction in the following terms: "Every day, we experience the kindliness of the Council Fathers towards us and the concern of the Secretariate for Christian Unity."

In a climate of mutual confidence, feeling very much at home and relying on the fact that Cardinal Bea, the great champion of ecumenism, had invited them to express freely their positive and negative reactions to the Council, Professor Skidsgaard took the liberty of offering certain suggestions to the Holy Father: "May I be permitted," he said, "to draw attention to a fact which strikes me as being extremely important. I refer to the great importance of a biblical theology based on a study of the history of salvation in the Old and the New Testaments. The more progress we make in understanding the secret and paradoxical history of the People of God, the more clearly do we understand the Church of Jesus Christ in its mystery, its historical existence and its unity. Nevertheless, Your Holiness, permit me to express our lively hope that the specialists in such concrete and historical theology, namely one built on the Bible and the teachings of the Holy Fathers, may play an ever increasingly important role in the work of this Council."

Paul VI accepted the suggestion, calling it "worthy of further study and examination." He then repeated the celebrated maxim of John XXIII, namely that greater emphasis should be placed on what unites us than on what divides us, and that we should pay more attention to the present, and especially to the future, than to the past.

An Our Father *Together*

Nevertheless, this ecumenical spirit does not aim to create confusion, as if it aimed to give the impression that since we all admit and recognize the same God, we should be satisfied with this, as though there was no further point in seeking after visible unity in one Church. This would not be ecumenism, but would lead to a kind of irenicism which has already been so frequently condemned in the history of the Church.

In this connection, it would be in order to cite a passage from Jean Guitton, a layman who assisted at the First Session of the Council by virtue of a special personal concession, and who was joined by twelve others as Auditors in the Second: "I think that there are certain ideas on Church unity which are absolutely false and that attention must be called to this openly: the idea that Catholics and Protestants intend to unite under a kind of least common denominator, simply ignoring everything which divides them. This ecumenism, which I would call minimistic, is altogether blameworthy for us Catholics. In fact it would lead us to throw overboard everything which makes the Church what it is. A Catholic must be ready to have his head chopped off rather than deny a single article of his Creed. But what I want to stress now is that if Catholics rule out that kind of ecumenism which we have called minimistic, it is also rejected by the great consciences of the Protestant and the Anglican world. In other words, one of the most admirable signs of our time consists in this, that the search for unity undertaken by the separated Churches does not demand that union among Christians should be achieved by bartering over doctrine and dogma. . . .

"We Catholics ask the Protestants to review their positions in the light of Church history. On their part, the Protestants ask us to review, not our positions but our formulas, in the light of this same history. . . . Consequently we must make every effort to speak the same language. Language is not the truth, but it is the outward garb of truth. We must ask ourselves if the habitual, usual and traditional language in which we express the eternal truths may not contain certain historical elements which cause useless clashes, give scandal, and brusquely hold people at a distance."

When a language has been found which is acceptable to all, then there is no further discussion. The *Our Father*, for example, continues to be recited by all of us, just as it is. For this reason, Paul VI wished the audience for the Council Observers to close with the Lord's Prayer, recited by the Pope and by each one of the forty-eight Observers in his own language.

The preceding remarks should not be interpreted in the sense that efforts for unity have already reached a happy conclusion. This would be exaggerated and dangerous optimism. Paul VI added to his discourse words eloquent with realistic good sense and complete sincerity, with which, according to the expression of Hans Küng, "He called white white, grey grey, and black black."

"We are aware," said the Pope in his inaugural Allocution, "that there are still serious and complicated questions to be studied, discussed, and resolved. Because of the love of Christ which 'urges us,' We would hope that this could be realized immediately. But We also realize that these problems presuppose many conditions which are as yet premature. Hence We are not afraid to await patiently the blessed hour of perfect reconciliation.

"Meanwhile, We wish to affirm before the Observers here present certain points in Our attitude towards reunion with Our separated brethren, in order that they may pass them on to their respective Christian communities. May Our voice also reach other venerable Christian communities separated from Us, which did not accept the previous invitation to attend the Council, even though this involved no commitment of any kind. We believe these points are already common knowledge, but it will be useful to repeat them here.

"Our language towards them is friendly, completely sincere and honest. We are setting no traps; We are not motivated by temporal interests. To Our faith, which We believe to be divine, We owe the firmest and most candid devotion, but at the same time We are convinced that this is no obstacle to the understanding We hope for with Our separated brethren, precisely because it is the truth of the Lord and therefore the principle of union, not of division and separation. At any rate We have no desire to make of our Faith an occasion for polemics.

"Secondly We look with reverence upon the authentic religious patrimony We share in common, which has been preserved and in part even well-developed among Our separated brethren. We are pleased to note the study undertaken by those who seek sincerely to make known and to honor the treasures of truth and genuine spirituality possessed by Our separated brethren, in order to improve our mutual relations. It is Our fond hope that with like desires they will endeavor to study our doctrine more carefully and its logical derivations from the deposit of Divine Revelation, as also our history and our spiritual life.

"Finally We wish to say that, aware of the enormous difficulties still blocking the way to desired union, We humbly put our final trust in God. We shall continue to pray. We shall try to give clearer witness of our efforts at genuine Christian living and fraternal charity. And when the realities of history might tend to disappoint Our hopes, We shall recall the comforting words of Christ: 'Things that are impossible with men are possible with God' " (Luke 18:27).

Beholding Immense Harvests

The Church is a reality of world-wide proportions, since she is the continuation and the extension of the saving mystery of Jesus Christ on behalf of all men. The Christian cannot remain cooped up in his churches or his sacristies, because he must be the leaven of the entire world, the light pointing out the true path of ascent to God. Recent Popes—We refer particularly to those of our century—have enjoyed ever-increasing and far-reaching prestige. But in this connection We are pleased to recall an item of particular importance in these recent years, namely the Encyclical of John XXIII *Pacem in Terris,* which had such precedent-shattering echoes resounding far beyond religious boundary lines, because it was directed to all men of good will. The special stamp of this pontifical document recalls to mind the precept of the Gospel: *Go and teach all nations,* without exceptions of any kind.

Just as the Good News first announced by the Apostles was joyfully welcomed by the men of the first generation fortunate enough to hear them, thus the Encyclical of Pope John signalled a real rebirth. "The world has awakened," was the comment of the Holy Father, as he noted the positive reaction produced in the great majority of nations, and he expressed his satisfaction with the wave of confidence and tranquillity which this historical document had aroused in the entire world.

All men of good will regarded themselves as involved in this great cause and welcomed enthusiastically the program of international order traced out by the Pope with a master's hand. Of course, not all answered his appeal. The battle, the entire battle must be reduced in the last analysis to a test of strength between good and evil. This is one of the characteristics of our earthly pilgrimage. Along with men of good will there are others whose wills are sickly, weak or ill-intentioned. Paul VI took note of this saddening side of human reality within the great framework of his inaugural discourse for the Second Session of the Council:

"We must be realists, not hiding the wound which for many motives reaches even into this Universal Synod. Can We be blind and not notice that there are many vacant seats in this assembly? Where are Our brethren from nations where the Church is opposed, and what is the condition of religion in those territories? Our thoughts are saddened because of what We know, and even more because of what We cannot know, about the sacred hierarchy, Our religious men and women, Our countless children subjected to fear, persecution, privation and oppression because of their loyalty to Christ and the Church. What sadness We feel in the face of such sufferings and what a cross it is to see that in certain countries religious liberty, like the other fundamental rights of man, is being smothered by principles and methods based on political, racial, or anti-religious intolerance! It grieves Us to see how in the world today there are still so many injustices against goodness and the free profession of one's own religious faith. But, rather than in bitter words, Our lament must be expressed in a frank and human exhortation to all those responsible for these evils to desist honorably from their unjustified hostility towards the Catholic religion, whose followers should be considered neither as enemies nor as disloyal citizens, but rather as upright and hard-working members of the civil society to which they belong. Finally, to those Catholics who are suffering for their Faith We send once more Our affectionate greetings and for them We invoke special divine assistance."

Paul VI was clearly referring to the Churches living in difficult times in the countries of eastern Europe. We have already mentioned how the Polish government refused passports for Rome to twenty-five Bishops. But numerous also are the "impeded Bishops" in other countries of central Europe. In Czechoslovakia, for example, few Bishops can exercise their pastoral ministry with any degree of liberty, although the population is two-thirds Catholic. Nevertheless, during the Council, the announcement came of the liberation of Archbishop Beran and of other Bishops on October 2, 1963. Archbishop Beran thus emerged from an internment which had lasted twelve years.

"On March 7, 1951," the illustrious prelate narrated, "several representatives of the government presented them-

selves at my episcopal residence, and obliged me to follow
them, without giving any reasons. Perhaps they thought I
might cause trouble." Once liberated, Archbishop Beran
awaited the decision of the Holy Father before resuming
his functions, although the Communist authorities had lost
no time in letting him know that he would not be allowed
to exercise his ministry freely "at least for the present."
"Archbishop Beran," reported a news agency which had
interviewed him, "was wearing his pectoral cross and his
pastoral ring. His eyes were sparkling as he spoke with a
strong and firm voice." He did not come for the Second
Session of the Council. "I prefer to wait," he said, "until
the dust settles and the situation clears." His liberation was
quite similar to that of Archbishop Slipyj, the Ukranian
Metropolitan of Leopoli, who had been released early in
1963.

The general public is aware of the trips to Budapest
by Cardinal Koenig for discussions with Cardinal Mindszenty, another "impeded Bishop," unable to exercise his
ministry in Catholic Hungary since the very first years of
the post-war period. In a visit to the College of Propaganda
Fide on the evening of October 20, 1963, Pope Paul VI
voiced his regrets publicly that such a noble nation as
Hungary was not represented among the fourteen Bishops
whom he himself had consecrated that morning and that
its pastors had been forced by circumstances to leave vacant
the places assigned to them in the Council.

Facts such as these cast dark shadows over the work
for peace which the Church has always carried on and
which in recent years has been particularly intensified. In
our days, when it can be said that human liberty has been
fully recognized in the vast majority of the countries of the
world, it is saddening to have to record those violations
which, in the name of an ironclad ideology, are committed
against the most sacred rights of the human person, which
becomes a victim sacrificed to the cult of purely material
progress, a progress which will never succeed in satisfying
the most intimate and deepest aspirations of man.

Our Lord declared that "man does not live by bread alone." Today, quoting the words of Saint-Exupéry, we could find a new proof for the words of the Gospel and say that "man does not live on frigidaires and salaries." This does not imply any contempt for technical progress, but echoes a desire for the elimination of that universally recognized disproportion between the marvelous technical progress of our time and the anemia of genuine spiritual values in our standardized culture which is set before us "just as we would set before an ox a supply of fodder prepared according to all the rules of culinary art"—to quote Saint-Exupéry again.

Should this lead to despair? By no means. Rather, Christians must endeavor to revivify spiritual values. The vastness of Paul VI's ideas on this point really knows no limits:

"We look upon our times and upon their varied and conflicting manifestations with immense tenderness and with an equally immense desire to offer to the men of today the message of friendship, salvation, and hope which Christ has brought into the world. 'For God did not send his Son into the world in order to judge the world, but that the world might be saved through Him.' (John 3:17)

"Let the world know this: The Church looks at the world with profound understanding, sincere admiration, and the sincere intention not to conquer it but to serve it, not to despise it but to appreciate it, not to condemn it but to strengthen and save it.

"From the window of the Council, opened wide on the world, the Church looks towards some categories of persons with particular solicitude. She looks toward the poor, the needy, the afflicted, the hungry, the suffering and those in prison. In a word, the Church looks to every human being who suffers and weeps. The human race belongs to the Church by the right which the Gospel gives her and she likes to repeat to all men: 'Come to me all of you.' "

That these were not mere empty words will be clear in subsequent chapters, as the reader becomes aware of the intense social activity in which Paul VI engaged in all the different periods of his life. For the present it will suffice to recall his fatherly gesture on the day of his coronation, when he arranged for all the inmates of Italian prisons to have a special dinner at his expense, setting aside for the poorest among them a sum of money to be invested so that on their release they might have the wherewithal to live with a certain degree of independence.

Among his many meetings with the sick, there is the incident of his first trip outside the Vatican, the very day after his election, to visit Cardinal Pla y Daniel, who was confined to bed in the Spanish College in Rome, as also Archbishop Slipyj. By this act, the Holy Father gave a first proof of his fatherly character, which was later manifested on repeated occasions during the Second Session of the Council in his various visits to sick Bishops. When receiving a pilgrimage of children afflicted with polio from Palermo, Paul VI surprised all those present by affectionately kissing one of the little patients, a deaf mute, who was held up alongside his portable throne. Moving also was the audience granted to a group of blind children, to whom the Pope addressed a few words, "because," he said, "words are the only things you can see."

During his summer stay at Castel Gandolfo, the Pope was seen distributing Holy Communion personally to hundreds of children in the nearby villages. His first trip out of the papal villa was to a house of suffering, the Clinic of the Daughters of St. Paul at Albano. With special emotion, the Pope visited a young Sister who was dying of cancer and who was happy to tell him that she was from Brescia, the same province as the Pope.

"The Church," continued the Pope in the inaugural discourse of the Second Session, "looks towards men of culture, students, scientists, and artists, for these also she has great esteem and an immense desire to profit by the fruit of their research, to strengthen their intellectual life, to defend their liberty, to increase joyously in the luminous spheres of the Word and the Grace of God the liberation of their troubled spirits.

"The Church looks towards workingmen, towards the dignity of their person and their efforts and the legitimacy of their hopes, towards the need of social betterment which still afflicts them, and the mission which can be theirs, if it is good and Christian, to create a new world of free men and brothers. The Church, as mother and teacher, is at their side.

"She looks to the leaders of nations, and in place of the grave words of warning which the Church must often address to them, she speaks today a word of encouragement and confidence. Take courage, rulers of nations. Today you can give to your people many of the good things necessary for life: bread, education, work, order, the dignity of free and peaceful citizens, provided only that you truly recognize what man is—and only Christian wisdom can show this to you in its full light. Working together in justice and love, you can create peace, that greatest good which is so yearned for and which the Church has defended and promoted so strenuously, and you can make of the human race one single city. God be with you."

Such words could not fail to make a deep impression on the Diplomatic Corps present at the ceremony. Certainly the diplomats then recalled the unforgettable audience which John XXIII had granted them a few days after the opening of the Council, when he had charged them—these men whose life is protocol and official couriers—to take home an embrace to their children, "the embrace of the Pope." If politicians thought out and lived the intimate problems of their people, especially their family problems, then they would not so easily take those tragic decisions which bring so many tears to innocent children, who deserve only embraces. Paul VI had already addressed much the same ideas in his audiences on June 24th and July 1, 1963 for the Diplomatic Corps accredited to the Holy See and for the eighty-one Extraordinary Missions which had assisted at his coronation.

Lastly, the Church, called by its very nature to universal expansion, tends to take in all panoramas, pushing beyond all frontiers and endeavoring to find basic points of universal agreement among all men, without exceptions or distinctions. "The Church," insisted Paul VI, "looks beyond her own sphere and beholds those other religions which have preserved the sense and notion of one God Creator and Sustainer, supreme and transcendent, which worship Him with acts of sincere piety and on these beliefs and religious practices base their moral and social life. It is true that the Catholic Church, with sorrow, sees in such religions some gaps, insufficiencies and errors in many expressions of religion like those indicated, yet she cannot fail to turn her thoughts to them and she would have them know that for everything in them which is true, good and human the Catholic Church has due appreciation, and that for the conservation in modern society of religious sense and the worship of God, which is both a need and a duty of civilization itself, she is in the front line as a most vigorous defender of God's rights over mankind.

"The searching eye of the Church also takes in other vast fields of humanity: the new generations of youth growing up with the desire of life and self-expression, the new peoples now acquiring national consciousness, independence and civil organization, and the countless men and women who feel isolated in a troubled society that has no message of salvation for their spirit. To all, to all without exception she proclaims the Good News of salvation and hope; to all she offers the light of truth and life and salvation, for God 'wishes all men to be saved and to come to the knowledge of the truth' (I Tim. 2:4)." These thoughts could be illustrated with a long series of concrete facts. Among these, a few might be chosen, as, for instance, the interest in the

Catholic Church demonstrated for the first time by religious confessions which up to yesterday ignored her or showed open hostility for anything smacking of Christianity.

The death of Pope John, which marked a peak of ecumenism in the broadest sense of the word, profoundly troubled the souls of Jews, Buddhists, and Moslems, united in admiration of the work for peace and mutual understanding which had been carried on by this great Pontiff. In the presence of a large gathering of Christians and Moslems, the Grand Mufti of Lebanon delivered a long eulogy of the deceased Pope, holding in his hand the Encyclical *Pacem in Terris*, reading from it and commenting on its most important passages, and classifying that document among the most inspiring messages ever to come to the human race.

Today there is talk of an open dialogue between Catholics and Moslems, as has been stated by Bishop Plumey, Bishop of Garoua, in North Cameroun. In his diocese, schools are open to all and, without carrying on among the Moslems any kind of direct apostolate, which would be to no purpose, efforts are being made to use indirect influence and, in the first place, to establish friendly and sincere relationships, eliminating once and for all the age-old hatreds which lined up the followers of these two religions into two armed camps. At Christmas, 1961, Bishop Plumey addressed a message to the Moslem chiefs, listing the points common to Christianity and Mohammedanism: Abraham, the Bible, the common vocation to be witnesses of God in a world tending constantly to lose its sense of the divine, the same human ideal to lead man to eternal life, and to build up here below a society founded on the order willed by God.

The reaction to such a message and the first results which followed from it exceeded all expectations, especially among the Moslem élite, which was amazed to learn that, especially with reference to the Bible, there were so many points of contact between them and the Christians. Thus

they were able to reflect with greater clarity on the maxim
of Mohammed: "Whoever among you does not love his
brother as himself, will not be a believer." Certainly, for
the present, there is question only of setting up contacts
based on initial tolerance and mutual understanding. Rank-
ling prejudices which have remained unchanged for centuries have not yet disappeared. But the important thing
is that a start has been made. "The Council," wrote *Le Pen-
sée Chiite*, published by the Iranian Center of Islamic Formation in Europe, "should seek out points of contact with
the heads of monotheistic religions in order the better to
combat the invasions of materialistic Marxism."

Thus, the Council has had the effect of arousing interest
even beyond the confines of Christianity. Paul VI has
created a Secretariate for Non-Christian Religions. This
represents the vastness of the program of the Sovereign
Pontiff, which he set forth solemnly in his discourse at the
beginning of the Second Session of the Council, and which
these pages have endeavored to reproduce and comment on.

A Session Less Spectacular
But More Dense in Meaning

Following the directives given by the Holy Father in
his opening discourse, the Council Fathers set to work
willingly, adopting a crowded schedule calling for five
working Congregations weekly. Saturdays and Sundays
were free days, as also certain others set aside for liturgical
solemnities or special commemorations having some connection with the over-all theme of the Council. Every morning large and small busses brought to Piazza San Pietro
groups of Bishops in violet mozzettas and rochets, adding
a special glint of color to the Roman mornings. At noon,
on the border line between Italian territory and Vatican

City, a considerable throng of people was always waiting
to watch the Fathers come out of the Basilica on their way
home after three hours of work. The piazza, transformed for
the time being into a temporary parking lot, began to move.
The outside steps of the Basilica were soon flashing with
countless violet cassocks, also the scarlet ones of the Cardinals, the grey and black robes of the religious and the special garments of the Orientals. Then began the procession of
automobiles carrying on the windshield the special identification disc: *Second Ecumenical Vatican Council*. This was
a kind of special pass procuring certain advantages in the
always intense and sometimes chaotic traffic of the Italian
capital. Not a few Fathers preferred to return home on
foot, with a burst of youthful zeal recalling their student
days in the universities of the Eternal City, and they fanned
out over the city in all directions to satisfy their thirst for
new artistic and historical knowledge. They could sometimes be seen walking along the Tiber for long distances,
engaged in animated conversations, greeting all who sa-
luted them. At the exit from the piazza, curious crowds
could greet the Fathers passing on foot with briefcases under their arms, containing material which would call for
hours of study in the evening on topics that had been discussed that morning.

The Second Session of the Council was less spectacular
but more "substantial" than the first. This, at least, is the
judgment suggested by the results of two long months of
General Congregations, which witnessed the discussion of
some of the most important themes on the agenda of
Vatican II.

The assembly of the Council Fathers in Saint Peter's
on December 4, 1963, was held in what was a feast-day
atmosphere. After a year of work, they were about to gather
the first fruits of their labors. Earlier, on November 22nd
and 23rd, the Fathers had approved by substantial margins
(2,149 votes out of 2,178) the schemas on the Liturgy and

on the Media of Social Communication. On this latter document there were 1,598 affirmative votes and 505 negative. The only element now lacking was the definitive approval of the Holy Father, with the promulgation of the Liturgical Constitution and the Decree on the Media of Social Communication.

In the Public Session of December 4th, in the presence of the Holy Father, the final voting took place. The schema on the liturgy received 2,147 favorable votes, as against 4 negative. The voting on the Media of Social Communication brought out 1,960 votes in favor, and 164 against the proposed text. Paul VI approved both these texts and promulgated them with the following formula: "In the name of the most holy and indivisible Trinity, Father, Son and Holy Spirit, the decrees read in this sacrosanct and universal Vatican Council II, legitimately assembled, have been accepted by the Fathers. And We, by the apostolic power given to Us by Christ, together with the venerable Fathers, in the Holy Spirit, approve, decree, establish, and command that the decrees thus approved in Council should be promulgated, for the greater glory of God."

December 4, 1963, will pass into the annals of history along with that other date of December 4, 1563, which marked the closing of the twenty-fifth session of the Council of Trent. The promulgation of these first two Council documents will give the theologians new subjects for study and will be an invitation to patient waiting for those individuals who had become so accustomed to the Council atmosphere as to pay no more attention to it, and also for those who were accusing the assembly of not getting anywhere. The Council was not born under the sign of haste. Pope John XXIII had already stated this on the unforgettable night of October 11, 1962: "The Council has begun, but We do not know when it will finish. Certainly, We will not be able to say in a short time everything we want to tell each other. Perhaps We will not be in complete agreement on everything in the beginning."

From the human view point, the best guarantee for the Council is the seriousness with which its themes are treated, without sparing time or effort. All things considered, it must be said that Vatican II is moving along with the times, rapidly. Rapidity, yes; haste, no.

At times the Fathers feel as though they would want to finish off the work at once, but the importance of the themes under discussion demands hours and hours, months, and even years of work. The Holy Father declared to the Bishops: "You have already been a long time away from your respective sees, where the sacred ministry calls for your presence, your counsel, and the work which, as zealous pastors, only you can do. Serious, assiduous and long has been the work created for you by ceremonies, study, and meetings during the conciliar period. . . . But now We must, for the second time, interrupt the course of these magnificent Council meetings. We must exchange with one another the greeting of fraternal peace. We must once again experience the inexorable onward movement of things which time both engenders and devours. We must part after having enjoyed days and events marked with stupendous fraternal contacts."

The Council is little by little working out its program without air-tight divisions or absolute deadlines. December 4, 1963, will be linked up with September 14, 1964. The Council sessions will follow one another until the agenda has been completed.

Forty-three General Congregations and Three Solemn Commemorations

Figures tell us very little in the face of spiritual facts like the Council. There is an immense field which escapes control by statistics. The reader must be satisfied with the cold data of certain figures, a kind of statistical account, leaving to the future the joy of tasting deeply the burst of life coming from Vatican II. Paul VI expressed himself in almost the same terms in his closing discourse: "... Many aspects of this Council belong to that field of grace and to that interior kingdom of souls where it is not always easy to enter, just as many results of the work accomplished are not ripe at the present time but, like seed sowed in the furrows, must await the future and the new assistance of divine grace in order to produce their effects and unfold as they should."

The Second Session was long and counted seven more Congregations than the first. Between General Congregation No. 37 and General Congregation No. 79 there were forty-three working sessions. Of these, twenty-three were devoted to the schema on the Church, nine to the document on Bishops and the government of dioceses, and eleven to ecumenism. There were also two Public Sessions, the first on September 29th, for the re-opening of Vatican II, and the second on December 4th, the day it closed, both occasions being marked by discourses of His Holiness.

Ninety-four votes were taken by secret ballot and some ten by a show of hands. Among other provisions, fifty-eight amendments were voted into the schema on Sacred Liturgy. Five general questions were proposed to find out the viewpoint of the Fathers regarding the fundamental theme of the collegiality of the Bishops and allied questions. A vote was also taken on the insertion of the schema on the Blessed Virgin into that on the Church. This vote was called for after a discourse by Cardinal Santos, of Manila, in favor of a separate schema and another by Cardinal Koenig, of Vienna, who argued for treating of the Blessed Virgin in chapter 5 of the schema on the Church.

Three dates stand out particularly in the recollections of the Council Fathers, even though they concern meetings which were in one sense only marginal to the Council. On November 28th there was the solemn commemoration of the fifth anniversary of the election of John XXIII as

Sovereign Pontiff. Cardinal Leo Joseph Suenens, Archbishop of Bruxelles, in the presence of the Pope, delivered a moving panegyric of the great Pontiff. The truth of the matter is that the figure of John XXIII has not been shunted into the background and that on the contrary it seems to be hovering over everything connected with *his* Council. Then on November 4th, the Council solemnly commemorated the fourth centenary of the founding of seminaries. A numerous gathering of seminarians brought a note of color, good spirits and hope; from them must come the prelates who will carry out the decisions of the Council. The discourse on this occasion was delivered by Cardinal Wyszynski, with the Holy Father presiding. Cardinal Urbani marked the fourth centenary of the Council of Trent.

The Themes of Session II

The topics discussed in the two months of the Second Session have already been listed. Now is the moment for a bird's-eye view of what took place in the Council Hall and of the salient points emerging from the discussions. As had been the case in the First Session, all discussions were marked by a spirit of holy freedom and fraternal charity. The very fact that the Council had met to study and discuss delicate problems meant at the outset that there would be divergent trends in evaluating and emphasizing the individual problems themselves. But it is absolutely certain that all those taking part in this imposing assembly were basically in perfect agreement. Bearing this in mind, certain episodes which marked some of the discussions, and the clashes which to the superficial observer might seem to reflect antagonism on matters of principle lose all their significance. The Pope had emphasized this long-range view: "We might call attention here to a twofold aspect of this activity, namely that it was very trying and at the same time completely free in the expression of opinions. It seems quite in order to call attention to the twofold claim to merit which characterizes this Council and which will leave its mark on history. Thus does the Church work today in the highest and most significant moment of its intense and spontaneous activity."

The point most debated in the schema on the Church was without doubt the collegiality of the Bishops. This term raises the question whether the general government of the Church is reserved exclusively to the Pope or is to be shared in likewise by all the Bishops. In the Council Hall two conflicting currents became evident in the First Session. Some Fathers regarded collegiality as a danger or a downgrading of the monarchical character of the Supreme Pontiff. This was really not the point at issue, because everyone agreed on the absolute necessity of respecting the decisions of the First Vatican Council on the Primacy. The only difference now was one of perspective. Previously, attention had been centered on the relation of the Pope with each individual Bishop, and the problem was resolved on an essentially juridical level. Attention today is shifted to the relations of the Pope with the episcopate as a body. The fundamental approach is pastoral. A strong trend is developing to put the concept of authority into evangelical context. Whereas the emphasis previously was on *power* and *domination*, today it is on *service*.

In one of his discourses in the Council Cardinal Liénart, Bishop of Lille, declared: "There is no opposition between the Primacy of the Roman Pontiff and the College of Bishops. Instead of concentrating on finding New Testament quotations for one or the other of these theses, as though they contradicted one another, it would be much more useful to read and to meditate on the whole Gospel, with the desire to understand the authentic thought and will of Christ. Christ assembled around Himself a College of Apostles. To one of them, Peter, he entrusted the Primacy, that is, the mission to confirm his brethren. Among them He wanted charity to reign and He wanted them to avoid clashes and disputes. After the Ascension, the Apostles themselves acted as a body. Assembled in the Cenacle with Mary they completed the membership of their College, replacing the Apostle who had turned traitor. On the day of Pentecost, they began their preaching all together. Together they governed the Church, instituting the deacons by common agreement and assembling in Council in Jerusalem. Thus Christ instituted both the collegiate union of the Apostles and the Primacy of Peter. The two realities are not in contradiction, because authority in the Gospel and consequently in the Church cannot be understood in terms of power, but in terms of service. The return to collegiate union will make the catholicity of the Church more visible to the entire world and will better serve the expansion of the Catholic Church."

In this sense the proposal was made to create a body composed of Patriarchs, residential Cardinals, and other residential Bishops who, under the presidency of the Supreme Pontiff, would be the visible expression of the lasting exercise of the universal authority of the Bishops, even outside the Council sessions. This would be a kind of super-Congregation or permanent Senate of the Church, in which all nations or Episcopal Conferences would be represented.

The Church has enjoyed marvelous growth, as was foretold in the parable of the grain of mustard seed. In order to co-ordinate all the manifestations of its life, no one man is now sufficient. For centuries the Popes have understood the necessity of surrounding themselves with collaborators and organisms competent to exercise the universal government of the Church. Christ Himself entrusted to twelve men chosen by Himself personally the mission to guide and extend His Church. According to an expression very common in the entire Orient, Peter was to be the "coryphaeus," the co-ordinator, of governing action in the whole of the Apostolic College.

Christ chose the twelve Apostles, not through Peter, but directly. They were empowered to exercise the jurisdiction He had given them, and without any special permission from Peter. Thus did the Apostles act. Up to this point, everyone agrees. There is likewise unanimous agreement that the Bishops are the successors of the Apostles, but not as to whether this is as individuals or as a body. This is the point at issue. Many times, and not merely when there was explicit discussion on this point, the remarks of the Fathers came back unfailingly to this basic question. That is why, at one point in the discussion, it seemed clearly evident that some way had to be found to sound out the mind of the Council Fathers on this burning issue.

During the fifty-seventh Congregation, on October 29th, the same day on which insertion of the schema on the Blessed Virgin into that on the Church was decided, the Council Moderators proposed to the Fathers a vote on the following five points: 1) Does episcopal consecration constitute the highest grade of the Sacrament of Orders? 2) Does a Bishop legitimately consecrated, in union with the other Bishops and with the Supreme Pontiff, who is their Head and the origin of their unity, become at once a member of the episcopal body? 3) Does the body or College of Bishops succeed the College of the Apostles in the mission of evangelizing, sanctifying and governing, and when it is united with the Roman Pontiff, its Head, and never without him—because he preserves intact his right of supreme authority over all pastors and all faithful—does the body of Bishops share in his supreme and full power over the entire Church? 4) Does this power belong by divine right to the episcopal body united to its Head? 5) Is it opportune to restore the diaconate as a distinct and permanent grade of the sacred ministry, according to the necessities of the Church in various countries?

The Fathers were not being asked to approve or disapprove any determined text, but only to make known their viewpoints on the five questions proposed. Consequently, the procedure was something of a straw vote, even though everyone was fully aware of the importance of the results. As a matter of fact, in subsequent discussions, many of the Fathers supported the decisions taken as a result of this voting.

On October 30th, the Council Fathers voted as follows on the individual points: 1) 2,123 for, 34 against; 2) 2,049 for, 104 against, 1 null vote; 3) 1,808 for, 336 against, 4 null votes; 4) 1,717 for, 408 against, 13 null votes; 5) 1,588 for, 525 against, 7 null votes. Thus each one of the five points was answered in the affirmative and with a majority comfortably beyond the two-thirds required for the approval of Council texts.

The next step was to work out an adequate formulation for such far-reaching questions. This work was turned over to a competent Commission which would do its work during the interim period before the Third Session. But it may be taken for granted that the final answers to these questions cannot differ from the viewpoints expressed by the vast majority of the Council Fathers. October 30, 1963, was a key date in the evolution of Vatican II.

The Mind of Paul VI

The preceding pages are not a thoughtless digression. The story they tell may seem to wander from Paul VI but in reality it does not, because the Council is really the great work of Pope Paul VI. He himself declared in his first address to the Sacred College on the day after his election that the Council would be "the pre-eminent part" of his pontificate. Thus there can be no complete biography of Paul VI without at least a cursory account of what went on in the Council Hall.

On the other hand, the Pope's mind on these questions was already well known beforehand. In one of his discourses, in the First Session, the then Archbishop of Milan had remarked that the schema on the Church did not attribute the necessary importance and scope to the role of Bishops in the Church. Once he became Pope, he announced in various discourses, as in the one delivered on September 21, 1963, to the Roman Curia, that the theme of the central administration of the Church had become very timely, and he emphasized the importance of consultations with Bishops. Finally, he decided to open the second Council session with the schema on the Church and, as has already been observed on several occasions, in his opening discourse he dedicated one of his central points precisely to the episcopate, inviting the Council Fathers to probe deeply into this important aspect of the Church, and declaring himself ready to accept the doctrinal and practical criteria which would come from these discussions.

As though this were not enough, Paul VI expressed himself still more clearly in his closing discourse of the session: "Other questions stay open for new study and new discussion, which We hope the Third Session, to be held next fall, will bring to completion. We are happy that there will be time for reflective study of such serious problems and that the various commissions, in which We have such confidence, taking into account the mind of the Council Fathers as expressed especially in the General Congregations, may prepare for future Council meetings formulas which have been carefully studied, vigorously formulated, opportunely condensed and abbreviated, in such a way that the discussion, while remaining always free, may be easier and briefer.

"Such, for example, is the question of Divine Revelation.... Such likewise is the other very complex question of the episcopate, which has priority both for reasons of logical order and because of the importance of this theme in this Second Vatican Council which, We can never forget, is the natural continuation and complement of the First Vatican Council. Consequently, not in contradiction to but in confirmation of the supreme prerogatives derived from Christ and recognized for the Sovereign Pontiff, prerogatives provided with all the authority necessary for the universal government of the Church, this Council wishes to put in its proper light, according to the mind of Our Lord and the authentic tradition of the Church, the nature and the function, both divinely instituted, of the episcopate, clarifying the nature of its powers and the mode of their exercise either as regards the individual prelates, or in regard to the entire body, in order that the exalted position of the episcopate in the Church of God may be set off in proper focus. This would not be as an autonomous or separated body, or much less as one in opposition to the Supreme Pontificate of Peter. Rather, with Peter and under Peter, the episcopate would be collaborating for the common welfare and the supreme goal of this same Church, in order that the hierarchical structure of the Church may thereby be strengthened instead of weakened, and that its internal collaboration may be increased and not slackened. Likewise, there would be an increase rather than a lessening of apostolic efficiency, a re-enkindling instead of a cooling of mutual charity. On a theme of such importance We expect the Council to speak its clarifying and strengthening word."

Pope John had followed the Council discussions by radio in his private apartment. Nothing has been said as to how Paul VI decided to follow developments in the Council Hall. But it is certain that he did follow closely all the different phases of the Council's work. During the Second Session, he usually received the four Council Moderators every Saturday. There were eight of these audiences in which the Moderators explained for the Pope the progress of the Fathers' discussions during the week. In addition Paul VI received forty-nine groups of Bishops, usually national but sometimes regional groups, with whom he could discuss special points connected with the Council. Lastly there were numerous other priviate audiences for the Secretary General of the Council, Archbishop Felici, and many other Bishops.

On November 16th, at the close of an intense week which had witnessed the most lively discussions of the Second Session, Paul VI presided at a special gathering of the Cardinals of the Presidency Council, the Moderators, the Secretary General, the Under-Secretaries and the Co-ordinating Commission.

In the First Session John XXIII had intervened on two occasions, with great tact and at the right moment. These occasions were during the election of members to the Council Commissions, and likewise in the vote to remand to the Theological Commission the text of the schema on the sources of Revelation. Paul VI maintained consistently an attitude of deep respect for the Council, and intervened indirectly through suggestions to the Moderators. At the end of the Session he voiced enthusiastic approval of the work of the Council Fathers: "The Council has done good work. As you are already aware, it has faced up to many questions for which solutions have been virtually decided upon in authoritative form and which, after the completion of the work on the matters to which they refer, will be duly published."

From the very beginning of his pontificate Paul VI gave assurances that he was not guided by any ambition for domination and, in complete harmony with this principle already laid down by John XXIII, he allowed the Bishops the fullest possible freedom and initiative. On some occassions, he even anticipated some of their requests.

Along with the question of collegiality, there were other important debates on points like the diaconate as a permanent rank in the Church, having its own finality and not serving only as a step towards the priesthood, as it is today. The Fathers voted favorably on the principle of a permanent diaconate.

Another of these points dealt with Episcopal Conferences in the schema on Bishops and the Government of Dioceses. But it would perhaps be more exact to say that, instead of just discussing, the Episcopal Conferences acted. Never before had there been such a clear understanding of the enormous power wielded by the episcopate of an entire nation or region in the solution of problems of common interest. Many such meetings were held during the Council at times when the Fathers were free. They discussed, among other topics, the lists of members for the various Commissions, and the collective viewpoints to be brought to the attention of the Council Fathers. Several Cardinals and Bishops addressed the Council in the name of dozens and even hundreds of other Fathers. This greatly facilitated and simplified the work of the Council, because it cut down on the number of speeches and was able to influence the group thinking of the majority. A characteristic instance was that of Cardinal de Barros Camara, Archbishop of Rio di Janiero, who in his four speeches on the schemas on the Church and on Bishops, spoke in the name of 153, 133, 91, and 110 Council Fathers. Similarly, Cardinal Silva Enriques, Archbishop of Santiago, Chile, on one occasion was spokesman for 44 Fathers, and on another day for 80. Cardinal Landázuri Ricketts, Archbishop of Lima, Peru, spoke in the name of 95 Latin American Bishops, and Cardinal Arriba y Castro, in the name of 60 Spanish Bishops. Numerous Fathers were spokesmen for all the Bishops of a region, a nation, or a rite, especially among the African and Oriental Fathers.

"The Church In the State of Mission"

This is the title of a well-known book by Cardinal Suenens and is an exact expression of what the Church must be in reality. We usually picture "mission lands" as virgin forests, deserts, countries of witch-doctors and savages. If anyone were to call our country "a mission country," we would feel offended, because this would be tantamount to calling us uncivilized, under-developed barbarians. As far as we are concerned, missionaries are only those front-line heroes, the pioneers, who push the first paths through territories which are impassable and impossible.

This is a very narrow mentality. *Mission* comes from a Latin verb meaning *to send*. This concept served to express the most marvelous and most divine reality which ever happened in our world. Jesus Christ was announced as "the one sent" by the Father. The Church is the continuation and the fulfillment of Christ: "As the Father has sent Me, so also I send you," He declared to His Apostles as He bestowed upon them their supreme mandate to go out to all the peoples of the earth to convert them to Himself and to evangelize them, that is to say, to announce to them the Good News, the glorious announcement of the Redemption. Carrying out this divine mandate, the Church must be always on the march, in a state of siege, a state of *mission*. All its members must be missionaries, not only those on the front line or those doing service under a particular flag. All Christians must be the leaven mysteriously at work in the world. This function cannot be restricted only to the hierarchy. On this vital point also the Second Vatican Council is clarifying many unprecise and actually erroneous ideas. All of us are "the Church."

The schema *De Ecclesia* which was discussed so thoroughly in this Second Session had been revised on this point also and it laid great stress on the position of the faithful in intimate union with the mystery of the Church and the pastoral ministry of the Bishops. This emphasis produced a marvelous vision of the Church, corresponding to the biblical concept of the Chosen People, the people consecrated to God, as opposed to profane peoples.

"The Church is a People, not a Mass"

Baptism is not merely a blessing, but an authentic consecration of the individual. According to the theology of the sacramental character, the indelible seal of Baptism makes us acceptable to God, because it shows us to be brethren of Jesus Christ, His Son, and sanctifies us. By the grace of the Son of God Himself we participate in His own dignity and are able to perform most noble and holy functions. This doctrine is not well-known, but it is basic if we are to have an exact concept of the Christian's dignity. Prescinding from any eventual discussion of the extension of the Mystical Body, all those baptized are united to Christ in a most personal manner through a kind of hypostatic union, and they constitute a living organism in which there can be nothing passive. To use the striking expression of Pius XII, the Church is a people, not a mass.

The invitation of recent Popes to all the faithful to collaborate vitally in the mission of the Church marks one further step towards re-structuring and re-evaluating the role of the laity. In the language proper to social problems, it might be said that the faithful have been made profit-sharers and have been urged to realize that they also have a share in ownership. The profound truth is that, as Saint Paul puts it, all the faithful are called to "build up the body of Christ." In such terms we can measure the difference between saying that an individual begins to share in profits and saying that he begins to be a vital part of a body. The difference is basically in life.

It would lead too far afield to offer a panoramic view of this unfortunate split, of that movement towards "flight from the world" which has given rise to a regrettable confusion and the identification of the world of evil with the Christian world. Since the end of the last century there has been evident a growing movement of return which has recently developed into a trend of irresistible renewal. Vatican II opened just in time and intends to make a definitive contribution to this awakening of the Christian world, leaving aside the pessimistic concepts of the past. There can be no identification of the biblical concept of the "world" with the geographical and demographic framework of what is found outside religious houses and churches. Christ did not wish to pray for "the world"—identified with evil, but not with the vital space in which we live—and on the other hand He prayed His Father fervently for all those who would believe in Him throughout the centuries. Hence these two terms cannot be confused. The early Church offers the spectacle of a community profoundly united, whose members—Apostles and disciples—each one in his own position, without clear-cut juridical distinctions, "had one heart and one soul." The bonds uniting the members of the Church are like family bonds. It is meaningful that the Christian message has as its distinctive mark the revelation of divine fatherhood shared in by those who live in the Church. It is a share in fatherhood, not in power. We may be sick sons, even prodigal sons, but we are always sons, not servants.

The layman is an authentic member of the People of God. The layman also has his own priestly mission, which consists in the sanctification of the world from within, starting out with the integral consecration of his own person. He has also a mission of expansion, which is that of the good leaven. Each one of the faithful is a living witness to the necessary co-ordination between religious interests and those which are profane, without confusing the two, and without even clearly separating one from the other. In one of his letters Saint Peter speaks of "the kingly priesthood" of all the faithful. "All the members of the Church," declared Cardinal Ritter in the Council, "absolutely all, and not only the hierarchy, have the right and the duty to preserve, save, defend, propagate, and even, at least in a certain measure, to interpret the deposit of the Faith. This right comes to them not by special indult, but by Baptism."

For the first time in the history of Councils, representatives of the laity were present in the Council Hall.
Halfway through the First Session, acting on the suggestion
made by the then Cardinal Montini, John XXIII had
authorized Jean Guitton, member of the French Academy,
to be present as a special Auditor. Paul VI extended this
privilege to thirteen other laymen representing the millions
of the faithful who make up the body of Christians. It is
the mission of the hierarchy to guide and direct the faithful, to co-ordinate them, not merely to drag them along like
trailers.

These few observations can be appropriately concluded
with the words pronounced by Pope Paul VI on September 1, 1963, in the nearby cathedral of Frascati: "...Today,
the hierarchy itself is calling upon the laity for collaboration. The hierarchy is no longer exclusive or jealous—in
reality it never was—but its plea is really impressive.
'Come with us,' the hierarchy calls out, 'let us try to work
together: let us see how we can arouse harmony of ideals
and programs, in order to distribute the work to be done.'
The hierarchy itself wants the laity at its side as a co-
worker. It summons all and reminds all that this is the
hour, yes, this is the hour of the layman."

A Schema Which Took Courage

On November 18th, in its 69th General Congregation,
the Council took up the sensitive theme of ecumenism,
undoubtedly the topic most eagerly awaited by those following the progress of the Council from the outside. This
does not mean that the theme does not have its own profound importance but, because of its ramifications and its
transcendence, it is likewise within the reach of the man
in the street. In fact, now that efforts are being made to

find a new organic structure for the Church, anyone who is not interested in these problems and does not live them, will have a hard time understanding eventual changes.

On the contrary, ecumenism has penetrated today into all circles, because everywhere it is felt that this is a question of world-wide importance. Everyone understands unity without difficulty; it is like a gilt-edged stock. The Council Fathers understood this truth and several of them proclaimed it in the Council Hall. Bishop Elchinger, Co-adjutor of Strasbourg, expressed himself as follows: "The decree on ecumenism can be regarded as a grace. Concern for ecumenism should be for pastors and for the faithful of the Catholic Church a real duty in conscience. Sincere ecumenism inevitably calls for a change in mentality among many Catholics. We must not be afraid of the truth and we must be disposed to accept it even when it hurts. God does not need our weakness in order to defend the truth. To be afraid of understanding the truth means failing in trust in the Holy Spirit. Besides, we must free ourselves from all preconceived underrating of the religious positions of non-Catholics and we must recognize honestly the treasures of truth which they also possess. Bearing in mind the teaching of Saint Paul on the diversity of gifts in the same Holy Spirit, we must avoid confusing unity and uniformity. Ecumenism does not mean compromise on dogmas or rejecting the rules of pastoral prudence, but neither does it mean demanding of our separated brethren that they get in step with us."

Cardinal Frings began one of his discourses in the Council Hall with the following words: "The Council has aroused in the entire world, especially in regard to ecumenism, an atmosphere of great expectation." Cardinal Silva Enriques emphasized the special importance of the ecumenical argument, drawing attention to the fact that it is a symptom of our times, and stating that any efforts not in keeping with ecumenism are out of date. Later Paul VI used very significant words, words which were strong, peremptory, and unequivocal: "It is by this time clear to everyone that we cannot evade the problem of unity. Today this desire of Christ is pressing upon our minds and obliges us to do with wisdom and love everything possible to bring to all Christians the immense benefit and high dignity of sharing in the unity of the Church."

The schema treating of this theme at first comprised four chapters. Later a further chapter was added, between chapters 3 and 4. The first chapter sets forth the general principles of ecumenism. The second treats of the practice of ecumenism. The third, divided into two parts, examines in detail the relationships between the Catholic Church and the Oriental Churches and the other Christian communities which arose after the Reformation. The fourth chapter studies the special situation of the Jewish people and, lastly, chapter 5 takes up the problem of religious liberty.

After approving the schema as a whole—this approval did not include the two special chapters above mentioned—and thus accepting it as a basis for fruitful discussion, the Fathers examined and discussed the first three chapters. One of the trends favorable to the schema was expressed by Bishop Flores, of Barbastro, Spain: "It can be said that this schema is opening up an era of Catholic ecumenism, concerned not with the condemnation of error, but with the calm and secure explanation of doctrine, in order to promote unity, the "ut unum sint" willed by Christ. . . . This dialogue must be undertaken fearlessly, with a clear and objective explanation of our teachings, without holding anything back, while emphasizing the elements which unite us and seeking out a solution for those which divide us." An Argentinian prelate, Archbishop Juan Carlos Aramburu, Archbishop of Tucumàn, declared that "ecumenism must not be treated as a simple problem, but elevated to the dignity and nobility of a mystery." "Unity," concluded the Maronite Archbishop Ignace Ziadé, "must be achieved without the suppression of legitimate differences. History teaches us that divisions arose whenever an attempt was made to eliminate all diversity."

The basic norm of all ecumenism is found in the phrase of Saint Paul: *"Veritatem facientes in caritate,"* which means "setting forth the truth with charity." The only problem is determining the starting-point. Some would want first of all to present in a block all those truths which are unchanging. Others want to begin with charity: "Here you are on the right track," emphasized the Chilean Cardinal Silva Enriques, "because love creates union." We must begin with the fact that we cannot walk away from this magnificent opportunity which God has provided for our age. Hence, the question is to pose the problem practically in such a way as to assure the best results.

Some Council Fathers felt strongly that the schema was defective in its treatment of the Primacy: "The Holy Roman See must not only preside in charity, but also in authority," declared Cardinal Bacci. There was criticism also of the fact that the text speaks of our separated brethren "not in perfect communion with the Catholic Church." The objection was raised that "by the very fact that they are outside the Church, there can be no discussion of perfect communion or of imperfect communion."

Other Fathers recognized that in the Christian communities which arose out of the Reformation, and with still greater reason in those of the Orient, there are sufficient elements to justify calling them churches, following the oft-repeated maxim: "Concentrate more on what unites us—Baptism, the priesthood, the Eucharist—than on what divides us."

In this connection several of the Fathers stressed that the best means of achieving union is common prayer: "Common prayer is a manifestation of faith in one Christ. Frequently Catholics and Orthodox live in the same family or at least in the same locality and the prohibition against common prayer is offensive and gives scandal to our separated brethren. Non-Christians cannot conceal their wonderment. How is it possible to recommend union and collaboration in the solution of social and labor problems, if we are forbidden to take part in sacred ceremonies, without prejudice of course to divine law and the danger of scandal or indifferentism?" This position was expressed by Father Hilary Capucci, Superior General of the Order of Saint Basil the Great. His attitude was shared by many others, among whom were Monsignor Jean Webber, Prefect Apostolic of Parakou, Dahomey, and the Bishop of Thebes, Egypt. There was special stress on the question of the validity of marriages celebrated before an Orthodox priest.

"Willy-nilly, They Are Our Brothers"

Bishop Edward Mason, Vicar Apostolic of El Obeid, Sudan, asked for at least the joint celebration of feasts like Christmas and Easter. This would be an excellent means of initiating the long-desired dialogue. Basically, since we are all convinced that the Church "by its inmost nature is on the way towards unity," as was stated by the Archbishop of Saragossa, one of the under-Secretaries of the Council, since promoted to the new Archbishopric of Madrid, "the real point at issue is the method or, rather, the methodology for establishing this dialogue."

In the history of the Church one may find several methods of treating with those outside the fold, but they may all be reduced to two. The first approach is "hard," while the second is "mild but forceful." A predominantly apologetical rigidity had found expression, for example, in Saint Irenaeus and in Tertullian. The second method, which is more approachable, characterizes Saint Augustine. In his controversies with the Donatists and the Pelagians, the Bishop of Hippo stands out as a genuine "master of dialogue." In either method logic rules out all irenicism or compromise. But care must be taken to clear away all bias, to review and correct certain historical "versions" which are unduly tendentious or one-sided.

In this connection a very significant speech was delivered by Bishop Stephen Leven, Auxiliary of the Archbishop of San Antonio, Texas: "These discussions point up the necessity of having dialogue not with our separated brethren but also among the Bishops themselves. Many Fathers have insisted too much on the Scripture text of the foundation of the Church on Peter, as though this were the only important passage in Sacred Scripture. They speak as though John XXIII had never quoted Saint Augustine: 'Willy-nilly, they are our brothers.' They speak as though recognizing the charisms of the Holy Spirit in others were a denial of the Faith. They look upon non-Catholics, whom perhaps they have never seen, as children in a catechism class. Those prelates who are promoting ecumenism are not disobeying the Pope. God wills union. Those who are not against us are for us. Let us make an end of name-calling and let us lend a hand to the providential movement towards that unity for which Christ prayed." The Auxiliary Bishop of Bordeaux concluded: "Remaining passive in the presence of the ecumenical movement or, which would be still worse, opposing it, would be a sin against the Holy Spirit."

There is no doubt that if the unity of Christians were achieved, there would be a tremendous increase in the moral force of the Gospel and its leavening power throughout the entire world would reach undreamed-of limits, not only in the religious field, but likewise on the international level, in political and social fields. "The grave and urgent problems of our times," declared Bishop Guano, of Livorno, Italy, "such as the problem of daily bread for everyone, of religious liberty, social justice, human dignity and peace, could be solved more easily if all Christians were united with all men of good will. Many also look to the Church with sentiments of hope which it would be dangerous to disappoint."

Why should not the Church begin right at this point, lining up with those colossal undertakings which are today so necessary and urgent, such as the war on misery and hunger, illiteracy, and other similar evils. This was the thought suggested by many African Bishops.

On the other hand, attention was called to the genuine dangers which can arise from this constant exchange of ideas and association between Catholics and non-Catholics. Cardinal Bea, himself, President of the Secretariate for Christian Unity, had this to say: "The term 'ecumenism' might perhaps be changed to something else less equivocal. In the hands of persons who are imprudent and not well prepared, the ecumenical movement can encourage religious or inter-confessional indifferentism. It is the duty of the diocesan Ordinaries to supervise the doctrinal preparation and the prudence of those active in this movement. The Directory to be prepared on this topic must make allowances for the innumerable differences between countries. This is why the implementation of this Directory will always be the responsibility of the local Bishop. Only in this way will we avoid the dangers of false ecumenism, that is to say, an ecumenism which will not stop short even of doctrinal compromise in order to reach union. . . . Non-Catholics want to know the true Catholic doctrine, not doctrinal formulae which have been watered down for their benefit. Nothing is farther from true ecumenism than false irenicism." Cardinal Frings made the same observations, with reference to such concrete cases as teaching in Catholic schools, Catholic education, mixed marriages, and others.

Today's new impetus to biblical studies takes us back, in some sense, to the early days of Christianity and shows us that, side by side with the articles of Faith, as was stated textually by a Bishop from Poland, we have a multitude of theologians, schools of thought, customs, opinions, and traditions, which, no matter how venerable they may be, are not immutable.

The fact that the movement towards unity is set in a framework of charity and the rejection of centuries-old prejudices is a stimulus to a greater and deeper instruction, not merely in relation to others, but likewise in the whole sphere of Christianity. To cite an example, we must have a better knowledge of traditions and the liturgies of the Oriental Churches, and must appreciate the difficulties encountered by non-Catholics in accepting our teachings: "The aspects of Catholicism which are most difficult for our separated brethren, according to the testimony of several converts," declared Abbot Benedict Reetz, O.S.B., Superior General of the Benedictine Congregation of Beuron, "are a complex and sometimes acrobatic theology, an undue accentuation of Scholasticism, an exaggerated juridical sense which makes one fear for the liberty of the faithful, certain new forms of Marian devotion, and excessive facility in granting indulgences. In the light of our experience along these lines, the things which attract them are our Catholic liturgy, so severe and solemn especially in its chant, the monastic life, priestly celibacy, Confession as a source of interior peace, and very particularly the magnificent unity of the Church in its languages, rites, discipline, the exercise of Faith, the Eucharistic Sacrifice, and the authority of its Bishops around Peter."

Ecumenism tends to sweep out over the entire world. The growing number of lapses from the Faith and the tendency to indifferentism, especially in countries which have reached a high degree of economic progress, or among large numbers of emigrants, raises a very difficult and burning problem. It is the task of authentic ecumenism to bring back these prodigal sons to the Father's house and, besides being a duty and a most urgent concern of the Bishops, it is, for each in his own way, the duty of all the faithful. Union depends exclusively on the good will of all Christians. "Christ did not give to His Church," declared the Auxiliary Bishop of Valencia, "a special gift to do away with divisions, but the commandment of charity and union. Division implies fault, and we must recognize that on both sides there has been and is some fault."

The Jews Are Neither
Perfidious Nor Deicides

In the 63rd General Congregation, on November 8th, a new chapter was added to the schema on ecumenism. This marked a gigantic step in the open-door policy encouraged by the Second Vatican Council. In his opening discourse, Paul VI had stated that the Church intended to busy herself also with non-Christians, with all men having some sense of religion.

The first outline of a genuinely universal dialogue is sketched in the chapter on the Jewish people, which epitomizes the stand of the Christian in regard to that people in whose history Christianity finds its own roots. The basic theme of the document presented to the Fathers—it is really an outline of a chapter rather than a definitive chapter—is this: "The part played by the Hebrew leaders contemporary with Christ in bringing about the crucifixion includes the responsibility of the entire human race. In addition, the personal sin of the Jewish leaders cannot be attributed to the Jewish people as a whole, neither then nor today. Consequently it is unjust to speak of the entire Jewish people as 'deicide' or 'cursed by God.' "

The document is based on truths known to all but not always applied in practice. Saint Paul states clearly that Christ "delivered Himself and died to expiate the faults of all men." Consequently no one can be exempt from responsibility for the tragedy of Golgotha. This same Saint Paul, with explicit reference to the Jews, notes: "God has not rejected his chosen people." Hence it is evident that we cannot open an unbridgeable gap between the Church and the chosen people of the Old Testament. The roots of Christianity are Jewish. The Apostles were Jews, the first Christians on Pentecost morning were largely Jews, the Blessed Virgin was a Jewess, Jesus Christ Himself, as man, was a Jew. The New Testament is the continuation and the crowning of the Old: "The Church" declares the Council schema, "can never forget that its roots reach down into the Covenant of God with Abraham and his descendants. The plan of salvation culminates in the coming of Jesus Christ, Son of David and offspring of Abraham according to the flesh. The divine call, at one time directed to the Chosen People, is now, through Christ, extended through the Church to the entire world."

Apart from such considerations, the document draws its inspiration directly from the will of Pope John XXIII who "with respect and universal love" had deleted from one of the most solemn prayers of the Good Friday liturgy the expression "perfidious" Jews, with which the priest, perhaps with an excess of charitable understanding, invited the faithful to pray for those very ones who had crucified Christ.

The significance of the document comes exclusively from the universal charity of John XXIII. It absolutely cannot and must not be given political implications. This document is not a *mea culpa* of the Church for the furies of anti-Semitism. No accusations of this kind can be lodged against the Church. On the contrary, even in recent history, both Pius XII and other outstanding ecclesiastics, among whom the then Cardinal Roncalli, gained particular distinction for their charitable activities in alleviating the sufferings of persecuted Jews. The Council's motive in taking up this study was mainly doctrinal. The biblical passages which voice condemnation of the Jews, and especially the account of the crucifixion of Christ, should not give rise to contempt, hatred or persecution against the Jews as such, but must give food for serious meditation on the share all of us have had in the death of Christ. The history of the Chosen People is in some way our own.

Many of the Fathers were opposed to inserting this fourth chapter in the schema on ecumenism. It was not that they rejected the comments on our relationships with the Jews, but they felt that the presence of this chapter at that particular point would interfere with the unity of the discussion. Many others felt that the chapter would be better situated in the schema on "The Presence of the Church in the World." The chapter on the Jews prompted a flood of suggestions that there should be discussion also of other religions such as Islamism, Shintoism, Buddhism and so forth. The Bishops acquainted with these religions from their contacts with them in their respective countries described their own personal efforts to establish' dialogue with the faithful and the leaders of these religions in which, as is increasingly clear, people are recognizing new points of contact with Christianity, a sense of common values, and positive efficacious aspects. Efforts along these lines are numerous and consoling. There is an extraordinary atmosphere of search after anything which can unite, almost a kind of magnetism in the ideal of unity.

THE PILGRIM POPE

This was the most decisive and most far-reaching step towards unity in the flock of Christ in nine centuries of separation. The following pages were written under the emotion of that icy Roman morning of January 4, 1964, when for the first time in history a Pope boarded an airliner and, likewise for the first time in history, the same Pope started on a pilgrimage to that blessed land which was the geographical setting for the drama of our redemption. This emotion made it difficult to maintain clear perspective and, in the recounting of such an extraordinary event, made it hard to distinguish between mere news and history. But perhaps in an event of this kind the distinction between news and history does not exist, because the news of Paul VI's pilgrimage to the Holy Land rose to the heights of real history even before it took place.

In the closing discourse of the Second Session of the Council, Paul VI had expressed his satisfaction with the work accomplished. His Allocution had to all appearances been concluded and was complete. The Fathers who had followed the translation in copies provided by the Council Press Office were putting the pages back in order and getting ready for the final blessing. Still, the Pope continued to read and started on a new section which had not appeared in any translation.

Everyone listened attentively: "And now allow Us a last word, to inform you of a project which has for some time been maturing in Our mind and which We have decided to announce today in the presence of such an elect and significant assembly. So convinced are We that prayers and good works are necessary for the final happy conclusion of this Council that, after careful deliberation and much prayer, We have decided to make a prilgrimage Ourselves to the land of Jesus Our Lord. In fact, with God's help, We intend to go to Palestine in January, to honor personally in the Holy Places where Christ was born, lived, died, and ascended to heaven after His Resurrection, the first mysteries of our Faith: the Incarnation, and the Redemption."

The moving commentary on these words which appeared in an outstanding weekly can spare us a task whose results would perhaps not be quite so brilliant: "One part of the audience caught on immediately, but did not applaud at once. Surprise brought to their lips first of all a collective 'Ah!' followed by applause and great excitement in the benches, while the Basilica resounded with a long ovation. 'Long live the Orient!' cried out a young Auxiliary of the Patriarch of Antioch. A Bishop near him, who had not at first grasped the significance of the Pope's announcement and who found himself being hugged enthusiastically by his brother Bishop, continued to ask: 'But what has happened?' *Palestinam petit, Palestinam petit!'* repeated the Bishop from Antioch. Then the other Bishop also understood, returned the embrace of his neighbor as his mitre

91

fell off his head, and applause continued. Pope Paul, looking out over his glasses, beheld with a tired smile the joy
of the Cardinals, Patriarchs, Bishops and Abbots, and the
festive re-action of Anglicans, Lutherans, and Orthodox, as
well as the amazement which was spreading through the
rows of the invited guests in formal dress."

Then, as though he were already experiencing the deep
joy of beholding the land where Our Lord was born, lived
and died, the Pope continued: "We shall see that blessed
land whence Peter set forth and whither not one of his
successors has returned. Most humbly and most rapidly
We shall return there as an expression of prayer, penance,
and renovation, to offer to Christ His own Church, to summon to this one holy Church Our separated brethren, to
implore the divine mercy for peace among men. . . "

All these reasons belonged exclusively to the spiritual
order, in view of the great goal of the Council, which in
the second interim period of nine months, would be called
upon to carry on intensively the work it had set for itself
and to take key important decisions on the general theme
of the Church. In this connection, the mind recalls instinctively the triumphal journey, undertaken for exactly the
same purposes, by John XXIII to Loreto and Assisi. This
similarity is another expression of the continuity of one
same policy in the two pontificates, a line which is always
going farther and receiving new impetus, with holy audacity and enthusiasm.

In fact, all the first commentators spoke of audacity and
enthusiasm, after the press agencies, the teletypes, the radio,
and television had flashed this sensational announcement to
the entire world. Up until that day there had not been the
slightest indiscretion to give grounds for suspecting any
decision of this kind. Only the radio and television an-
nouncers broadcasting the closing ceremony directly from
the Basilica, as well as the Press Officers for the different
languages, had learned of this historic plan a little ahead

of time, so as to be ready to make the formal announcement to the world at the precise moment determined by the Holy Father.

Not even the Oriental Bishops had been informed of the Pope's plan. The Latin Patriarch of Jerusalem, Archbishop Alberto Gori, was one of the first ones out of the Basilica as soon as the ceremony was over, and hurried to give the news personally to his fellow religious in the Holy Land Delegation in Rome. On his arrival, he learned that the news had already reached the monastery. He later recalled, however, that in an audience not so long before, Paul VI had asked him numerous questions on the situation of the 47,000 Latin Catholics in Jerusalem. Now, the purpose of the queries was clear!

The Greek Catholic Bishop of Galilee also then saw the full significance of a remark made to him during the First Session of the Council by the then Cardinal-Archbishop of Milan, who had said to him: "The dream of my life is to visit the Holy Land!" Bishop Hakim had replied happily and with a knowing smile. "Fine! Perhaps it will be all the better when you are Pope!"

But all this was hindsight because in reality, although arrangements for such a trip are anything but easy, all plans had been studied with great prudence and perfect secrecy, without even an inkling of what was under way. Accustomed as they were to the years of John XXIII, who had the habit of telling people in all simplicity about his plans, the so-called "Vaticanists" had not suspected anything in a single detail of ordinary Vatican routine. No suspicions had been aroused by special audiences or unexpected announcements. Around mid-November, the Egyptian press spoke of a secret Vatican mission to Tel Aviv "to prepare the way for the recognition of Israel by the Holy See." At the beginning of November the Chargé d'Affaires of Israel to the Italian government had called on the Pope. No one had even noticed the absence of the Pope's private secretary, Don Pasquale Macchi, or that of a French prelate of the Secretariate of State, Monsignor Jacques Martin, an expert Orientalist. These two individuals had really gone to Tel Aviv on a secret mission, though it was not exactly the one indicated by the Egyptian newspapers. After the announcement of the Pope's intended pilgrimage, the above details were recalled and acquired special significance. But before the announcement no one had succeeded in piecing together all these scattered details.

By the irony of fate, or perhaps by an unfathomable mystery, the land where walked the one and only Prince of Peace has for many years been an inferno of fierce political passions, which could at almost any time explode into war in that boiling cauldron which is the Middle East. Within the recollection of this generation, that is to say, since the end of World War II, Palestine has been the scene of bitter hostility between Jews and Arabs. The result of this antagonism is the actual unsteady political situation, based on an artificial division of territory and a lack of security which creates difficulties for pilgrims going to the Holy Places.

John XXIII had visited Palestine while Apostolic Delegate in Turkey. With his customary nonchalance he recounted that he "had been escorted by English soldiers up to the residence of the Apostolic Delegate in Jerusalem," who was the now Cardinal Gustavo Testa. The frontier between Jordan and Israel is normally closed, and it is only at a time of great throngs of pilgrims, such as Christmas and Easter, that passage from one State to the other is assured with a certain facility. The Holy Places themselves are politically divided. Bethlehem and the Holy Sepulcher are in Jordan, while Nazareth, Cana, the Lake of Tiberias, Capharnuum, and the Cenacle are on Israeli territory. From the very beginning of Arab-Jewish hostilities, the Holy See favored internationalizing those lands, principally the city of Jerusalem, which is today split into two zones.

Hence, it was logical that the plans for the Pope's trip should have been made with great secrecy, so as not to arouse unfavorable reactions. On September 20, 1963,

Paul VI wrote to the Cardinal Secretary of State, Cardinal Amleto Giovanni Cicognani, a letter which was published only at the beginning of January, 1964, asking His Eminence to see to it that the pilgrimage was studied in all its details, with precise timetables and itineraries.

Likewise, the motives impelling the Pope to such an exceptional journey had to be stated very clearly. The Pope listed them in the same discourse which announced his pilgrimage to Palestine, and he seized every occasion to repeat them. In his Christmas Message, after wishing for all men in the light of Christmas "bread, progress and peace," he stated clearly: "We repeat again that Our pilgrimage is motivated exclusively by religious aims and aspects. Ours will be the journey of the confession of Peter. We want to express in Our own faith all the faith of the Church and We want to affirm to Christ, as Peter did at Caesarea-Philippi: 'Yes, Lord, You are the Christ, Son of the living God.' It will be a journey of offering. For like the Magi from the Orient, the figurative precursors of all the peoples of the earth, so We also, coming from the West, wish to take to Christ the offering of His Church, to recognize in Him her Founder, her Teacher, her Lord and her Savior.

"This will also be a journey of search and hope, the search after all those who are Our sons and brothers in Christ. In the very center of the Gospel scenes as provided by that blessed land, We cannot fail to ask Ourselves: 'Where is the integrity of the flock of Christ? Where are the lambs and the sheep of His fold? Are they all here? And those who are missing?' We cannot fail, consequently, to beseech Jesus the Good Shepherd and with His very own words, that there may be but one fold and one shepherd.

"Our heart shall reach out also beyond the fold of Christ and We shall have kindly and noble thoughts for every nation on the earth, for those near and those far, with feelings of reverence and love, and with hope for all good things and for peace. All those whom We shall meet along our path, of whatever race, especially those in authority, and peoples, pilgrims and tourists, We shall greet them respectfully and cordially, but without slowing Our hasty steps and without distraction from the uniquely religious scope of Our journey.

"Hence it will be a journey of prayer, carried out in humility and love. The whole world will be in Our heart and no one will be forgotten.

"Asking pardon of Our Lord, of Him who shows mercy for Our every failing and for every weakness, We shall have the courage to invoke mercy, peace and salvation for everyone."

After this discourse, no other purpose could possibly be attributed to the Pope's pilgrimage. Nevertheless, it was not long before someone summed up the Pope's three days in the Holy Land by saying that Paul VI had gone to "take incense, myrrh, and politics," alluding to fantastic compromises which no one in his right mind could have thought up. Such writers resembled an individual who is unwilling to look out the window to admire the panorama, and consequently simply peers through a hole through which he sees everything deformed.

The style of this Christmas Message is as clear as the noonday sun. Nevertheless, it can be usefully complemented by the discourse in which Paul VI replied to the Christmas greetings of the Cardinals on the morning of December 24th:

"We must, Venerable Brothers and Beloved Sons, bring the great Ecumenical Council to a happy conclusion, just as it has just happily concluded its Second Session. This final phase of Our Universal Synod strikes us as being the most difficult, as also the most important. Thus, while We thank you sincerely for your generous efforts in the two Sessions already held, We urge you to still greater efforts for the Third Session, which under many aspects will be grave and decisive. . .

"In order that the great purposes of the Council may be achieved, We shall be leaving in just a few days in humble and rapid pilgrimage to the land of Jesus, Palestine, the country which was the scene of Bible history, the land of the Patriarchs, the Prophets, the Apostles, and of Our Lord Himself, as if to draw from the very roots the certainty and the strength of which the Church feels profound need in its great epiphany of unending vitality amidst the conflicts and the needs of the world in her regard. We shall set out in joyous and awesome wonderment at being the first Pope to go back over the path which Peter the Apostle was the first to walk, and which led him to set up in Rome and to seal with his blood his firm and unshaking testimony of Faith.

"What is this journey? A tourist excursion? A political ruse? An escape from the duties which require Our presence and bind Us here? No. If this were the case, We would fear that from Our very first steps there should befall Us what one day—whether it is historical or not, it is certainly symbolic—happened to Peter. In his famous discourse against Auxentius, Saint Ambrose recounts that the Apostle Peter was in grave danger in Rome at the beginning of the first persecution. The saint continues: 'Generous Christian souls begged him to go away for a while. Although he was anxious to face death, nevertheless, out of deference for the pleas of the people, he yielded. He was being asked in fact to save himself so that he might be available later to instruct and strengthen his Christian community. But what happened? One night, he set out on his way outside the walls, but near the city gate he soon saw Christ coming to meet him. He asked: *'Domine, quo vadis?* Lord, where are You going?'* Christ answered him: *'Venio iterum crucifigi.* I am coming to be crucified again for you.' Peter then understood that this divine answer referred to his own cross, and without a moment's hesitation he turned around and retraced his steps.

"We shall go to Him, and We shall ask of Him pardon for all Our weaknesses. We shall tell Him of that Faith which the Father inspires within Us and makes invincible, and We shall express to Him Our humble and entire love: '*Tu scis quia amo Te*. You know that I love You.' We shall offer Him His Church, the one built on the rock chosen by Him and made firm as the foundation of His mysterious edifice. We shall beg of Him to give Us the great favor to welcome there all our brothers in Christ, including those who are perhaps on the threshold, as well as all nations and those far removed from Us, for the perfect unity of His same Church and for Our peace."

Pope Paul VI and the "Jet Church"

Rumors had been circulating about possible trips by the Holy Father, but no one was expecting a journey of the Pope to the Holy Land. As the Pope remarked himself, this would be the first time that a Successor of Peter would return to the land which had beheld within its confines the unfolding of the unspeakable mysteries of the human-divine existence of Jesus Christ. It was likewise the first time that a modern Pope would go beyond the limits of the Italian peninsula. The last instance had been that of Pius VII going to Paris to crown Napoleon who, in 1809, a few years later, repaid this act of courtesy by making the Pope his prisoner!

Times have changed completely. Paul VI could go out of his "little Vatican kingdom" by his own choice, cross the borders of Italy, fly over the Mediterranean and reach the Holy Places, not to crown a king-emperor, but to beg of the King of Kings the great Christian renewal which the entire world is expecting from the Second Vatican Council.

What John XXIII once said of himself was already beginning to come true: "I am ready to cross not only the little Lake of Galilee, but all the seas of the world." This phrase, in a certain sense, could be taken literally. Peter made the first crossing from Jerusalem to Rome. Paul traveled the vast reaches of the Roman empire. The Apostles spread over the world of the known earth. After thus setting a precedent through his pilgrimage in Palestine, Paul VI may perhaps follow these examples. The only difference will be in the means of transportation. Peter's barque has been replaced by a powerful DC-8, literal devourer of space and distance, which can streak from Rome to Amman in less than two hundred minutes of flying time.

When the Pope's trip was first announced, it was taken for granted that it would be by plane, since he had spoken of a "most rapid" pilgrimage. Twelve days later, on December 17th, *L'Osservatore Romano* announced January 4th to January 6th as the period for the journey, while the Alitalia airline began to get one of its spacious airliners ready to welcome the pilgrim Pope and his party.

Not so many years ago, when the Pope went walking in the Vatican gardens, even access to the dome of Saint Peter's was barred, since it afforded a vantage-point for viewing practically all the nooks and corners of the gardens. John XXIII did away with this ruling: "But why should my faithful not be allowed to see me! There is nothing scandalous about me!" Neither is it strange that the Pope should leave the Vatican. No one should be surprised that he should want to travel by train. Paul VI ventured further than mere trains and went in one stretch to the very well-springs of Christianity. A pilgrimage to Jerusalem is practically a duty, or at least a very common and logical gesture for all Orthodox Patriarchs, Anglican Primates, and certain other outstanding personages of the Christian world. Why should the Pope be the only one unable to visit that land whence all things radiate and towards which all things converge? As a matter of fact, there is no question of going to an unknown destination or to some unexplored region, but rather of a "return." "We shall return" Paul VI had said, because it was from there that Peter had set out.

Archbishop Alfonso Carinci, the oldest of the Council Fathers, died at the age of 101 on December 7, 1963, after almost eighty years in the priesthood. During those years it had been his constant dream that he would one day see a Pope go to the Holy Land. Just before his death, he learned of the decision of Paul VI, which thus came as the crowning of his long and heartfelt wait. Eighty years of prayer and almost twenty-five thousand Masses to obtain the grace of the three hours of flight time from Rome to Palestine!

A *Voice Echoing Over the Whole Earth*

The enthusiasm of the Council Fathers over the announcement of the Pope's Holy Land pilgrimage spread out through the whole world. Newspapers splashed headlines across entire front pages. "Peter came; Paul returns" wrote an English daily. Favorable comment poured in from all countries. The governments of Israel and Jordan informed the Vatican immediately that this unusual guest would be received with all honors. King Hussein sent an olive branch from Gethsemane, which was presented to the Holy Father on the feast of the Immaculate Conception, during his traditional visit to the statue of the Immaculate Conception in Piazza di Spagna.

The Secretary of the United Nations, U Thant, offered full cooperation in facilitating the Holy Father's pilgrimage and termed the journey "a historic event." Non-Catholic Christian centers, whether Orthodox, Anglican, or Protestant, echoed this same enthusiasm. The significance attributed to the papal journey saw in it a courageous gesture on behalf of world peace and Christian unity. These two highlights had been expressly pointed out by Paul VI himself.

All the world comments on ecumenism were intended to prepare the way for the most impressive gesture towards unity which has yet been made. The Holy Father's pilgrimage to the Holy Land brought the world face to face with the fact of ecumenism. This fact is almost universally welcomed, notwithstanding efforts in certain quarters to fan the fires of long-standing antipathies by quibbling over the fact that instead of proposing that Rome and Orthodoxy should meet together, Paul VI had merely issued an invitation to them to come to him. The Pope's answer was dramatic. He went to meet the Patriarch of the East in Jerusalem. To that very spot, to the city which had witnessed the death and resurrection of Christ, Paul VI and Patriarch Athenagoras would journey toward a memorable meeting which has placed a question mark overflowing with hope on almost a thousand years of history.

The initiative for this meeting came from Paul VI. The mild Patriarch Athenagoras stated: "For me, my meeting at Jerusalem with the Pope was more than just the realization of a fact or of a dream coming true. Just two months ago, who would ever had thought this possible? It is from His Holiness the Pope that the idea of our meeting at Jerusalem first came. Otherwise, we would probably have met in Rome, but this meeting in Jerusalem, the center of Christianity, was entirely unexpected."

"After Centuries of Silence . . ."

The first feelers for this historical meeting were put out at an early date. On December 9, 1963, Father Pierre Duprey, of the Council Secretariate for Christian Unity, went to Constantinople with a letter for Patriarch Athenagoras. The Patriarch later let it be known that he was very ready to meet with the Pope. There then followed weeks of doubt and uncertainty until, on December 28th, Metropolitan Athenagoras of Thyatira, Greek Orthodox Archbishop of Great Britain, arrived in Rome as an official representative of His Holiness Patriarch Athenagoras and of the Holy Synod of the Orthodox Church of Constantinople. That same day he was received by Pope Paul VI. Just the

fact of this visit was in itself a gigantic step forward, because it represented the first official contact between Rome
and Constantinople since 1439. Other prelates had visited
John XXIII and Paul VI, but these visits had never been
official. Metropolitan Athenagoras spent close to two hours
in the Vatican, some thirty minutes being devoted to his
audience with the Pope.

"I am happy, extremely happy," he declared to a reporter after the visit. "This really was an historic hour." He
took out of the pocket of his flowing black robe a white
case bearing in gold the coat of arms of Pope Paul VI. He
opened it and showed the Pope's gift to him, namely a
large silver medal struck for the opening of the Second
Session of the Council. It bore on the face the profile of
Pope Paul VI, wearing his modern tiara, and a door opened
on the fire of Pentecost burning in the background. This
was the side of the medal which the Metropolitan admired
at length. "Was there a gift also for the Patriarch of Constantinople?" The Metropolitan smiled, his small blue eyes
sparkled over his gold-rimmed glasses, and he rapidly
stroked his well-trimmed grey beard. "It seems to me," he
remarked, "that it would hardly be necessary for me to
take gifts to the Patriarch. Would it not be more simple
if those gifts were presented to him directly?"

In his discourse at the beginning of his audience with
the Pope, Metropolitan Athenagoras had recalled that he
was fully aware of the historic significance of this meeting:
"After centuries of silence, the Latin West and the Greek
East, impelled by mutual love and by the respect inspired
by the Gospel in their Christian hearts, are moving towards
a friendly meeting for an exchange of viewpoints and fraternal greetings and, insofar as this may be possible, to ini-
tiate an understanding dialogue for the peace of the world
and the progress of the Church of God." The Orthodox
prelate, using a biblical comparison, declared that it seemed
to him that the Pope was called to go up the same mountain, the mountain of the Lord, on one side and the Ecu-

menical Patriarch on the other. All those who understand the significance of this twofold ascent, he added, are praying that they may meet at the summit "in the land sanctified by our common Redeemer, near His cross and empty tomb, and that they may henceforth proceed together, endeavoring to reconstruct in Christian solidarity the bridges which have been destroyed, in order that all men may be one, as Christ is one with the heavenly Father."

Metropolitan Athenagoras brought a letter for the Pope. This letter, sent in the name of the Holy Synod and of the other Metropolitans, contained expressions of good will, peace, and affectionate greetings. The step had been taken, the only thing left was to make the meeting a reality.

"And Rising Up, He Blessed Them . . ."

On Saturday morning, January 4, 1964, the Pope's day began a little earlier than usual. In fact at 5:15 the lights were already on in the Papal apartments. When Paul VI left the Vatican in a black Mercedes two hours later through the Arch of the Bells, thousands of persons were already waiting and shouting their enthusiasm. The Pope was standing up in the car and the air was cold. For some ten days an icy wind had taken hold of Europe and had now reached Rome. The night had been clear and starry. But now a slight mist hung on the outlines of the palaces and, like the crowd, it stayed with the papal cortege. Representatives of the Italian government greeted the Pontiff as his automobile entered the territory of the Republic. Then the cortege continued on immediately, accompanied by the uncontrollable applause of the waiting crowd, that nameless personage which never left the Pope alone for a minute until his pilgrimage was over. Passing in front of the Roman prison called "Regina Coeli," already known to the world because of Pope John XXIII's visit, Paul VI had the top of his automobile rolled back so that he might the more easily bless and greet a group of prisoners who had come to wish the Apostolic Pilgrim a pleasant journey, along with the Warden and other officials. The Pope wanted to distribute personally numerous medals to the inmates gathered around him and he left a package of medals with one of the chaplains for those who had been unable to take part in this significant meeting. Thus the Pope's journey began with a half-hour delay. This was not the last time that a delicate gesture of charity by the Pontiff caused delays in his timetable.

At the Leonardo da Vinci International Airport at Fiumicino the Pope was welcomed by the President of the Republic, Antonio Segni, accompanied by all the members of the government. There were brief discourses with good wishes, warm greetings to the Diplomatic Corps and the other high officials present. Paul VI had graciously invited all those present to keep their hats on because of the cold. Immediately the onlookers beheld the unusual, even unique, scene of a Pope walking with light step up the ramp of the airliner. Once again, he turned to greet the crowds and then blessed them from the window of the plane as his jet—it was exactly 8:57 A.M.—slowly pivoted on the runway and moved out for take-off.

At that moment the bystanders could not fail to be reminded of an unusual reporter named Saint Luke, and his account of the Ascension of Our Lord as paraphrased by the sacred liturgy: "And it came to pass as he blessed them that he parted from them and was carried up into heaven . . . and a cloud took him out of their sight." It seemed most appropriate to apply these words to Paul VI because during the whole of his journey in the Holy Land the faithful always beheld in his person that of the Divine Redeemer.

The Pilgrim of Peace sent messages of peace to the heads of all the States over which his jet made its way: Greece, Cyprus, Lebanon, Syria—all of them countries with biblical memories and which had likewise been traversed by the first Paul in his memorable apostolic journeys. On foot or on horseback Paul and Titus had made their way to Jerusalem in the year 50, to take part in the First Council, an historic meeting which first opened the door definitively towards Christian liberty. The points of comparison between these two events—two Councils, two journeys, two identical names—open up vast horizons before the imagination. But the white jet launched off into the sky was by this time, *I-DWS-AZ* 1820 *Papal Flight*, a tiny comet with its nose pointed towards the Orient.

As the Pope's plane flew into Jordanian air-space an escort of fighters came out to meet him. Already Amman, the capital of Jordan, could be seen in the distance. There had been reason to fear for a while that fog might force the papal jet to change its route, but as the DC-8 came in over Amman the fog was lifting and the landing was effected without incident. King Hussein directed the landing operation personally from the control tower, and when the DC-8 touched down on the runway he was the first one out to greet the Pontiff, to extend a welcome to his country and then to present all the members of his party. The air shook with a 21-gun salute, as the Arab Legion presented arms. It was 1:30 P.M., local time. The trip had lasted about three hours. A military band struck up the papal hymn and the Jordanian national anthem, while little girls in regional costume offered olive branches to the Pope. Then, in the spacious waiting room of the airport, the official welcoming ceremony took place. King Hussein spoke briefly: "I express to you my gratitude for your visit to our country, in the name of all the Arab people and of all those who believe in God."

In his reply Paul VI emphasized once again the religious character of his trip and recalled a quotation from Psalm 33 as used by Saint Peter in speaking of peace: "Who is the man that desireth life: who loveth to see good days? ... Turn away from evil and do good: seek after peace and pursue it."

The Pope's arrival in the Holy Land was hailed by an immense throng, acclaiming the Vicar of Christ with expressions most characteristic of the Orient—from the biblical "Blessed is he who comes in the name of the Lord" to the popular "Yaja baba!" or "Hail, father!" and the Islamic "May Allah bless you!" The entire scene seemed to have been taken right out of the Gospel.

The Holy Father's party set out for Jerusalem, the Holy City of Christians, Jews and Moslems. Before the eyes of the Pope there opened up the picturesque panorama of the hilly land of Jesus: the Jordan, Jericho, Bethany. All these localities called up countless memories, and in some of them Paul VI was able to make brief stops. On the banks of the Jordan, in the very spot pointed out by tradition as the one where Jesus was baptized by John, the Pope recited aloud the *Our Father*. At Bethany he visited the little church built on the ruins of the house of Lazarus. Immediately after, in the enchanting beauty of a golden sunset, Jerusalem loomed up before him with all its walls, towers, cupolas, minarets, and its splashes of green across stretches of rocky land. The welcome for the Pope had been prepared with great care, but everything was turned topsy-turvy by the uncontrollable enthusiasm of the crowd. No one had expected anything like what actually took place. The police force was inadequate, along with the stockades set up to control the crowd. The military trucks which tried to open a path through the throngs were unequal to the task, as were also the police wielding heavy clubs and trying to make order with rifle butts. In just a few minutes anything like ceremony, protocol, or anything which could be called "official" was swept completely away by the onrushing mob. The Pope was soon hemmed in by the noisy crowd, protected by only a few husky policemen and some persons in his party.

Paul VI went on blessing, greeting, lifting his arms— this was all that could be seen above the swirling sea of heads—and he was literally swept off his feet by that tumultuous mob. It had been said that although the Moslems would go out to see the Pope, they would keep their distance. Instead, the over-all picture was like a scene of wild enthusiasm and mass delirium right out of the Bible. Even the burly soldiers of the Arab Legion, completely lost in the crowd in their characteristic uniforms and with the traditional *chepir* on their heads, were trying to touch the Pope with one hand, while with the other they were doing their best to hold back the crowd. In chaotic confusion the air was streaked with palms, olive branches, and muskets. Orders and counter-orders flew back and forth, as also whistled military commands, acclamations in all languages, guttural cries and the chanting of the *Lauda, Jerusalem, Dominum.*

Paul VI Could Not Hold Back His Tears

No one knows if the Pope had time to pray and meditate, because he had to be constantly on the alert for everything happening around him. He had to be careful where he stepped, be on the lookout not to bump his head against the rifle butts being brandished in the air, and not to lose contact with the small "bodyguard" which remained at his side. His pale face was etched by a smile, and his lips were murmuring a silent prayer.

The background of this unusual scene was the Damascus Gate, celebrated both in the Old and the New Testaments. This Gate had witnessed the departure of Paul, his heart brimming with hatred against the first followers of Christ, and through this Gate he set out for his unexpected encounter with his marvelous destiny. The human torrent was winding its way in and out through narrow lanes of the Via Dolorosa, narrow, twisting, crooked streets, heavy with the drama of a thousand years. The Pope would have wanted to walk this road alone, in recollection, absorbed in meditation on the first Good Friday. On the contrary, in a certain sense, it was his lot to climb up to Golgotha, tired and almost smothered by the crowd.

"This was a tremendous trial for the Holy Father," was the remark made later by Cardinal Tisserant, who had also been lost in the crowd. He had been pushed and shoved around along the whole route of the Via Dolorosa. "I am certain that the Holy Father could not see any of the things he had wanted to contemplate with holy devotion."

At the Sixth Station, the rumor got around that the Pope was not feeling well. As a matter of fact, he stopped for a moment in the chapel of the Convent of the Little Sisters of Jesus, but no one knows whether it was to rest or to pay homage to the poverty of those heroic Sisters who spend their lives with the poorest of the poor in that wretched street. The procession got under way again almost immediately, moving only inch by inch at times and at others at almost a breakneck pace. Noticing that the Holy Father had "disappeared," many persons tried to retrace their steps. But he was still there, locked in the embrace of that immense human crowd, enroute to the Basilica of the Holy Sepulcher. At long last he was able to begin the celebration of Holy Mass, mercilessly hemmed in and imprisoned by the crowd which hardly left him enough freedom of movement to perform the ritual actions of the Holy Sacrifice.

At the Gospel, which recounts the finding of the empty sepulcher, the stone rolled back, the young man clothed in white seated on the tomb announcing the Resurrection, Paul VI was unable to keep back his tears. He was celebrating Mass on the precise spot which had witnessed the basic event of all Christianity. The name "Basilica of the Holy Sepulcher" gives an erroneous impression of something funereal and mournful, brightened only by the shining light of the scene of the Resurrection. But the sepulcher of Christ is not just like any ordinary tomb, and its epitaph, dictated by the voice of angels, proclaims clearly: "He is not here!"

The Basilica of the Holy Sepulcher also rises over Calvary, or Golgotha, that is to say, the place of the Crucifixion. Paul VI here pronounced a discourse of elevated lyricism, inviting all those present to ask pardon for the sins of all ages and to beg for the unity of the human race: "Lord Jesus, our Redeemer and our peace, Who have made known to us Your supreme desire that 'they may all be one,' hear this prayer which we make our own and which becomes here our prayer: '. . . that all may be one.' "

This was a dramatic dialogue prayer: "O Lord Jesus, we have come, as do criminals to the scene of their crime. We have come here like those who have followed You but who have also betrayed You. Unfaithful faithful we have been so often! We have come here to recognize the mysterious bond between our sins and Your Passion, between our deeds and Yours. We have come to strike our breasts, to ask Your pardon and Your mercy. We have come because we know that You can pardon us and want to pardon us, because You have made expiation for us and are our redemption. You are our hope."

A First Day Rich in Emotion and Significance

In the crypt of the Basilica, Paul VI remained a long time prostrate in prayer, silent and recollected, on the very spot corresponding to the tomb which received the dead body of Jesus. It is the most sacred spot of the entire earth. The Pope prayed with fervor and left there a golden olive branch.

The Pope's day continued immediately, with a meeting with the Greek Orthodox Patriarchs, who had been invited

to the Apostolic Delegation. Present were the Patriarch of
Jerusalem, Benediktos, as also the Armenian Patriarch, Der-
derian. Paul VI was most happy and grateful for the welcome accorded him by the clergy and the faithful, and with
evident pleasure he remarked on the collaboration of the
Greek, Armenian and Catholic communities in the reconstruction of the Basilica of the Holy Sepulcher: "It is Our
dearest wish that charity may always reign in an increasing
degree among all men, a true charity, a charity without
tension, that charity which was the sign whereby in the
ancient Church the followers of Christ were recognized:
'See how they love one another!'" Then the Pope emphasized the significance of this meeting for ecumenism and
unity: "One aspiration is making ever greater headway in
Christians hearts. It is the desire to achieve what the Apostle
of the Nations recommended when he urged the faithful
to forget the past and to throw themselves into what awaits
them in the future, with their eyes fixed on Jesus, the
Author and Finisher of our Faith."

These aspirations towards unity became still more
meaningful in the significant background of the Church of
the Agony, on the same spot where in all probability Our
Lord pronounced part of His marvelous discourse after the
Last Supper, as recorded by Saint John in chapter 17 of
his Gospel and which contains the burning plea for unity:
"Yet not for these only do I pray, but for those also who
through their word are to believe in Me; that they also may
be one in us, that the world may believe that Thou hast
sent Me. And the glory that Thou hast given Me, I have
given to them, that they may be one, even as we are one:
I in them and Thou in Me, that they may be perfected in
unity and that the world may know that Thou hast sent
Me, and that Thou hast loved them even as Thou hast
loved Me." (John 17:20-23)

The Garden of Olives had beheld the most mysterious
scene of the human-divine existence of the Man-God when,
alone and abandoned by all, He begged His Apostles to

keep Him company, and then was afraid, sweated blood, and begged the Father to remove the bitter chalice far from Him. On his knees before the Stone of the Agony, Paul VI made an Hour of Adoration to which he gave the symbolic significance of a desire to keep company with Christ in that tepid night after a day of intense cold.

A group of Lectors read in different languages extracts from the Gospel describing Christ's dramatic vigil on the eve of His death. Once again the Pope issued to all Catholics a call to unity, to all Christians, and to the entire world: "Let us not forget that our neighbor, the neighbor whom we must love as we love ourselves, is not only our Christian brother." About midnight Paul VI withdrew, to spend the night on the Mount of Olives, not far from the place where Jesus had taken leave of the world on the day of His ascension.

Thus ended the Pope's first day in the Holy Land, a day which had been very crowded, but which had been at the same time rich with emotion and significance.

"Welcome, Splendor of Your Glory"

With this ancient expression the President of Israel, Zahman Shazar, greeted the Pope as he crossed the Israeli-Jordan frontier through the Tannach Gate, which had been closed for fifteen years, and set foot in Megiddo. This spot is famous in sacred history for the death of the pious king Josias, who had come to block the path of the Egyptian army on its way to take help to Syria. Rarely in history has the death of one man made such a deep impression on the soul of an entire people as to be considered a national tragedy. Even today Megiddo lives under the threat of smouldering war. Paul VI went there to bring the balsam of peace: "Shalom! Shalom!"—Peace! Peace!—said the Pon-

tiff in reply to the greeting of the Israeli President. "From
this land which is unique in the world for the grandeur
of the events of which it was the theater, Our lowly prayer
rises up to God for all men, believers and non-believers,
and We gladly include in this prayer the sons of 'the people
of the Covenant' whose share in the history of the human
race We cannot forget. As a pilgrim of peace, We beg above
all for the great grace of reconciliation of man with God
and the further grace of profound and sincere harmony
among all men and all peoples. May God grant Our prayer,
that God who, as the prophet proclaims, has for men
'thoughts of peace and not of affliction.' "

Paul VI was beginning a new day. He had left the
Apostolic Delegation at about 6:00 A.M. Stretching out before him was the smiling Galilean countryside, evoking
countless memories of the Gospel, because these were the
spots most loved by the Man-God in the years of His
public life. Nazareth, Capharnaum, Caesarea, Cana, the
Lake of Tiberias—all these names bring back holy memories,
idyllic peace, and the soothing echo of the Sermon on the
Mount.

At Nazareth the Holy Father celebrated the Mass of the
Annunciation. In this Church, which is hardly more than
a grotto, was written the prologue of the Christian religion,
the overture of the majestic symphony of Christianity: "Now
in the sixth month the angel Gabriel was sent from God to
a town of Galilee called Nazareth, to a virgin betrothed
to a man named Joseph, of the House of David, and the
virgin's name was Mary . . ." Thus Saint Luke begins his
description of the Annunciation scene, which closes with the
humble consent of the Virgin: "Behold the handmaid of the
Lord, be it done to me according to thy word." These
words are then echoed by those others describing the ineffable event which was taking place at that very moment:
"The Word was made flesh." The Redemption had begun.

But Nazareth also has another message for the world.
Alongside the Grotto of the Annunciation is another small-

er one, almost a catacomb, which tradition points out as the sleeping quarters of the Holy Family. From this lowly spot rises the message of poverty and work. The Word Incarnate willed to spend thirty of the thirty-three years of His mortal life in recollection and manual labor, so much so that He was known as "the carpenter's son." This was one of the symbolisms of the trip of Paul VI particularly because there had been much talk in the Council on the subject of poverty.

John XXIII had opened the way with his trip to Loreto, where tradition says the angels transported the lowly house of Nazareth, and to Assisi, the homeland of Lady Poverty. Perhaps not too many grasped the full significance of these two destinations. Pope John's trip was followed by the Council, and Cardinal Lercaro held the Fathers spellbound with a discourse on poverty, affirming that the time had come when, fearlessly and without half-way measures, the Church would have to limit its use of material things and modify the external splendor of its prelates. Jean Guitton, of the French Academy, in his discourse in the closing days of the Second Session of the Council, did not hesitate to address the Holy Father directly and to treat of this argument with a touch of audacity: "The Church," he said, "must give up all its useless ornaments and all its vestiges of antiquity, so that all men may be happy to meet within its sublime simplicity." Paul VI wanted his pilgrimage to be "most humble," with no splendid corteges or luxurious residences. But it must not be forgotten that in the Holy Land the Pope was a guest, and a guest cannot lay down conditions.

Paul VI's discourse at Nazareth unveils a canvas setting forth this very basic theme. After a filial invocation to the Virgin Mary, in which he addresses her as "Lady of the House," along with her strong and humble Spouse Saint Joseph, in intimate union with Christ her human and divine Son, and after calling Nazareth "the school of intro-

duction to the understanding of the life of Christ," Paul VI
dwelt on the lessons of silence, family life and recollection
as taught by Nazareth.

At the end, speaking of work and poverty, the Pope
described them in eloquent terms: "O Nazareth, O house
of 'the carpenter's son,' how We should like to understand
and to honor the austere but redeeming law of human fatigue. Here We should like to acquire a new awareness of
the dignity of work, to recall how work in itself cannot be an
end, and to show how its freedom and nobility will be
measured, much more than by its economic value, by the
values which give it meaning. Here also We should like
to greet all the workers of the world, pointing out to them
their great Fellow-Workman, their Divine Brother, the
Prophet of all their justice, Christ our Lord!"

Recalling the Sermon on the Mount in which Christ
set forth the principles of the New Law, the Pope continued: "Blessed shall we be if in poverty of spirit we know
how to free ourselves from deceitful confidence in temporal
goods and how to put our first desires in those of the spiritual and religious order. Happy also shall we be if we respect and love the poor as our brothers and as living images
of Christ!"

The Gospels speak repeatedly of the concern of the
God-Man for the poor, of the pleasure their companionship
brought Him, in their anxiety to hear His divine words and
to enjoy being with Him. In fact, they surrounded Him and
pressed so hard around Him that on more than one occasion the Apostles began to fear for His safety and even
Saint Peter felt obliged to scold Him for allowing the
multitude to close in around Him.

"*Lazarus Had a Thousand Faces*"

Experts on protocol severely criticized the frightful disorder and the incredible neglect of those who left the Pope alone in the midst of a shouting and screaming crowd of unknown people. Paul VI's entrance into Jerusalem the day before had presented in its own way a contact with the poor, an episode taken literally from the Gospel. Of this scene and its impact for the poor, an Italian journalist had written as follows: "They witnessed the most glorious procession the Catholic Church has ever recorded in the calendar of her feasts. Although he was dragged, shoved, pulled by the sleeves and by his red mozzetta, the Pope was never more sure of himself, never more at ease, never more in the right place than in those malodorous streets, surrounded by milling throngs of the poor who wanted to touch him to make sure that it was really true that the Pope was breathing the same foul air as themselves, was looking at them and smiling at them. . . . Here the Pope was confident and triumphant, almost unbelievably so, as though he were on his portable throne. Surrounded and carried on by the mob of poor towards the Holy Sepulcher, he was aware that he was making history for generations to come and that he was hastening the Church on the road of progress. Here was the Pope among the poor, the Catholic Church restored to its first and exclusive mission. Here was the man who was closing the 'Constantinian' era of agreements with temporal powers, putting Christianity back into the front-line of the battle against the poverty which has been called 'the disgrace of our world.'

"The spectacle of that first day's tumultuous welcome and of the scene in the grotto of Nazareth will be unforgettable memories and will give us a clear insight into the problems of our world, the paradoxes existing among the two-thirds of the population who go hungry, and the thorny questions raised in the world of work, with its injustices, its miseries and its suffering. Consequently, when this world

of the wretched sees a symbol of salvation, it goes out to
him unrestrainedly, battering down every barrier and
sweeping through even the most efficient cordons of police."

Our Italian journalist continues: "When Paul VI appeared in the piazza, when amidst that vast throng of
people there flashed the white of his skull-cap, it was as
if the wind had wanted to play tricks by upsetting all preparations. All of a sudden the Pope disappeared. From every
side, shouting, applauding, weeping, there rushed towards
him in commotion and despair that 'person' who had not
been assigned a place in any ceremonial preparations and
who had no official place at all, that 'person' who had
been ignored until just a moment before and who a moment
later already had the Pope in his power. That person was
Lazarus!

"Lazarus, not the man from Bethany raised from the
dead by Jesus after His conversation with Martha, but
rather the Lazarus of the Gospel parable recorded by
Luke. This was Lazarus the beggar, reeking with sores,
lying at the entrance to the house of the rich man and
waiting hungrily for the crumbs falling from the banquet
table. On the afternoon of January 4, 1964, Lazarus went
out to meet the Pope as he arrived from Rome for the
first time in history. This Lazarus had a thousand faces.
He came from the noisome caves of the old city, where
one small door leads into a tiny room which is an approach
to other little rooms without windows, getting always smaller
and darker and with hardly room for a bed, and on the bed
there is almost always some sick person covered by yellow-
ing sheets. Lazarus is also the unfortunate group of refu-
gees from the Palestinian war (1,200,000 between Jordan,
Syria and Lebanon, which the U.N. and a Pontifical Mission are endeavoring to defend against the ancient plagues
of hunger, insanity, leprosy and blindness). Lazarus is the
citizen who scrapes the dry clods of earth with his plow,
that earth on which the rain falls only to run off and which
in summer is cracked and burned by the sun."

Doors are swinging open before Lazarus. John XXIII was called "the Pope of the works of mercy." Just a few days before his pilgrimage, Paul VI went to celebrate one of his Christmas Masses in one of the poorest quarters of Rome. "I want to go somewhere where people would like to see the Pope, people who need him," he said to the Vice-gerent of Rome, a well-built Venetian prelate, Archbishop Cunial. "Go to Pietralata," Archbishop Cunial had answered the Pope, "because no one prominent would ever go there!"

Paul VI went, celebrated Mass in the parish church, and personally distributed Holy Communion. He accepted the gifts offered to him: a lamb, a bottle of wine, a basket of fruit, lifting them up for all to see amidst the enthusiastic shouting of the children. He patted the heads of a thousand babies, and shook as many outstretched hands. He went into a little one-story shack, consisting only of a kitchen and one room with eight persons crowded into it. In the bed lay a young woman bed-ridden for many years with deforming arthritis. The Pope leaned down, made the Sign of the Cross on the forehead of the patient, recited a *Hail Mary* with her and asked her what she wanted for Christmas. Paul VI then made another visit. He called on "the little cripples" of Don Gnocchi, and was most affectionate in his visit with them. He took them in his arms, sat them on his knees, while speaking briefly to them and promising to return. This was the Christmas of the Vicar of Christ just a few days before his pilgrimage to the Holy Land, just a few days earlier than his visit to the grotto-church of Nazareth, the school of the Gospel, the most effective apologia for poverty.

"In all truth," to quote François Mauriac, "something new has happened in the Church, a far-reaching event of which this return to the origins of the Chief of the Apostles will be only one phase. It also makes clear to the eyes of the world that the death of Pope John did not interrupt his miraculous pontificate. Everything is continuing as before. The same spirit which hovered over that elderly diplomatic prelate—whom I knew well at the Nunciature in Paris, who was so shrewd and delicate and, could I say, so whimsically humorous, and who gave no one any ideas of greatness, so much so that I never had the slightest idea that he would one day become the inspired man, the revolutionary, the saint that he was—this same spirit had laid hold of Paul VI with a force which is supernatural and 'literally divine.' Before our very eyes we have seen the onward progress of history become the onward progress of grace."

Yes, history marches on. This was later stressed by Paul VI in his Allocution to the patricians and nobles of Rome on January 14, 1964: "We are no longer," he said, "the temporal sovereign who was in past centuries the rallying-point of the social classes to which you belong. We are no longer for you what We were yesterday. Perhaps this has hitherto not been too clear because the fall of the temporal power of the Popes took place in circumstances which are well-known and because, during almost six decades of refusal to recognize the situation thus created, the Holy See preserved, along with its insistence on its ancient rights, the external and traditional forms of the sovereignty it had lost. . . . But, We were saying, history marches on. Although the Pope finds today in the sovereignty of Vatican City the shield and symbol of his independence from all other authority in this world, he cannot and should not in the future exercise any other power than that of his spiritual keys. Before you, heirs and representatives of the ancient families and ruling classes of Papal Rome and of the Papal States, We now stand with empty hands. We are no longer in a position to confer upon you offices, benefices, privileges, or advantages deriving from the organization of a temporal state, nor are We able any more to use your services in civil administration. In your regard We feel Ourselves humanly poor.

"We should also add that the Papacy today, entirely taken up with its spiritual functions, has determined on a program of apostolic activity which We can call broader and new in comparison with previous times. Its religious mission is developing along lines which cannot fail to modify those aspects of its practical structure which the needs of other ages had proposed as necessary and opportune.

"The duty of the Holy See to busy itself with the government of the Universal Church and to establish apostolic dialogue with the modern world, today so agitated by rapid and far-reaching changes, forces the Church to a realistic vision of things, one which obliges her, even at the cost of suffering, to make distinctions and to prefer in the institutions and customs she has inherited from the past, whatever is essential and vital, not to forget but rather to rejuvenate genuine traditional commitments."

Language could hardly have been clearer. Still, Paul VI was fearful that his words might not be fully understood. Consequently he went on: "We say this with some hesitation and, to speak frankly, with some misgivings, fearing to be, or at least to seem to be, not sufficiently devoted to tradition or sufficiently grateful for your services. But this is certainly not the case."

"Welcome, Angel of Peace!"

The Pope left Nazareth as if setting out on a quiet country excursion across the green fields of Galilee and around the blue waters of the Lake of Tiberias. It was a kind of imposing audience for the people, all open-eyed with wonderment and enthusiasm along the more than two hundred miles of his journey for the day.

Capharnaum, the Man-God's adopted city, was there with the impressive ruins of its imposing synagogue, where Jesus had preached so often and had worked miracles. Farther on was the tiny church built on the scene of the multiplication of the loaves and fishes. Then there was Tobga, where Peter became a fisher of men and where, after the Resurrection of Christ, he received his mission to feed His flock. The Pope went down to the shores of Tiberias, put his hand into the water and blessed those present. Behind them rose the Mount of the Beatitudes, a hill dominating the Galilaean panorama. This was a stopping-place for the pilgrim in white. The Little Sisters in charge of this sacred spot offered him fish from the lake, that same kind that had filled Peter's net, the same kind that Jesus Himself had prepared on the glowing coals on a morning after the Resurrection. Lastly, in the opalescent light of twilight, there was Mount Thabor, the Mount of the Transfiguration. On the way back to Jerusalem the Pope passed through Ein Karem, the little village which was the birthplace of John the Baptist, and where the Blessed Virgin intoned her *Magnificat* as she arrived to visit Elizabeth.

At the gates of Jerusalem, the Mayor of the city, accompanied by several important personages from the Israeli government, welcomed the Pontiff, offering him the traditional gifts of bread and salt. The Pope expressed his thanks and gave his blessing to an enormous throng. Then, going up Mount Sion, he entered the Cenacle, which was flooded in an other-worldly light. Paul VI knelt down on the floor in prayer and meditation. This was the place where the Eucharist had been instituted. In this same room Peter had made his profession of unshaken faith in the Master, and the Master affectionately, but with a touch of sadness, had foretold his cowardice. After His Resurrection Christ had passed through these walls, bringing joy to the afflicted hearts of the Apostles. Here they had awaited the coming of the Holy Spirit promised by the Redeemer. Here Peter had preached his first sermon. Here the Church was born.

The Holy Father then went down to the underground chapel, called the "Crypt of the Dormition," where the Mother of Christ, as recorded by tradition, closed her eyes in death in the presence of the Apostles. In the meantime Cardinal Tisserant had stopped at the Shrine of the Israeli war victims and there had lighted seven symbolic candles.

Through the Mandelbaum Gate the Pope re-entered Jordanian territory, after receiving the farewell greeting of the President of Israel: "Blessed be this new guest, in the moment of his departure." This phrase was an echo of the "Baruch Bocha Leshalom" or "Blessed be your peaceful coming" with which the Pope had been welcomed in the morning.

The bells of the two zones of the city blended their joyous ringing over the barricades and over the ill-fated no man's land. The Magi—it was in fact the vigil of the Epiphany—had brought to people living under the terrors of war the silver sound of a message of love. The common people, simple and sincere, showed that they had understood the significance of this event, and they greeted the Pope with joyous expressions such as "Welcome, angel of peace!" or "With you comes a smile!" Certainly the happiness, plus the warm and noisy enthusiasm of the Arabs, along with the order and respectful silence of the Jews were but one same expression of a joint desire for peace.

A Historic Meeting

The Apostolic Delegation in Jerusalem is a new building set in gardens on the dusty slopes of the Mount of Olives. It is really too confined a setting to serve as a stage for the great event which took place within its walls. The Pope had just ended his journey across Galilee. About 9:00 P.M. a murmur of feverish activity indicated the imminent arrival of Patriarch Athenagoras, the "first among equals" of the entire Orthodox world. The outlines of the Mount of Olives took on an air of mystery in the night. The

city below, swathed in fairy-like lights and fluttering with
flags, seemed far removed from this spot so heavy with
destiny.

The Patriarch arrived at 9:15, accompanied by his
party. At the entrance to the Apostolic Delegation he was
welcomed by Cardinal Tisserant and then accompanied to
the reception hall where the Pope was waiting. The meeting
between the Pope and the Patriarch was most cordial. There
was an affectionate and prolonged embrace which served as
a seal on their mutual longing for a meeting which had already been prolonged for over five centuries. After ex-
changing greetings, they took their places in two identical
armchairs, since Paul VI had preferred not to use the small
throne which had been set up for him. Then they conversed
privately for forty-five minutes.

Afterwards came the official discourses. Paul VI declared: "Great is Our emotion, deep Our joy in this truly
historic hour in which after centuries of silence and waiting,
the Catholic Church and Orthodoxy become present once
more in the persons of their highest representatives."
Athenagoras replied: "In all truth, this event is an occasion
for the fullness of joy. With a foretaste of this joy, with a
heart filled with satisfaction and animated by fraternal
sentiments, we have come to this meeting with your beloved Holiness, and we now greet you with happiness in
this holy spot."

Both Paul VI and Patriarch Athenagoras manifested
their deep mutual gratitude, first to God who had prepared
this day of grace for the whole of Christianity, emphasizing
the marked improvement in relations between the Catholic
and Orthodox Churches in recent years. "For centuries the
Christian world has been living in a night of separation.
Its eyes are weary from straining in the dark. May this
meeting mark the dawn of a blessed day of light in which
future generations, sharing in the same chalice, in the same
sacred Body and Blood of Our Lord, may praise and glorify

in charity, in peace and unity, the one Lord and Savior of the world." With these words the Patriarch addressed his "most holy brother in Christ, the Pope of Rome."

Paul VI then dwelt on the lovable figure of John XXIII, who had opened the door to these meetings and had offered his life for the realization of the desire of Christ "that all may be one." "Undoubtedly," added the Pope, "on both sides, the paths leading to union may be long and strewn with difficulties. But the two roads converge on each other and finally meet at the well-springs of the Gospel. . . . With these sentiments We tell you not 'farewell' but, if you will permit it, 'good-bye.' " The two personages then recited together the *Our Father* in Greek and Latin and embraced once more.

The next morning Paul VI returned the visit of Athenagoras in the summer residence of the Patriarch of Jerusalem, Benediktos, which is also located on the Mount of Olives. This time the meeting lasted two hours. Paul VI had celebrated Mass at Bethlehem and in his message to the world had affirmed: "It is now clear to all men that no one can evade the problem of unity." Immediately after, addressing himself to Athenagoras, he had stated: "It was fitting that in this spot which is always so sacred and so blessed, we pilgrims from Rome and Constantinople should have been able to meet and join in common prayer."

Gifts were also exchanged. Athenagoras offered to the Pope a precious "engolpion" which is for the Orientals a symbol of priestly power, and Paul VI offered to the Patriarch a stole, which has the same significance for Catholics. Then he put around his neck the gold chain on which hung a silver medallion with the image of the "Panaghia," or the Blessed Virgin. At the same time the Orthodox prelates broke into the cry which marks the election of a Bishop in their Church: "Axios! Axios! Axios!" which means: "He is worthy, worthy, worthy!"

Everything was done without previous planning, like the actions of two brothers meeting after a long separation.

This was possible because both the Pope and the Patriarch kept their eyes fixed on Christ. The first words addressed by Paul VI to Athenagoras were the Christian greeting: "Praised be Jesus Christ!" It is Christ who wants union. This was emphasized concretely by the Pope and the Patriarch when they alternated reading in Greek and Latin from Chapter 17 of the Gospel of Saint John, in a Bible printed by a Protestant publisher, and held by Paul VI and Athenagoras at the same time.

The visit which only the evening before had been regarded as "a courtesy visit" turned out to have far-reaching repercussions.

"What must we do now?" This was the last question addressed by Patriarch Athenagoras to Paul VI at the end of this second meeting. His question sums up an entire program.

After the First Step, the Future Is in the Hands of God

On his return to Rome, Paul VI declared that it was time to take action. It is not enough to have just some vague kind of good will or to speak nice words; all this must be translated into action. "The blessed hour of Christianity has sounded," affirmed Athenagoras, his eyes reflecting his emotion. "This was the most beautiful day of my life. It was the most beautiful day for the Church. It was the grandest day in the history of Christianity. I called the Pope my 'most holy brother' and in fact that is just how he struck me: a holy man, destined by God to bring about the brotherhood of Christians and all men, just as Pope Roncalli had seemed like John the Baptist sent by God to prepare new paths on which our divided past would come to an end. The Pope struck me as a brother, and both of us as sons in the same Christ, and in fact his embrace, his every act of thoughtfulness, his words, every one of his gestures, made me sense this great brotherhood which must unite 'the Church.'"

The sincerity of this statement by the Oriental Patriarch and the humility with which he gave credit to Pope Paul for the initiative and the merit of having brushed aside the veils of long-standing and deep-rooted misunderstanding, arouses in one's soul a feeling of deep emotion. "I was deeply impressed, moved and touched by the kindness, humility, knowledge, and wisdom of His Holiness Pope Paul VI. I was particularly struck by the fact that the Holy Father has completely forgotten the ugly past and has made a new era possible. Paul VI and I have been responsible for the opening of this new era. The future is bursting with promise, while hope and confidence stand out distinctly on the horizon."

Patriarch Athenagoras is a learned man, a man with broad views and devoid of resentment. Since 1948, when he took over the See of Constantinople, he had ardently desired a meeting with Rome, to begin "the journey of reconciliation." He is most approachable, an imposing figure—he is well over six feet tall, has a flowing beard and two sparkling and winning eyes—in many ways he resembles Pope John XXIII. In the seventy-eight years of his life he has acquired wide experience of men and things. He was born in a Turkish village, spent his ecclesiastical career in Greece, and then lived for eigheen years in the United States as Orthodox Archbishop of North America. He was a personal friend of Roosevelt and Truman, a great admirer of Kennedy and John XXIII, whose photographs he keeps on his desk. In 1948 he was elected Ecumenical Patriarch to succeed Maximos V. Some of his viewpoints recall the anecdotes and the delightful stories told about John XXIII, since he has always been ready to make people feel at home with one another and profit by their social contacts.

This, in a thumb-nail sketch, was the personage met by Paul VI. The joint communiqué published after their conversation states: "The two pilgrims, with their eyes fixed on Christ, the Author and Exemplar, with the Father, of unity and peace, beg of God that their meeting may be a symbol and a prelude to happy future events. After so many centuries of silence, they have met in the desire to realize the will of the Lord and to proclaim the ancient truth of His Gospel entrusted to the Church."

The dialogue had really opened. It is not our lot to know just what the future may hold in store. "The future," declared Athenagoras, "is in the hands of God, but God acts in men and through men. Consequently the future will depend on how men allow themselves to be guided by the grace of the Lord."

The Solemn Message of Bethlehem

On the feast of the Epiphany, one of the major solemnities of the liturgical year, at six in the morning, Paul VI once again left the Apostolic Delegation in Jerusalem to make his way to Bethlehem, a name meaning "House of Bread." There he celebrated Holy Mass at the altar of the Crib, where the Infant Jesus was laid by His mother on the night of His birth two thousand years ago. The chapel is only a narrow grotto some forty feet by ten, and in it Paul VI could really enjoy a moment of peace and genuine recollection. The entrance to this shrine is through a low narrow door, built in ancient times to keep out the Turks, who had been accustomed to ride into the church on horseback in order to beat the faithful. There is no other entrance, since the main door belongs to the Greek Orthodox. The interior of this church is adorned with distinctly Oriental decorations, which hide to some extent its natural squalor. From that august spot, where the angels announced the first Christmas, it was Paul VI's desire to address a solemn message to the world, as if to sum up the significance and the achievements of his journey. He wanted to proclaim before all men, first of all, the Church's profession of faith, a profession of hope and love, because this had been the inspiration of his pilgrimage to the Holy Land.

Recalling the marvelous days spent in the country of Jesus, the Pope declared later in an audience that "the impression arising in one's heart spontaneously in those spots described in the Gospel is that of a meeting between Him, the Divine Master, and ourselves. The feeling is accompanied by the need to establish and demonstrate the relationship existing between Jesus and ourselves. Then a question confronts the soul, a silent but haunting question: 'Are we real Christians? Is our life with His?' . . . ." Paul VI concluded that, thanks to the grace of God, the comparison comes out favorably, even though not completely so, as though to spur us on to continued effort.

The very fact of the Pope's pilgrimage was part of the framework of this good will, just as the Council is progressing in an effort to meet and go beyond the more stringent requirements demanded by an ideal as infinite as is Christ.

The second part of Pope Paul's discourse on the feast of the Epiphany, 1964, was dedicated to the Church. On many other occasions he had stressed the burning theme of unity: "This is the historic hour in which the Church of Christ must live its deep and visible unity. It is the hour in which we must heed the wish of Jesus Christ: 'May they be one in unity and let the world recognize that You, O Father, have sent Me. . . .' We repeat that we are disposed to consider every reasonable possibility to smooth out the path of understanding, reverence, and charity, as preparation for a future and, God grant, early meeting with the brethren presently separated from Us. The door of the fold is open. All are waiting sincerely and anxiously. The desire for this meeting is strong and patient. There is abundant room. The step to be taken is preceded by Our affection and can be carried out with enthusiasm and mutual happiness. We shall refrain from requiring any acts which may not be free and based on conviction, that is to say, moved by the Spirit of the Lord, who breathes where and when He wills. We shall await this happy hour. For the present, We shall merely ask Our most beloved brethren to do what We propose to Ourselves: may the love of Christ and His Church inspire every eventual gesture of reconciliation and dialogue. We shall see to it that the desire for understanding and union remains watchful and sleepless, and We shall put our confidence in prayer, which, although it is not yet common, nevertheless can at least be simultaneous and rise in parallel lines from Ourselves and Our separated brethren, to meet in the heights of heaven and form an arch in the God of unity.

"We are profoundly happy that our meeting in these blessed days with the Ecumenical Patriarch of Constantinople took place in the spirit of the greatest possible affability and has proved to be a source of most encouraging hopes. . . . May the Lord who inspired in Us this good work of peace and union deign to bring it to a good end."

Lastly Paul VI addressed himself to the entire world:

"We understand by the term 'world' all those who look at Christianity from the outside, as if they were or seem to be strangers to it. We would like above all to take Our place once more in this world in which We live. We are the representatives and the promoters of the Christian religion. We are certain that We are furthering a cause which comes from God. . . . We desire to work for the welfare of the world, for its best interests and its salvation. We feel likewise that the salvation which We offer to the world is necessary. . . . We look upon the world with immense understanding. Although the world may feel itself a stranger to Christianity, Christianity does not regard itself as a stranger to the world. . . . This means that the mission of

Christianity is a mission of friendship among men, a mission of understanding, encouragement, betterment, elevation, We will even say of salvation.... The Christ whom We bring to humanity is the 'Son of Man' sent by God, not to condemn the world but to save it."

The Pope then greeted also those who profess faith in one God outside the Christian religion, and to the peoples among whom the missionaries of the world are carrying on their activities: "Our greeting cannot have limits. It goes beyond all frontiers and wants to reach all men of good will. Still more, it goes out likewise to those men who do not now give proof of good will towards the religion of Christ and who are endeavoring to shackle the spread of the faith and to persecute its followers. Also to those who persecute the Church and who deny God in Christ We turn Our sorrowful thoughts and Our calm question: 'Why? Why?'"

Paul VI's day in Bethlehem diffuses a universal light just as the choir of angels on the first Christmas night begged for "peace to all men of good will," and like the mysterious Magi who turned the stable of Bethlehem into a communications center with lines reaching out even over the remote paths of the desert.

Paul VI's last appeal was to the rulers of nations: "In this place of purity and calm, where there was born twenty centuries ago He to whom we pray as the Prince of Peace, We feel a compelling duty to repeat to the heads of states and to all who share in responsibility for nations Our insistent appeal for the peace of the world. Let governments give heed to the plea of Our heart; let them continue their generous efforts to assure to humanity that peace for which it yearns."

Many details have certainly been omitted from this rapid account of the unusual pilgrimage of Paul VI. These pages, for example, could have mentioned the young couple at Cana who invited the Pope to baptize their baby daughter and could have related how His Holiness, working under the pressures of a tight schedule, especially in Israel, could not accede to the request as he would have wanted to. Yet, as though in compensation for this, he was able to find a few minutes, just enough to visit a paralytic in a poor house in Jerusalem and to receive in that same city a child polio victim who had not been able to see the Pope on the evening of his dramatic entrance into the Holy City through the Damascus Gate. Special attention could have been called to the unusual welcome accorded by a Moslem sovereign, who followed the journey of the Holy Father through his country, personally piloting his own helicopter. The same could be said of the acts of courtesy showed by the Israeli President. Then there was the episode of the two Moslems who held the Pope by the arm as he started to slip down the banks of the Jordan, as also the fatherly gesture of the Pope who, as a souvenir of his pilgrimage, offered to the sanctuaries where he celebrated Holy Mass the vestments used on those occasions. One Arab wanted the Holy Father to walk on the waters of the Lake of Tiberias!

Incidents such as these, and numerous others of their kind belong in news accounts rather than in a book, but they are none the less significant. They are the sparks of the immense flame which was the Pope's journey. They were his epiphany.

A Symptom of the Continuation of the Council

At the Amman Airport, the DC-8 was waiting to take the Pope back to his See of Rome. He left behind him certain unbeatable "records," one can in all truth begin to speak of a new era.

Before boarding his jet, the Holy Father once more greeted the crowd which had never abandoned him, pronouncing two words in Arabic: "Salam Ailekum," which means "Peace be with you," thus arousing wild enthusiasm and applause.

King Hussein seemed also to find it hard to take leave of the Pope. He spoke with His Holiness earnestly on the way to the ramp of the plane and betrayed evident emotion. But the pilgrimage was coming to an end at the moment in which the papal jet took off and then gradually disappeared in the clouds dotting the blue sky. The Holy Land became once more a dream far away from reality, and it was all the fault of these ultra-powerful jets! When would another Pope return to Palestine?

In an audience after his return to Rome, Paul VI stated that his journey had made a most unusual impression on him: "It was like a new telling of the old fable about the individual who fell asleep and when he awoke a hundred years later, thought that he would find the world around him just as he had left it. On the contrary, he soon found that he knew no one and no one knew him."

Will there be a repetition of this thousand-year dream? No one can penetrate into the secrets of the future. No one can even foretell what the possible repercussions of the Pope's pilgrimage will be on the Council. One thing is certain, and that is that the Third Session cannot ignore this extraordinary precedent. Things have definitely changed.

The Holy Father reached the Vatican, very tired after the long hours of the unusual welcome accorded him by the people of Rome, who had poured out on the streets along the papal route, as though to emulate his triumphal welcomes in the Orient. Speaking from the window of his apartment to an immense throng in St. Peter's piazza the Pope dropped the solemn "We," to use the simple "I": "Thanks, thanks again, my children, for this welcome which is something memorable and incomparable by itself. I want to express my warmest thanks to all the citizens of Rome, to the city authorities, and to all who were on duty along the route of this immense cortege. I really would have wanted not to inconvenience anyone and to complete my journey home simply and quietly. On the contrary, your intelligence and your kindness prepared an extraordinary welcome of which we have all been witnesses.

"I bring you greetings from Bethlehem where I celebrated Holy Mass this morning. I bring you the peace of the Lord; I bring you what you already have in your hearts and what you have showed you understood, namely, the truth that there is a direct wire between Christ, Peter, and Rome. This wire has vibrated with all holy emotions, and now it transmits to you all my blessings.

"You have understood that my trip was not merely an isolated and spiritual event. It was one which can have tremendous historic importance. It is a link binding itself to a tradition which is centuries old; it is perhaps the beginning of new events which can be great and beneficial for the Church and for humanity. Tonight, I shall say only that I had the great fortune this morning, after centuries and centuries, to embrace the Ecumenical Patriarch of Constantinople, and to exchange with him words of peace, brotherhood, desire for union, concord, honor for Christ, and helpful service for the entire human family. Let us hope that these beginnings will bear good fruit. May the seed which has thus been planted germinate and ripen. Lastly, let us all pray, because these hours and these events are certainly great and are stamped with the seal of the providence of God. So now receive my blessing, in the name of the Father, and of the Son and of the Holy Spirit. Praised be Jesus Christ."

For an instance, it seemed to be the voice of John XXIII. The only difference was that at the end he did not say "Good Night!" But everyone went away quietly or still better, deeply and joyously moved. As his plane came in over Rome, the Pope had asked the pilot to circle twice around the city. From the heights of heaven, he wanted to get a panorama of the Church on earth.

WORKING CLOSELY
WITH TWO GREAT POPES

It has been said of Giovanni Battista Montini that he was "born Pope." This is evidently a paradox, but one which can be explained by the life story of this son of an obscure Brescian town, a life providentially dedicated to impassioned service of the Church, from within the shadows of an intense but unassuming spirit of work.

The testimony of many close acquaintances has made it possible to reconstruct the first fifty years of the life of today's Pope—from Concesio, where he was born, to Brescia, where his dream of the priesthood came true, to the Eternal City, the main scene of his total dedication to the Church.

Giovanni Battista Montini was born on September 26, 1897 at Concesio, Province of Brescia, not far from Milan or from the tiny hamlet of Sotto il Monte, Province of Bergamo, the birthplace of his immediate predecessor. He was baptized on the 30th of the same month in the parish church of Sant'Antonio, the only one in the town, receiving the names of Giovanni Battista Enrico Antonio Maria, as is recorded in the parish books over the signature of the pastor at the time, Don Giovanni Fiorini.

Giovanni Battista's parents were Giorgio Montini and Giuditta Alghisi. Giorgio was a lawyer but had also devoted a great deal of time to journalism, as editor for twenty-four years of *Il Cittadino*, of Brescia, and had also been active in national politics as a Deputy of the Catholic Party. Among her closest friends the future Pope's mother was called "Little Judy" because she was so tiny.

The example of his parents, whose deep mutual affection and strict living of the Christian life contributed no less than their words to guide their son from his earliest years towards self-discipline and understanding, impressed on him the lesson that in every aspect of life spiritual considerations had to have first place over those having merely material and passing value.

Giorgio Montini, whose name in all official documents is always prefixed by the official title of "Avv." or "Lawyer," left a vigorous imprint on all those Catholic activities in the Province of Brescia in which he had a part. Before very long, he found it necessary to move into the town of Brescia itself because of his editorship of the Catholic daily *Il Cittadino*. This paper was then nothing but a modest country paper, short on financial means and sober, sometimes too sober, in its make-up. It came out daily around noon. But the same criticism cannot be voiced of its contents, especially of the editorials signed by the father of the future Pope. The reader should not forget that this was a period of conflict and polemics in the political history of Italy and the position of the Church was precarious.

135

The simplest description of the father of young Montini comes from Pope Paul VI in his audience to the press on June 28, 1963, the day before his solemn coronation: "... Above all We cannot keep silent on one point which would naturally call for further comment on Our part. Our father, Giorgio Montini, to whom, along with Our natural life, We owe so much of Our spiritual life, was, among other things, himself a journalist. He was a journalist of the old school, and was for long years editor of a modest but fearless provincial daily. But if We wished to show how he was sustained by an awareness of his profession and by the cultivation of moral virtues, We feel that easily, even without any prodding from filial affection, We could in those words sketch the profile of one who recognizes in the press a splendid and courageous mission in the service of truth, democracy, progress, in a word, of the public welfare."

Certain words in this quotation deserve to be emphasized. Among these are "a fearless provincial daily" as also the other longer expression: "We could sketch the profile of one who recognizes in the press a splendid and courageous mission in the service of truth, democracy, progress and, in a word, of the common welfare." Attention should be called to these words because they seem to be a perfect description of this unassuming but courageous paper, and of the perfect integrity of its editor. The description comes from one who was best able to understand and appreciate Giorgio Montini.

No sooner had Pius X abolished the *non expedit* of his predecessors, Pius IX and Leo XIII, and permitted Italian Catholics to engage in politics, than Giorgio Montini announced his candidacy for the post of municipal and provincial Alderman. He was elected. In 1917 Benedict XV evidenced his high confidence and esteem for Giorgio Montini by offering him the presidency of the Catholic Voters Association. Montini was elected to Parliament, precisely because of the team-work of Catholics in the Provinces of

Brescia and Bergamo—a team-work for which the greater share of the credit belongs to the father of the future Pope. Some five or six years earlier this collaboration had induced the Sovereign Pontiff to make his first exception in the abstentionist policy hitherto imposed on Catholics. Giorgio Montini tells the story himself in a letter to a friend: "For many years I was a town alderman and engaged in other civic and Catholic activities. For twenty-five years I belonged to the Council of the Province. From 1913 to 1920, I was town alderman in Brescia in the war administration. In 1917, because of the high authority by which it was offered to me, I could not turn down the office of President General of the Italian Catholic Voters Union, then one of the great sectors of Catholic Action in Italy. But this was a task not tailored to my strength and temperament, and I could not divide my time between Rome and Brescia, where I was tied down by inescapable obligations. Consequently, I resigned in 1918. In 1919 I was elected to Parliament and remained there for three sessions, earning neither distinction nor disgrace."

The story of Donna Giuditta Alghisi is less rich in externals. Perhaps this is only normal. She was engaged in her own important activities, as she was Diocesan President of the Catholic Womens' Association of Brescia. But the principal field for the practice of her own uncommon Christian virtue was her own home life, assisting her husband and looking after the Christian education of her children.

Four Bishops and a Pope

At Concesio a stone plaque records the names of the illustrious sons of the town. Among these names are the names of Bishops Francesco and Sebastiano Lodrone, who were born respectively in 1600 and 1643. In the same town and in the same year in which Paul VI was born, there was born also Giovanni Battista Bosio, now Bishop of Chieti. Just a few days after Concesio's most illustrious son had been elevated to the Chair of Peter, it was still possible to read on this plaque, alongside the name of Giovanni Battista Montini, the title "Cardinal." In the meantime this inscription has been replaced by another which, with the baptismal name of Concesio's famous citizen, proudly proclaims that he is "Pope Paul VI," with the dates of his election and coronation, namely June 21st and June 30th, 1963.

On the front wall of the Montini home, which goes back to the beginning of the seventeenth century, there is an old sundial with the inscription "Aeternitatis horas labentes indico," that is to say, "I mark the fleeting hours of eternity." In the shadow of this sundial Paul VI was born and spent the first years of his life.

Taking into account the then current ideas on the Sacrament of the Eucharist, it will not be surprising that the son of Giorgio Montini and Giuditta Alghisi was not admitted to First Communion until he was ten. The date was June 6, 1907, in the chapel of the Sisters of the Child Mary at Brescia. He was confirmed on the 21st of that same month by the diocesan Bishop, Giacinto Pellegrini. If chronological details have any importance, it is interesting to point out that the Holy Spirit, who on that day took possession of the soul of this young boy, exactly fifty-six years later, on June 21, 1963, guided the Sacred College in the choice of that same child as Universal Pastor of the Church.

The ceremony of Giovanni Battista Montini's confirmation took place in the "Collegio Cesare Arici" in Brescia, directed by the Jesuit Fathers. There young Montini followed his elementary and *ginnasio* courses, always working against odds because of his frail health. At one point he had to drop his studies at the college and carry on privately under the watchful guidance of his parents, later completing them by brilliantly passing his examinations in the "Istituto Arnaldo da Brescia."

Weak in body but strong in soul

In the records of the "Cesare Arici," the notation can still be found alongside the name of Giovanni Montini: "Dispensed from the examinations and promoted by unanimous consent of the professors." This decision of the college administration is no surprise. In fact, in the second semester of the 1909-1910 school year, young Montini had received the following marks: Conduct, 10; Diligence in Study, 10; Education, 10; Catechism, 10; Italian (written), 8; Italian (oral) 8+; Translations from Italian, 8+; Translations from Latin, 9—; Oral Latin, 8; Arithmetic, 8; History, 8; Geography, 8+; Penmanship, 7.

These are the finest marks obtained in that school of fifteen students. In that same year four other students, along with Giovanni Battista Montini, made the Honor Roll for catechism and diligence in study. Among these, according to the judgment of the professors, some had done better than young Montini as regards application to study. This was only natural because of the limitations placed on the young student by his poor health, which prevented him from studying as wholeheartedly as his other companions.

Those who were his companions and in a position to know him intimately—and they are still numerous in Brescia and Concesio—say that then, as today, he was physically frail but at the same time gifted with a strong soul and mind. Primo Savoldi who, with Domenico Pedersini and Margherita Peretti, was a school-mate of the future Pope, still recalls very clearly the day when, in the summer of 1916, while World War I was raging, he accompanied Giovanni Battista to the Brescia barracks for his physical examination. Young Montini was exempted from active service because of poor health.

The "Collegio Arici" published for its students a school paper called "La Fionda" or "The Sling." One of its most dedicated contributors was Montini. Among regular readers of the articles by the young student was probably Father Persico, who was also one of his professors. This priest, now almost a hundred years old, still recalls Giovanni Montini very clearly: "He was very fine, with surprising gifts as a writer and an eloquence based on facts and ideas, and was absolutely anti-rhetorical. I taught him only physics and philosophy, but I know that he wrote well because he often brought me the articles he was preparing for our little school paper. He would have made his reputation as a famous journalist, had he not chosen another way of life. In his father he had an excellent teacher."

May 29, 1920: *a priest forever*

At a date around 1917, which cannot be determined with any precision, young Giovanni Battista Montini decided to inform his parents, or more probably his mother, of his desire to be a priest. Neither of them placed any obstacles in the way of their son's ideal. They may already have had some insight into his decision as they noticed how his general demeanor and conduct were different from those of their other children. Deeply Christian parents that they were, they knew that when God asks for a son all for Himself, whoever wants to make his son happy must co-operate generously with heaven's plans, even though these may run counter to long-cherished human plans, especially when this call from God demands sacrifice and renunciation.

Thus free to follow the call of the Lord, Giovanni Montini was admitted to the diocesan seminary of Brescia. He was enrolled as a day-student, living at home with his parents, who had taken up residence in this city in order to make it easier for the lawyer-father to look after his professional interests.

One of the details connected with the priestly vocation of Giovanni Battista Montini has been recounted by another priest, Don Luigi Benassi, today pastor of a little town in the diocese of Brescia: "One day when we were at our house, my grandmother, as she waited on table, let it out that I wanted to become a priest but that my family was not well enough off to send me to the seminary. In the general silence which followed, Don Battista was the only one to speak: 'Grandma Margarita, don't forget Providence.' Then, taking advantage of a moment when our table companions were busy with other things, he whispered into my ear: 'Get everything ready; you'll be leaving for Brescia.' Two days later I received a letter from the students' boarding-house, informing me that I had been accepted with all expenses paid. Later I found out that the president of the organization was the Honorable Giorgio Montini."

Don Benassi is today a humble country pastor, who can hardly believe that his old school-chum from 1915 to 1920 has now reached such heights. But it is fortunate that Don Benassi is still alive, and with his clear memory, to tell of other incidents in the life of Paul VI which otherwise would remain unknown. This good priest continues: "I really do not think I was the first one to receive Montini's confidences about his priestly vocation. Just imagine, when no one as yet knew anything at all, I learned that a future Pope was going to the seminary! Some years back I went to visit Don Battista, who was already a very important personage. I happened to be at Brescia at the Sanctuary of Our Lady of Grace. I had hardly gone into the sacristy when I heard a rustling of priestly vestments.... I was about to leave when a strong voice called to me. It was Montini. 'Don Benassi, how is Grandma Margarita?' I blushed, because emotion had confused my ideas and tied my tongue. Then he said: 'I understand. She has gone ahead to wait for us in Paradise.' Then the prelate took me off to one side and asked me lots of questions about my ministry, our mutual friends, our old schoolmates who were then working their land. It seemed to me that we were making a trip together back to our old farm."

Don Benassi provides one last reminiscence: "From his mother he had received great wisdom and deep faith. On one occasion, at Verolavecchia, at three in the afternoon, the bells began to ring to recall the death of Christ. At that sound, Battista stopped playing and recollected himself in quiet prayer. If sometimes he happened to hear the *Angelus,* then at once, without any human respect, he invited those present, big and small, to recite this prayer with him."

From the year 1919, when Montini donned the cassock and received Tonsure from Bishop Defendente Salvetti, of Brescia, there is a photograph showing the seminarian Montini with a group of other university students at Rome for a FUCI congress. This detail, though apparently insignificant, shows how far back he was linked with an organization which was destined to exert such deep and lasting influence on the priestly and human formation of the future Pope at the very outset of his ecclesiastical life.

He received the cassock and also the Tonsure on November 29, 1919. Six months later, on May 29, 1920, he was ordained to the priesthood by Bishop Giacinto Gaggia.

For the celebration of his first Solemn Mass he chose the Sanctuary of Our Lady of Grace on the outskirts of Brescia. It was a quiet little shrine where the Montini family had long gone for excursions on Sunday afternoons and on other occasions, to ask for the blessings of their Heavenly Mother.

Some years earlier, according to an account published in *L'Osservatore Romano* on June 29, 1963, the young student Giovanni Battista Montini had gone to this sanctuary one evening to say his prayers to the Madonna, after receiving a prize for good conduct at the "College Arici." He had spent some moments in recollection and then, thinking that no one saw him, slipped up to drop his silver medal into the offering-box. It never occurred to him that he would be betrayed by his name on the back of the medal. In fact the rector of the sanctuary, who found this unusual offering among the others, decided to keep it in the treasury of the sanctuary. Time brought him his reward, because that medal has now become the symbol of the charity and piety of a Pope.

Don Montini's First Mass celebration was intimate and quiet, with only a very restricted number of persons present. One of these had a deeper share than the others in the joy of the new priest. This was Signora Giuditta who, while awaiting that day which meant so much to her and to her son, had made with her own hands a chasuble out of her wedding dress. Perhaps the most solemn note of that intimate ceremony was struck by the priest, whose name is not recorded, who was honored by the invitation to preach the sermon and to present to Don Battista the good wishes of all those present for his future ministry, according to a longstanding custom. Taking his inspiration from the name "Giovanni Battista" he expressed the wish that this new priest, like the Precursor of Christ, would fulfill his mission to proclaim to the crowds the Lamb of God whom on that day he was holding in his hands for the first time.

Montini is tops in everything

At the end of this school year Don Giovanni Battista obtained the doctorate in Canon Law with a thesis defended in the Pontifical Faculty of Law at the Metropolitan Seminary of Milan. At the beginning of the new school year his Bishop decided to send him to Rome to pursue higher studies in order to broaden his intellectual formation. The Lombard College had only recently been opened at Rome

under the rectorship of Monsignor Ettore Baranzini, now
Bishop of Siracusa. Don Giovanni Montini entered the Col-
lege on November 10, 1920. As a student of the Lombard
College he followed philosophy courses at the Pontifical
Gregorian University and at the same time registered at the
University of Rome as a candidate for a Doctorate in Letters.

The following year, 1921, Monsignor Pizzardo, who
was then Under-Secretary at the Secretariate of State,
summoned young Montini to the Ecclesistical Academy and
gave him his first introduction to Vatican diplomacy. As
early as May, 1923, he was sent as Attaché to the Apostolic
Nunciature in Warsaw.

This act of obedience to his direct ecclesiastical
superiors very likely cost the young priest no small sacrifice,
by putting him in a situation where he could no longer
satisfy his craving for broader culture. But the objections
voiced by himself and others against this abrupt interruption of his studies proved fruitless. Monsignor Pizzardo
answered them with a reply which has now become famous
from appearing the world over in all biographies of Paul VI:
"My heavens! What difference does one doctorate more or
less make? Do as you are told and don't worry!" Some claim
that the Monsignor then added: "The important thing is
to have the necessary qualities, and you have them."
Monsignor Pizzardo was well aware that this young priest
from Brescia had all the necessary qualities, since he had
been able to see them more clearly every day in the young
man's work with him, marked by intelligence and discretion.

Andrea Lazzarini, the well-known biographer of
Paul VI and of his immediate predecessor, has thus summed
up the Under-Secretary's evaluation of Montini from the
very beginning: ". . . I had at the very outset seen in him
all the makings of a diplomat, that is to say, tact, knowledge
of the law, knowledge of languages, but above all an inborn
political sense. Thanks to this sense, in whatever happened,
Don Montini was able to grasp at once the ideological implications of two opposed policies and in every individual,

even though he had known him for only a short time, he sensed clearly the precise role of this person in the vast drama of international life." Pizzardo was so convinced that Montini had the best possible qualifications that when Archbishop Lauri, Nuncio in Poland, asked the Secretariate of State for an assistant in whom he could have implicit confidence he was offered the twenty-five year old Don Giovanni Battista Montini. Thus, he was already a person to be trusted absolutely. The young priest obeyed. In that act of obedience there was perhaps a touch of the heroic because at that time Don Battista was much more interested in acquiring new knowledge than in taking his first step, perhaps a decisive one, in a diplomatic career.

His diplomatic career in Poland lasted only six months. In the October of that same year he was recalled to Rome and had to break off his work with the Nuncio, Archbishop Lorenzo Lauri, and the Auditor, Monsignor Carlo Chiarlo, both of whom later became Cardinals. At Rome he resumed his studies at the Ecclesiastical Academy until the October of 1924 when he entered the Secretariate of State as a *minutante*. From that moment on he alternated his hours of study with his work at the Vatican. People around him were already beginning to say: "Montini is tops in everything." But such praise, of which he was certainly aware, never disturbed his inner peace nor did it cause any slackening of zeal or any desire to rest on his laurels.

Contact with university students

At this point in his life Don Montini was recommended by Monsignor Pizzardo for a position of exceptional responsibility. In fact in May, 1924, Don Battista was given spiritual responsibility for the Roman circle of the Federation of Italian Catholic University Students (FUCI). This post

not only opened up before him a vast field for doing good,
but also proved to be a most useful contribution to his
priestly experience.

Because it was one of the busiest years, 1924 must
also have been one of the happiest and most fruitful of his
life, since it permitted him to work out a program of apostolic work in the twofold field of spiritual and moral assistance for young university students and the continuation
of his own studies, with the ever-growing realization that
he was thus contributing effectively to the rounding out
of his spiritual, cultural, and human training.

Good Giuditta Alghisi was worrying about her son's
health every time she learned of some new responsibility
placed on his shoulders. Her son made every effort to put
her at ease, assuring her that, thank God, his health was
actually improving with time. She could see this for herself
every year during the summer when Don Battista, between
one FUCI congress and another, found time to spend a week
in the quiet calm of the house at Concesio where he had
been born. The Montini family still maintained its residence
in the capital city of the Brescia Province, but spent the
summers in Concesio, where the friends of his early years
continued to greet Don Battista every time word got out
that he was home from Rome.

Don Montini was endowed with the courage needed
to face up calmly to all the duties imposed by his many
activities. To find the necessary time, he had to cut down
on his hours of sleep, which began at that time to be limited
to no more than four or five each night. His constitution
re-acted surprisingly well, so much so that the very ones
who thought he was overloaded with work, had to admit
that his health seemed much better than it had been three
or four years earlier when, in order to continue his seminary studies he had been obliged to live at home and take
advantage of his mother's loving care.

Don Montini's pastoral ministry was also expanding
under new forms. Every Sunday he celebrated Mass and

preached in the university church. He also frequently visited poor families, taking them whatever relief he was able to secure through his delicate sense of charity.

In October, 1925, after the Congress of Catholic University Students at Bologna, Pius XI gave Don Montini a new proof of his confidence by appointing him National Counselor of the FUCI, to replace Monsignor Giandomenico Pini, the fearless apostle of university students, who had resigned just before this Congress. The spiritual assistance of the FUCI was entrusted to Don Montini at a time when the national presidency of the association passed from the hands of Lizier to those of Igino Righetti, a young man of keen intelligence and good judgment.

The Vatican authorities had chosen Righetti to succeed Lizier after an incident which was in itself not terribly important but which had caused quite a commotion because of the special situation of Italian Catholics at the time. During the Congress at Bologna, the President of the FUCI had decided to send a telegram to the King. At Bologna this seemed a quite normal gesture, but in Rome it met with universal disapproval and even provoked a diplomatic protest by a foreign power. Consequently, it had been thought advisable for Lizier to resign.

From the very beginning Montini and Righetti agreed perfectly. Still, the life of the association was not easy, as can be seen in the memoirs of an eye-witness: "Wherever we went," he said, "chaos followed. The Fascists chased us and left us no peace. Ordinarily our meetings began in one city and ended in another. The most celebrated incident of this period took place at Macerata in 1926.

"The FUCI arrived at their meeting-place escorted by *carrabinieri,* lined up like prisoners, with Montini, Righetti and Pacchiani in the lead. The Fascists, hiding behind trees and bushes and armed with sticks, leapt out unexpectedly and blows began to fall. Many had to have medical care. One of the *Fucini,* Ugo Galli, now a dentist in Bergamo, came out of the fray with his head all bandaged.

Giving up, the Fucini returned to the railroad station to
go back to Assisi where, at least as they thought, there
was more freedom.

"After the meeting had adjourned as best it could,
we all went back to Rome to be received in audience by
the Pope, as was the custom. When Pope Pius XI came
into the room where the *Fucini* were waiting, his curiosity
was immediately aroused by the young man in bandages.
He asked the prelate near him what illness had stricken
the young man in the turban. 'That is the aftermath of the
incidents at Macerata, Your Holiness,' was the answer. Then
Montini and Righetti told the Pope what had happened.
It was Monsignor Pizzardo, the Under-Secretary of State,
who had to withstand the full outburst of the Holy Father's
anger: 'And you never told me anything about it?' thun-
dered Pope Pius XI."

The history of the FUCI at that time is one of the
most interesting chapters of the participation of Catholics
in Italian political life. It is certain that some characteristic
traits of Montini's personality cannot be understood except
in relation to the atmosphere of tension and opposition to dic-
tatorship which stamped the first years of his priestly ministry among the young members of the university association. Thus these years coincided with the period of Fascist
political domination, which had started just a few years
earlier, and which had not yet succeeded in quenching that
enthusiasm for open opposition which in the previous decades had animated the generous Catholics of the new Italy.

For a little more than half a century, Italy had achieved
her national unity at the expense of the temporal interests
of the Pope, with grave scandal for the numerous Catholics
who regarded the Papal States as essential to the life of
the Church. Garibaldi particularly had made his military
campaigns strictly anti-clerical affairs, spewing out vulgar
derision on whatever smacked of religion or Christianity.
Consequently, the soldiers who seized Rome and the Papal
States were considered by many Catholics, both in Italy and
abroad, as vulgar and sacrilegious usurpers.

Crispi and Count Cavour had taken advantage of the indecision of those foreign powers, which had always made the Holy See pay dearly for any protection accorded it, in order to achieve their dream of a united Italy, confronting the Papal forces, which were already beaten before the battle started. Their resistance was only symbolic, and was reduced to a few canon shots.

The years after the absorption of Rome and the Papal States into the Kingdom of Italy were a period of great uncertainty, which found expression in the Pope's voluntary imprisonment in the Vatican and in the prohibition against Catholics taking any part in national politics. In time, this prohibition was abolished as outmoded. Catholics were not only authorized, but even encouraged, to take an interest in public life and to seek out effective means of creating a Christian foundation for their nation. Nevertheless, the war-like spirit of previous years still perdured and was deeply rooted. Militant Catholics were viewed with suspicion and were attacked relentlessly. It was only natural that they also should have wanted to attack on their own, rather than be satisfied with trying to convince the opposition in unimpassioned discussion. Those who read today the press of that period can still smell the odor of gunpowder.

The future Pope had breathed this battle atmosphere and the spirit of Catholic reconstruction in his family circle, especially in contacts with his father who had battled courageously and suffered for those noble ideals. Now that the violence of the Fascists gave him a keener realization of his responsibilities, it was logical that Don Montini's family memories should confirm him in his resolute and clear-cut attitude.

"If it's a boy, give him Montini's name"

The results achieved by work carried out with equal intensity on the spiritual, charitable, and social levels were incalculable, as was demonstrated by subsequent years. The ranks of the FUCI sent forth top-notch men who later undertook to reconstruct their country after the collapse of Fascism. Aldo Moro, to cite only one example, met often with Montini and Righetti and bore the brunt of major responsibility during his years as national president of the association. Guido Gonella, Mario Scelba, Giovanni Gronchi and Mario Cingolani—significant names in the future of national public life as leaders of the Popular Party, which after the last war became the Christian Democrats—got their first experience in the ranks of the FUCI, as was also the case with Andreotti, Taviani, Spataro, Zaccagnini, Storchi and Vittorino Veronese and many others who later played a vigorous role in political life.

The English-speaking public will perhaps not be fully aware of the significance of the names just mentioned, but the varied sectors of public life which they represent show that, under Montini's guiding hand, the FUCI had worked well and in depth. The university students whom he directed in the '20s became the national leaders of the '60s. It may well be that no other spiritual director of young men on the university level has had such success in forming so many successful and respected leaders.

Aldo Moro is Prime Minister of the Italian government, having taken office in December, 1963. Giovanni Gronchi was President of Italy from 1957 to 1962. Mario Scelba was the hard-fisted Minister of the Interior, and later also Prime Minister, who held a tight reign on the national police and averted near-disaster after the attempted assassination of the Italian Communist leader, Togliatti, in 1948. Giulio Andreotti is Minister of National Defense, while Paolo Taviani is Minister of the Interior. Giuseppe Spataro, former Cabinet member, is now Senator of the Republic. Benigno

Zaccagnini heads the Christian Democrat group in the House of Deputies. Ferdinando Storchi is Under-Secretary for Foreign Affairs, while Vittorino Veronese is President of UNESCO, after having had an important role in the ranks of Italian Catholic Action. Few of them would have imagined in the 1920's that forty years later they would be occupying important positions in government, while their unassuming Assistant would be governing the Church of Christ.

"Monsignor" Montini—he had received this title at the age of twenty-eight—and his companion in responsibility, Igino Righetti, were at the head of the university association in the gravest crisis of its spirited battle against the Fascist youth organizations. The Fascist government was determined to swallow up in the Fascist university group all other student groups, suspecting and distrusting any other organization. Consequently, both Righetti and Montini often had to swallow some bitter pills, especially when they saw that Fascist party pressure was discouraging some of their members and inducing others, in their desire not to be bothered, to take out double membership cards. "Like us," states one of the *Fucini* of that era, "Monsignor Montini was skillful at finding the right word and the proper tone. We went to Sant'Ivo della Sapienza every Sunday morning at nine o'clock to listen to him. He held our attention with his quiet, calm and profound conversation. His personality was really a rallying-point for our souls."

Montini made constant efforts not to lose his calm, although his position was obviously most delicate. A policy of non-collaboration, passive resistance, watchful waiting for the future—that is to say, for the eventual fall of Fascism—all this was part of that patrimony of practicality which Monsignor Montini had learned at home and which was the basis of his attitude of prudence in moments of extreme difficulty. At home and within the circle of his friends, his lawyer-father had insisted on the policy of "preparation by abstention." A brother of the Pope, the

Honorable Ludovico Montini, recalls his father's advice: "When we were boys, our father used to repeat: 'We must get ready to see the light. We want no compromises. We must know just where we are going. When we have grown up, then we shall march.' "

Righetti was more impulsive and had no use for fence-sitters. He used to say: "You belong either to the FUCI or to the GUF (Fascist University Group)." To those who could not make up their minds he made it very clear: "Anyone interested in the GUF is out of place here."

These different character traits, which were in contradiction while really complementing one another, resulted in a deep cordiality and friendship between the National Counselor of the FUCI and its President. This friendship extended beyond the period of their collaboration, and ended only with death. Montini left his position as Counselor in 1932. Righetti, in whom everyone saw a future authoritative leader of Christian Democracy in Italy, died on March 17, 1939, at the age of thirty-five, in the arms of his closest friend. To his young wife who was then awaiting their second child, he whispered as he lay dying: "If it's a boy, call him Giovanni Battista, like Montini."

"Righetti was a leader without a trace of egoism or pride. He had the art of ennobling minds. He was strong enough to exert a commanding influence even on those higher than himself. The dictates of his conscience demanded both independence and resistance; he knew how to combine honesty in language and openness in conduct. He knew how to suffer without dishonor, and likewise how to win victories without claiming them for himself." This eulogy is from the pen of Montini himself, and was published by *Studium,* the magazine of the FUCI, which dedicated to its late president a special number with the very significant title: *The Virtues of a Leader.*

". . . with love and complete dedication."

It may seem that too much time has already been devoted to the events of 1939. Still, other details of this same period cannot simply be ignored, because they are at least very useful in filling out the picture of the activities of the future Pope and of their background.

First among these would be some of those frequent episodes which reflected the boundless charity of the Counselor of the *Fucini*. He was a convinced champion and tireless defender of Saint Vincent de Paul and worked enthusiastically to broaden the ideals and the activities of the Conferences named after this Saint of charity. One of the most abandoned areas in Rome at that time was around the famous Porta Metronia, which has now been completely rebuilt in the plan of urban development. Monsignor Montini would be seen in this section every week with his students, walking the rough and treacherous "streets" in order to devote himself to an activity which was charitable and generous, which brought him into contact not only with almost embittering poverty but also with blind and fanatical anti-clericalism. For this period there are numerous testimonies from persons closely associated with him.

One account comes from the memoirs of Enrico Zuppi, editor of *L'Osservatore della Domenica*, and of Ugo Piazza, a physician, but better known perhaps as a poet under the pen-name of "Puff." Professor Zuppi recounts that the first great gift he got from "Don G.B.M."—as the university students called Monsignor Montini—was his lessons on how to meet Christ by picking Him out in the midst of our superficial culture, giving Him real shape and form in what is at times almost an atmosphere of myth, carefully documenting His proper place in history, proving His divinity with logical arguments, describing Him in His humanity through the intelligent reading of the Gospel.

"Don Montini's other gift," continues this same professor, "more than in our unforgettable happy meetings, was through the abandoned shacks of Porta Metronia and the social and moral defeat which they represented. This section was located in an area where the Ministry for Tourism rises today. Don Montini guided our timid steps and took us into wretched hovels to discover suffering; he trained us to honest sympathy with our brother and to boundless charity. I can still see him preparing Christmas packages and gifts in 1925, if I recall correctly, in the parish offices of San Giovanni, where the pastor was Don Cartoni. He was surrounded by a choice group of *Fucini and Fucine*, all of them helping him generously in his task.

"He influenced us by example, and did not have to give orders. He persuaded with the simplicity of a word which reflected authority and he knew how to control the exuberance of youth. He gave us the satisfaction of doing good and of being, with him and like him, engaged in a great adventure. I recall how surprised I was at seeing how much at home he was with the poor. At first sight, he gave the impression of being a bit distant and aloof, I would even say on the cold side, but he definitely was not. He knew the secret of opening up hostile hearts and bringing pity to stony eyes, especially when his words (and his tears!) revealed the inner fiber of his charity."

Ugo Piazza's remarks, in turn, go back to the "Ritiri Minimi" or "Little Retreats" which Don Montini organized in the Benedictine Abbey of Saint Paul-Outside-the-Walls, with the collaboration of the then Abbot Ildefonso Schuster, O.S.B. From Saturday evening until Monday morning, groups of university students lodged in individual cells in the centuries-old abbey and were permitted to take part in the Divine Office. . . . Montini himself gave the conferences. None of us could ever have suspected that this invaluable spiritual project was bringing together two future Cardinals and Archbishops of Milan, and that in one of them the Lord had chosen His Vicar.

"But since faith without works is not real faith, those university students later followed Don Montini into streets echoing music which was anything but Gregorian. These "streets" were the dusty alleys of a huddle of shacks at Porta Metronia. This was the area lying between the Lateran Basilica and the Church of Saint John at the Latin Gate. It was a disgusting scene of embittered and rebellious misery. A zealous priest, Don Giovanni Contessa, who found Don Montini and his young students ready and courageous co-workers, was wearing himself out in the midst of these unfortunates. It was not merely a question of fighting hunger and illness, but still more of battling against immorality, the degradation of the family and the refusal of the Sacraments, even Baptism. Every week the gaunt priest from Brescia, with his markedly distinguished features and demeanor, moved in and around this depressed area, bringing material help, comfort and religious instruction. He was not at all perturbed if at times his first appearance at the edge of these squalid shacks provoked hostile whistles. There was always the 'thanks' of a sick person and the smile of a child to reward him amply."

Monsignor Montini attributed great importance to these contacts between his young university students and the social dregs of the suburbs, an importance, as well as an educational and social function, which went far beyond the practical effectiveness and immediate significance of the material and spiritual help they distributed. Little by little, the most prominent and most significant men of the Italy of today—all spiritual sons of Paul VI—felt the charm of their National Counselor's discreet insistence on the love of God through love of neighbor, on Christian responsibility and the pursuit of social justice.

Two other testimonies come from men who lived a long time in close intimacy with the future Pope and were thus in a position to observe his apostolate with the FUCI at close range. They are the more than eighty year-old friend of Paul VI, Father Giulio Bevilacqua, of the Oratory of Brescia, and Archbishop Sergio Pignedoli, presently Apostolic Delegate in Canada, formerly his Auxiliary in the Archdiocese of Milan.

"Montini," says Father Bevilacqua, "spoke to young people with a faith enriched with the treasures of the Gospel and the liturgy, and divine faith such as this always found expression in the whole man . . . because Don Battista is in love with the creative spirit of man under all its aspects: art, thought, culture, technical knowledge, and science. He worked with his young students in everything, following them with unflagging freshness and imagination in all the new discoveries of each succeeding day."

Archbishop Pignedoli emphasizes another aspect of Monsignor Montini's apostolate with young men: "The great prestige he had built up in the minds of these young students, whether in the solution of spiritual problems or especially in his confidence that he could solve them, flowed from his full and sure vision of Christianity. He saw Christianity in its complete and indivisible significance and before he saw it in its outside manifestations, he saw its role in the interior formation of conscience."

These remarks from friends have a value all their own. Nevertheless, they are less revealing than others coming from men who, after meeting Don Montini only once and experiencing directly the priestly warmth of his counsel have remained deeply impressed. Hence it will be useful to set down one further reminiscence from an old *Fucino*: "We loved him deeply," says this student, "even though he did not 'play' with us. He was always thin, distinguished, affable, and thoughtful, with those firm and transparent eyes which inspired confidence, and the charm of his northern twang which gave him dignity and authority. He was very precise in the celebration of Holy Mass, dignified, given to few but eloquent gestures, which seem to have remained unchanged because they are the natural expression of the language of the heart. . . . He was interested in our studies and liked to see us get good marks. He spoke to us in tones which were so delicately priestly that, notwithstanding our career as heirs of a faith which through the mercy of God has never known either weakness or crisis

or the uncertainties of suffering, we still keep that faith
in our hearts and ... have the strength to drag ourselves
back to the right path, to feelings of remorse and good
resolutions. These words were our salvation for many years
and God grant they may help us when our last hour comes.
Monsignor Montini dominates the scene of this fabulous
period of our lives."

Since the above lines have alluded to the Masses celebrated by the Ecclesiastical Assistant for his young students, it should be mentioned that these Masses were,
generally speaking, preceded or followed by discussions
which the young men still recall today as among the most
pleasant and most decisive of their lives. For Mass and
confessions, Monsignor Montini had chosen inside the Vatican a little church to which the people of Rome could have
access without going through the usual formalities with the
strict Swiss Guards. His friends always came in great numbers. They were all *Fucini*, but not all students; they were
joined by artists, professional men, and not a few girl
students.

On March 12, 1933, Monsignor Montini gave up his
work as Assistant to the FUCI, turning in his resignation
to Monsignor Giuseppe Pizzardo, who had been among the
first to discover and recognize publicly his excellent priestly
qualities and who in the meantime had left the Secretariate
of State to become Central Assistant of Catholic Action. The
future Cardinal addressed to his former protegé a letter
informing him that "the Holy Father Pius XI, in consideration of your growing duties in the Secretariate of State,
has accepted your resignation as Ecclesiastical Assistant of
FUCI, a post which you have filled with love and deep
dedication."

Those years had been happy ones for the young priest
from Brescia. They were also fruitful years, enriching his
soul both as a man and a priest. He said some twenty-five
years later that these were "wonderful years, rich in study
and reflection." It is extraordinary that even with all his

occupations, he could still find time for study and reflection. It could be said that there was only one main theme lighting and guiding his thoughts, namely, the Church.

"If anything comforts the heart of the Pope or his Bishops, it is a poor priest in a ragged cassock with buttons missing, surrounded by a group of boys who play with him, study with him, and meditate with him on their future, who are happy with him and believe him." These words Archbishop Montini spoke one day to his priests in the Archdiocese of Milan. But when he spoke in this fashion he could not fail to be thinking of the priest who, from 1925 until 1933, had been National Assistant of the FUCI and had always been happy to be surrounded by boys and young men who really loved him, even though, given his multiple duties in the Secretariate of State, he could not walk the streets of Rome in a ragged cassock with buttons missing. Certainly this was also his inspiration when he added: "This was a discovery. If I know anything at all, I owe it most of all to those dear friends of past years, because they were for me a stimulus, a living lesson, the kind that I could never have found in books and, I would say, not even in the example of the ecclesiastical world, which has so many other outstanding qualities."

He was glad to be dealing with young men and their problems, and when some of them were unaware of their problems, he brought them up! On the contrary, he did not like scatterbrained young men, perhaps because he could never stand superficiality, either in himself or in others. "Every surface," recalls a young man who knew him in those days, "was for him an invitation to look deep into the bottom.... I recall how shocked he was when he told me about a certain important individual who was working with young people but who was never given a problem to solve."

His worries as a priest seemed unjustified and exaggerated even to some persons very close to him. Perhaps the difficulty in understanding him was rooted, not in genuine misunderstanding, but rather in the desire to see him more at ease. Just the same, if people had been able to read in the depths of his soul, they would have seen that there calm and serenity always reigned supreme. "I always told Don Battista not to work so hard, to leave something for the others. I always told him not to stay up until two in the morning. I always told him that if he did, he would ruin his health. Lastly, above all, I always told him not to be so much of a questionmark." These remarks come from Father Bevilacqua. And yet this same priest concludes: "What can I tell you? A man like Giovanni Battista Montini, simple and reserved, always lived a life which was more on the inside than on the surface. I know, because we have been friends for sixty years." "He was a constant friend," another recalls, "in days of sadness and in days of joy. He was perhaps a severe friend, but approachable like few other men. For us, his name is inseparably linked up with the great moments of our life: marriage, the Baptism of our children, the last rites for the friends who have gone before us."

Among these friends there was especially one who was beside himself when he learned that Monsignor Montini would no longer be Ecclesiastical Assistant of the FUCI. This was Igino Righetti. To protest against such a "loss" he rushed to the Secretariate of State only to find the Secretary himself, Cardinal Pacelli, with a ready reply: "Monsignor Montini is so gifted that he is destined to render to the Church still more important service in much higher positions." The comment of Pius XI, when he learned of the resignation of the Ecclesiastical Assistant, had been no less eloquent: "Fine! Now We can have him exclusively for the service of the Holy See."

Tardini succeeds Pizzardo—
Montini succeeds Tardini

The name of a new publication, *Studium,* which had
been planned by the President of the university association,
Righetti, and the Assistant, Montini, had been suggested by
a magazine of the same name, which had been spokesman
for the university organization as far back as 1904. The
presses of this new publishing house were the first to pub-
lish the three essays written by the Assistant, mainly for
his young men. They appeared under the following titles:
1) *The Life of Christ*: Outlines of Lessons on the Precepts
of Catholic Morality for Students of Higher Schools, 123
pages; 2) *Introduction to the Study of Christ*: Outlines of
Lessons in Religion for the Students of Higher Schools,
178 pages; 3) *The conscience of a University Student*:
Notes for Students, 110 pages. As is indicated by the sub-
titles, these essays aimed principally to fill in a regrettable
gap in the spiritual and human formation of young men
on the university level.

This, however, was not his first experience with the
Catholic publishing world. For the "Morcelliana" of Brescia,
which had close ties with the Montini family, and for
"La Scuola," of which his lawyer-father had been president
for many years, he had already translated and published
Jacques Maritain's *Three Reformers*: *Luther, Descartes,*
Rousseau, as also an Italian version of Father Léonce de
Grandmaison's *Personal Religion*. He also suggested a com-
plete list of authors who might contribute to a series aimed
at a new awakening of Catholic culture.

Monsignor Montini was interested in "giving Catholic
thought a modern bent, a new cultural framework, a broader diffusion, a coherent and progressive application." The
era when the new publishing house was being organized
was a dark one in Italian history. The decision to resurrect
Studium implied a generous act of faith in the worth of cul-

ture, one which can exist even when the right of free association is outlawed. It was not so long before the congress at Macerata and the incidents already mentioned, as also the threat of suppression for the Catholic university association was already looming up darkly. "If tomorrow our ranks should be dissolved," wrote the university students' Don G.B.M. "they will be re-formed by themselves. We must try to find a recognized formula which can serve as our rallying-point." These were the circumstances in which the new publishing house was launched: "If the FUCI is to be really an association where ideas are discussed, not amateurishly and casually, but in a way which will contribute to formation and progress, and which will provide a training ground for those who tomorrow will give witness to Catholic thought, then we need an editorial organ."

To assure greater effectiveness to this activity in depth which was being organized for young men in the university, an important forward step had to be taken. The FUCI had to guarantee the continuity of its apostolate even when its members had left behind them the comparatively easy years of books and classrooms. This was clear to the young men themselves as, one after the other, they began to assume new responsibilities in life and society. Consequently, in December, 1930, that is to say two years before the official launching of the Catholic Graduates Movement, Monsignor Montini wrote in *Azione Fucina*, a paper of the association in which the signature of the Assistant alternated with those of Giulio Andreotti, who wrote articles on sociology, and Paolo Emilio Taviani, who was fascinated by poetry: "The university comes to an end, but there is no end to university education, that is to say, one which is scientific, deeply intellectual, and also speculatively and morally (not practically) professional—just as there is no end to that friendship which during our university years has given to our companionship the bond of the same ideas and that of memorable and unalloyed friendship. Consequently, the FUCI will have to discover the secret, that is to say, the

basis of an organization of Catholic graduates of which we
are not outlining here the organizational structure nor the
practical content, but only its necessity and possibility. This
organization does not cease, and will not cease, to insist
that its new members must remain faithful to their habits
of work, deep prayer, noble friendship and youthfulness
of spirit which they have contributed and are contributing
to the FUCI."

Two years later, as the result of the FUCI Congress
at Cagliari in the summer of 1932, there came into being
the Catholic Graduates Movement, which Monsignor Montini and Igino Righetti regarded as "an indispensable and
pressing ideal extension of the Catholic University Movement." The decade spent by Monsignor Montini in the
student apostolate reached a magnificent conclusion. Foun-
dations had been laid for a surer and more fruitful life for
the association.

From that moment on, he could dedicate himself entirely to the duties entailed by his responsibilities in the
Secretariate of State. These duties were supplemented by
his assignment to the Chair of the History of Papal Diplomacy at the Ecclesiastical Academy in 1931. To someone
who expressed some surprise that he could find the time
for such a task he replied simply: "I like to teach, because
this keeps me from neglecting my books."

For about five years Monsignor Montini succeeded in
keeping clear of new responsibilities. But in December,
1937, when Pius XI elevated to the Cardinalate Monsignor
Pizzardo, who had up until then been Secretary of the
Congregation for Extraordinary Ecclesiasical Affairs, he
was replaced by Monsignor Domenico Tardini. As successor
to Monsignor Tardini, Pius XI chose Monsignor Montini
who thus found himself for the first time in direct contact
with Eugenio Pacelli, who had been Secretary of State for
the last eight years.

When, on March 2, 1939, Cardinal Pacelli was elevated
to the Chair of Peter as Pius XII, Monsignor Montini was

re-confirmed as Under-Secretary of State, while the office of Secretary was assumed by Cardinal Luigi Maglione. At his death on August 22, 1944, the Secretariate of State, for all practical purposes, was taken over by Monsignors Montini and Tardini, since Pius XII—"his own secretary," as people were remarking—saw no need to designate a successor to the late Cardinal. It was more than eight years before the Pope named these two faithful collaborators Pro-Secretaries of State, turning over ordinary affairs to Monsignor Montini and extraordinary affairs to Monsignor Tardini.

From then on, because of the demands of his work, Monsignor Montini's visits to his native Brescia became increasingly rare. Still it was only natural that he should snatch a week during the summer months for a quick visit to Concesio, in order to rest and regain the strength of which he gave so generously in his trying work. But during the rest of the year, like Pius XII, he was a "prisoner" within the little circle of the Vatican. It was only with difficulty that, in 1943, he was able to perform his duty as a devoted son, hurrying to the deathbeds of his beloved parents who, only a few months from each other, left this land of exile.

Montini—Tardini

It is not without a touch of sly humor that someone has said that "a Secretary of State is like an all-powerful shadow, whose work is always on the increase while his credit for it decreases." Monsignor Montini and Monsignor Tardini, without being Secretary of State, were well able to recognize the truth of this definition. Monsignor Montini's work was killing, but his name appeared very rarely. He moved in the gigantic shadow of Pius XII, to whom he dedicated his services. This situation was very much in keeping with his personal tastes. He was passionately in

love with work, work for the Church, which was the great
object of his love. At the same time, through a kind of
instinctive modesty, he preferred to remain in the background where no one would be aware of his presence.

In the Secretariate of State his capacity for work was
proverbial. "When we reached the office at 9:00 A.M.,"
wrote one of his colleagues, "we not only found him already in his office but he had given out each one's work
assignments for the day." In an office near his, with a
tenacity and perseverance much like his own, Monsignor
Tardini, Secretary for Extraordinary Affairs, carried on his
work. Their capacity for work was equal, but their personalities were so different that certain individuals delighted
in emphasizing these contrasts with a little touch of malice.

A writer, Silvio Negro, who knew both these outstanding men intimately, wrote as follows: "The dissimilarity
between the two was already most noticeable in their
physical characteristics. Montini was tall and thin, while
Tardini was short and stocky. The first showed signs of a
marked tendency towards baldness, while the second had a
habit of cocking constantly to one side a bushy head of
grey hair. The man from Brescia was very susceptible to
drafts, while ever since the days of his youth, the man from
Rome spent his annual vacations at Chianciano taking the
liver cure. But their dissimilarity was still more marked in
their temperament and their features and also reflected the
different localities in which they had been raised, their
different family backgrounds, and the schools in which
they had been trained. One was an alumnus and the pride
of the Roman Seminary, while the other came from the
Lombard Seminary. One of them had a cordial smile for
the bore waiting in his outer office, while the other received
this same individual with ill-concealed annoyance and with
brusque words. The generosity of the first was expressed in
comprehension and confidence, and that of the second
pushed on hurriedly on the level of realistic evaluation
and violent disagreement. One was very precise in his man-

ners and careful about his speech, while the other was nonchalant, down to earth, famous throughout Rome for his ready wit.

Certainly, these two outstanding figures in the Secretariate of State were very different, and yet at the same time they shared too many noble characteristics not to find themselves in agreement on essentials. Both of them were generous, although they showed it in different ways. Each of them abhorred second-rate conformism, self-seeking, cheap tricks, and stupid remarks, but at the same time both were clear-eyed gentlemen and great servants of the Church. To speak of the one without recalling the other, after having so often seen the two of them close together at their work, would be an offense against both at this moment (Montini's appointment to Milan) when the Church is separating them. After all there is not much difference if one of them remains in Rome while the other goes to Milan, because right after the cupola of Saint Peter's comes the Duomo of Milan."

The diplomacy of Monsignor Montini

In a brief sketch of Paul VI, the above writer remarks: "The entire government of the Universal Church during the difficult years of World War II, went through the hands of Montini. To him and to his colleague Tardini belongs much of the credit for the pontificate of Pius XII." The deep realism of these words would perhaps not be so evident, had it not been necessary to compare the intense activity of the two Pro-Secretaries. Montini and Tardini together formed a pair and were the keystone of the intense activity of the Secretariate of State in a period made extremely trying and delicate by the horrors of war and the political revolutions which mushroomed out of the war.

By reason of his particular relationship with Pius XII, the work of the Under-Secretary of State had taken on world-wide proportions. In the first place, it was his task to assure contact with the Episcopate, even when the heads of certain dioceses were Cardinals. At the Secretariate, Monsignor Montini's tireless activity was well-known. At Rome it was said that in the Vatican only two windows remained lighted until the wee hours of the morning—the one in the office of His Holiness Pope Pius XII, and the other in that of his Under-Secretary of State.

During the war Monsignor Montini was the right arm of the Pope, as also the instrument and sometimes the organizer of the Pope's important charitable undertakings. He had an active role in organizing the Pontifical Relief Commission to provide urgent assistance to the most needy victims of the horrors of war. He also made a decisive contribution to setting up the ACLI (Italian Workers Catholic Action) to insure the Christian presence of work in the world, and of the Italian Catholic Womens Federation (CIF) to train women for social activities.

In those difficult years, Monsignor Montini bore up under his duties with humility and a spirit of dedication, even in the most dramatic moments of World War II when the Vatican, as Father Bevilacqua recalls, became "the throbbing heart of crucified humanity." Monsignor Montini was the main cog in this marvelous transformation. When, immediately after the bombardment of Rome, Pius XII left the Vatican to go, like a father, to help and ask mercy for his Roman children in the Tiburtina section still threatened by enemy bombardment, the Pope's faithful collaborator was at his side, a sorrowing witness of the ruins and the tears of the victims. Monsignor Montini was also on hand during the war when the Holy See multiplied its charitable efforts to relieve the sufferings of all peoples and when, at the end of the war, it was necessary to face up courageously to the immense task of reconstruction.

In his work as papal diplomat, Monsignor Montini knew how to keep a situation completely in hand, even in most touchy situations. It is related that on one occasion, at an official dinner, he found himself seated between the ambassadors of two nations at war with each other. Fully aware of how easily a similar situation could arouse suspicions of connivance or sympathy for one side or the other, Monsignor Montini maintained a dignified silence throughout the entire banquet, limiting himself to occasional observations at those moments of the conversation which could not be given sinister interpretations by even the most suspicious of the guests.

For a description of the activities and methods of Monsignor Montini at the Secretariate of State Silvio Negro provides interesting observations in an article written in 1958 when Archbishop Montini was appointed Cardinal: "The first surprise for anyone who felt he knew him well was to find in the very first meeting, that the Under-Secretary of State received every caller as a friend. This does not mean that it was easy to reach his office. Ordinarily there was a long wait which, among other advantages, provided an opportunity to meet and size up unexpected individuals, because it should not be forgotten that through the waiting room of the Under-Secretary, there passes the whole of the Catholic world and a good part of the rest of the world as well. But once a caller's turn had come, his wait was rewarded by most pleasant surprises, especially, that of being invited to sit down comfortably, of being treated with affable confidence, and having a prompt and courteous reply to every question.

"It was surprising also, not only to find a man who joined with the finesse of a diplomat a simplicity and a cordiality of expression absolutely opposed to any kind of formalism, but also a man who was alive and fresh, whose temperament had not suffered from the killing pace of an office routine which would have ruined anyone else. It seemed particularly incredible, in those surroundings where secrecy usually reaches the heights of the absurd even in insignificant things, to find such a high-ranking prelate always answering quietly, never beating around the bush, never take shortcuts, not averse to a bit of humor, and who did not mutilate and force questions, but rather expanded them on his own initiative, developing them with a richness of observations and information.

"He was a man who was alive and fresh but, most particularly, his culture was alive and fresh, and this was a surprise even more meaningful and special than the first one. Nothing can be more natural than for a high prelate to quote to you Dante and Saint Thomas. But it is really a surprise that he should also be able to quote just as easily Thomas Mann, Bergson and Schlegel. It may very well be that the formation of the man along these special lines came from the fact that Montini never followed the regular course of studies, that he was ordained priest at Brescia without having lived the common life of a seminary for more than a few months, that in earlier years he had not followed the *ginnasio* and the *liceo* because of poor health. Even in his later university studies at the Lombard Seminary in Rome he did not follow the regular courses because the authorities in the Secretariate of State were so anxious to avail themselves without delay of the talents of this slender and dark young man on whom they already had their eyes."

Long though it may be, this extract offers a living portrait of the man whom the author did not live to see Pope.

Giovanni Battista Montini was not yet Cardinal, but only Archbishop of Milan. Angelo Giuseppe Roncalli was not yet Pope, but Cardinal Patriarch of Venice. But they were old friends who grew even closer with the passing years.

Donna Giuditta Alghisi (above, left) and Don Giorgio Montini (right) parents of the future Pope. Donna Giuditta was President of the Catholic Women's Association of Brescia; Don Giorgio was a lawyer, for twenty-four years editor of a Catholic daily, and deputy in three sessions of Parliament. The photo below shows young Montini's report card.

"The priesthood is a service to society. It exists for others. Priesthood and egoism are contradictory terms. Priesthood and charity are synonymous." The words were written in later years by Giovanni Battista Montini, who was ordained priest on May 29, 1920.

Cardinal Alfredo Ottaviani, Cardinal Proto-Deacon, crowns Paul VI with the tiara in a service on June 30, 1963, in Saint Peter's Piazza, before an imposing throng. Below, the first Blessing Urbi et Orbi, an hour after his election, June 21, 1963.

The photos show Paul VI with three important members of the
Sacred College of Cardinals. In the first, with Cardinal Eugene
Tisserant, Dean of the Sacred College (above, left); in the second,
with Cardinal Augustin Bea, outstanding for his efforts at bringing about good understanding between the Church and her separated
brethren. The photo below shows His Holiness with the Primate of
Belgium, Cardinal Leo Josef Suenens, one of his closest friends and
also one of the most prominent of the non-Italian Cardinals.

John XXIII felt proud to have Giovanni Battista Montini as his "first Cardinal."

"*I have nothing but blessings to give*" (Paul VI). *Since the day John XXIII broke long-standing traditions by making frequent visits outside the Vatican, it is much easier to see the Pope. John XXIII introduced another winning custom, that of reciting the Angelus with the faithful, from the window of his apartment, on Sundays and holydays, and other special occasions. This is followed by the Holy Father's Blessing to the faithful in the piazza.*

*"Montini is a man who is at ease in our age,"
the Milanese said of their Cardinal Archbishop.*

"*Remember, O Lord, how he prayed, swiftly recollected, swiftly alone with You, in order to be before You and with You the Priest of the World. . . . He loved justice, he loved truth, and for this reason he tasted the bitter but exhilarating blessedness of persecution, aversion, and misunderstanding.*" (Montini in his funeral discourse for Pius XII).

"He made us see that the truth, religious truth first of all, is not by itself intended to divide men but to draw them to unity of thought, to serve them with pastoral concern, to infuse into their souls the joy of the conquest of brotherhood and divine life." (*Funeral discourse for John XXIII*).

Giovanni Battista Montini received his first diplomatic assignment in May, 1925, when he was sent to the Apostolic Nunciature of Warsaw. Perhaps because of his months spent in the capital of Poland Paul VI makes no secret of his affection for the heroic Primate of Poland, Stefan Wyszynski (photo above).

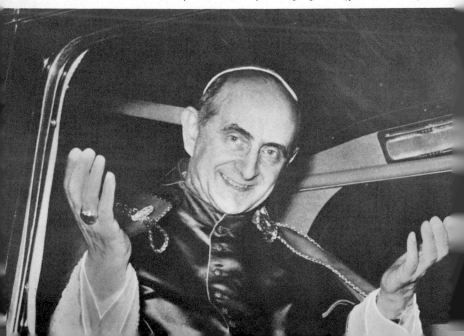

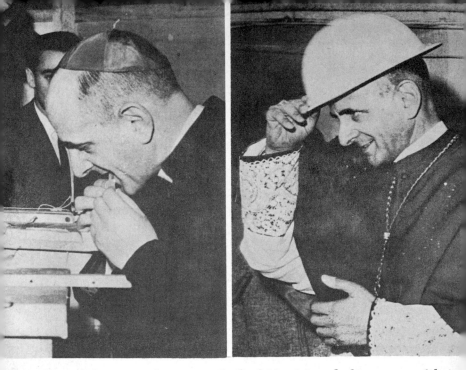

Through his pastoral activities Cardinal Montini made his presence felt in all the sectors of life at Milan. Because of the special social conditions of the capital of Lombardy, this was especially true of his contacts with the laboring classes. (Above, right). On the left, he performs his duty as a citizen, casting his vote in the national elections, while he was still Cardinal.

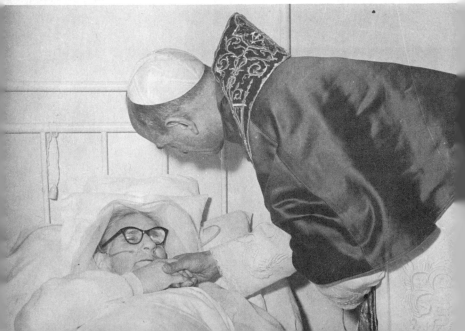

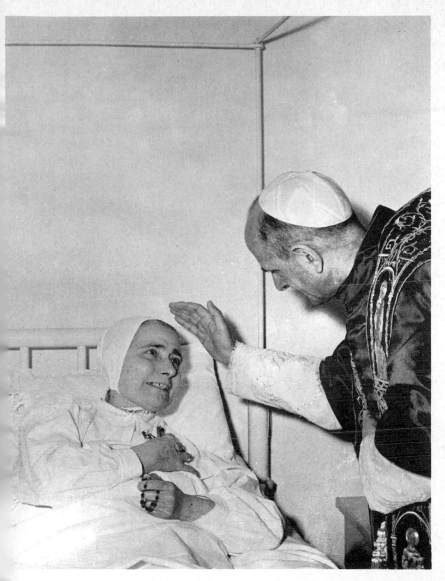

"One can suffer with rebellion in one's heart. One who does not believe, who does not pray, suffers in this way, even if he is silent. There is a second way to suffer, and this is with patience. But there is still another, namely to suffer with love and out of love. This can be done always, even when one has not the strength to say prayers or to make other exercises of piety. As long as the heart is alive, it is capable of this act, which is so sublime, and which sums up the whole of our spirituality; love." (Paul VI to the sick Sisters at the "Regina Apostolorum" clinic at Albano, conducted by the Daughters of Saint Paul.)

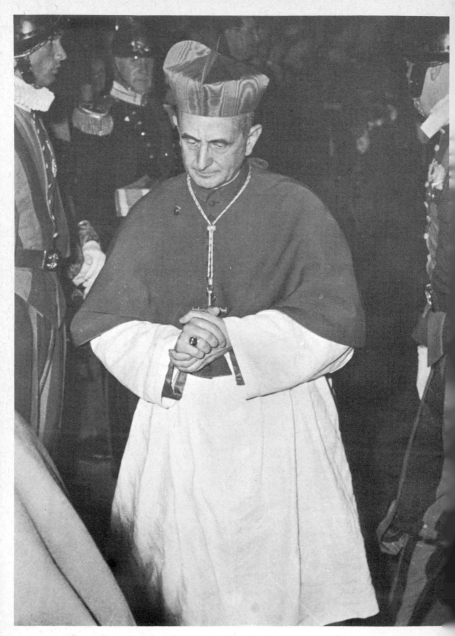

Recollected, strangely silent and detached from everything around him, Giovanni Battista Montini makes his way towards the Conclave. Among the eighty Cardinals present, he was candidate Number One. This dismayed the man who had said at the funeral of Pope John: "Can we stray from the path which, with such ardor, he opened up before the religious history of the future, namely that of a greater understanding of the universality of the Catholic Faith?"

**THE
SECOND
VATICAN
COUNCIL**

Pope John's heritage has passed into good hands. The continuance of the "Roncalli line" is guaranteed by the presence of him who stated in his first discourse: "The pre-eminent part of Our pontificate will be taken up with the continuation of the Second Ecumenical Vatican Council."—In the photos: Paul VI presiding at a Council Commission of Cardinals (above); the Observers from the separated Churches during a ceremony in Saint Peter's (below)

he Cardinal of Bologna, Giacomo Lercaro, is, among the Italian Cardinals,
he most outstanding representative of the pastoral approach. His discourses
i the Council Hall, both in the First and the Second Sessions, were to the
oint and were welcomed warmly. Particularly timely was his speech on pov-
ty in the ministers of the Church and his formula for the "qualitative uni-
rsalism" of the Church, which instead of concentrating on multiplying in-
ividual conversions, would strive to become the leaven of the world.

The Council favors useful exchanges of viewpoints even outside *actual encounters* in the Council Hall. It also helps the Fathers to meet old friends, as in the accompanying photos, with Cardinals Francis Spellman, Archbishop of New York, and Albert Gregory Meyer, Archbishop of Chicago.

Cardinal Amleto Giovanni Cicognani who, before becoming Secretary of State under Pope John had been for twenty-five years Apostolic Delegate in the United States, is highly esteemed by the hierarchy for his discretion and fidelity, which have won for him universal affection. The photo shows him in conversation with an old friend.

Cardinal Julius Döpfner, former Bishop of Berlin and now Archbishop of Munich, is one of the youngest and most dynamic Cardinals of the Church and, with Cardinals Alfrink, Suenens, Léger, Liénart, Lercaro, Bea and Wyszynski, is an insistent champion of the pastoral approach which dominates the Council. This, with the high esteem in which he is held, makes of his presence in Rome an excellent opportunity for the many Bishops anxious to consult him.

The Polish Cardinal Stefan Wyszynski, Archbishop of Warsaw, is the most prominent spokesman in the Council for a portion of the Church living under very special conditions. It is the Cardinal's greatest claim to distinction that he has been able to assure survival for the Church in Poland, under a government which is notoriously marxist and atheistic. With Cardinals Cushing and Suenens, Cardinal Wyszynski is one of the most popular Cardinals at the Council, even though each one's popularity is for different reasons.

The presence in Rome of the Observers from the separated Churches is one of the most significant characteristics of this Council which has unity as one of its principal aims. In his opening discourse of the Second Session on September 29, 1963, Paul VI himself outlined explicitly and clearly the aims of the Second Vatican Council: 1) a more exact and more explicit definition of the Church; 2) the internal renewal of the Church; 3) the return of separated Christians; 4) the dialogue of the Church with the world of today. In an audience granted to the Observers on October 17, 1963, Paul VI remarked: "We repeat to you once more, thank you for accepting Our invitation, thank you for coming, thank you for your presence in the Council sessions. Be assured of Our respect, Our esteem, Our desire to establish with you, in our Lord, the closest possible contacts." The presence of the Observers in the Council is largely the work of Cardinal Augustin Bea, formerly confessor of Pope Pius XII, who notwithstanding his age—he was born in May, 1881—has worked tirelessly with Pope John, as now with Paul VI, towards rapprochement with our separated brethren.

When General Congregations are held during the Council, scenes
like this are of daily occurrence. Twice a day, at the beginning of
the Congregation, towards 9 AM., and again at the end, around
12:30 P.M., the piazza fills with Bishops who, were it not for their
age and the colors of their robes, could easily be taken for the
students of the ecclesiastical colleges of the city. Some of them
pose for souvenir photographs beside a papal guard in uniform
(below, left) or before the "Pieta" of Michelangelo (below, right).

In the midst of the 2,500 prelates assembled in Rome for the Council identification is not easy In the photo at the left the prelate with glasses and a beard is Archbishop Felix Scalais, of Léopoldville, Africa. Below: a group of Oriental Bishops.

One day less than two months after his election, the clinic "Regina Apostolorum," belonging to the Daughters of Saint Paul and restricted to sick Sisters of all communities, was pleasantly surprised by a visit from His Holiness, who was spending a short period of rest at the nearby papal villa of Castel Gandolfo. The Holy Father was welcomed by Rev. James Alberione, Founder of the Daughters of Saint Paul and by Rev. Father Zanoni. Present also were Mother Thecla Merlo, first Superior General of the Congregation, with her Vicaress, Mother Ignazia Balla (photo below).

Contact with politicians is necessary for the Pope because politics is at the center of tension between God and Caesar. Thanks to exceptional preparation and experience, Paul VI is able to study the political aspects of problems with instinct and courage. Among the visits of prominent political leaders to Pope Paul VI were those of John Fitzgerald Kennedy (above), U Thant, Erhard, Antonio Segni, Giuseppe Saragat, and Aldo Moro (below), King Baudouin of Belgium and Conrad Adenauer.

On June 21, 1963, it was a little more than an hour since, in reply to the question of the Dean of the Sacred College, Cardinal Eugene Tisserant, Giovanni Battista Montini had accepted his election as Pope. The above photo shows the new Pope surrounded by the Cardinals. In the photo below, Paul VI with Cardinal Rugambwa, the Church's first Negro Cardinal, elevated to the Sacred College by Pope John XXIII; also the Pope in the Saint Paul Book Center in Milan while still a Cardinal.

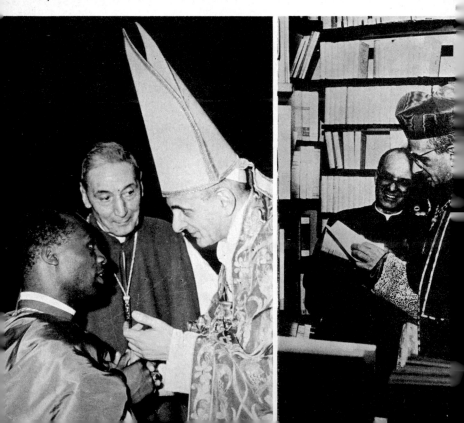

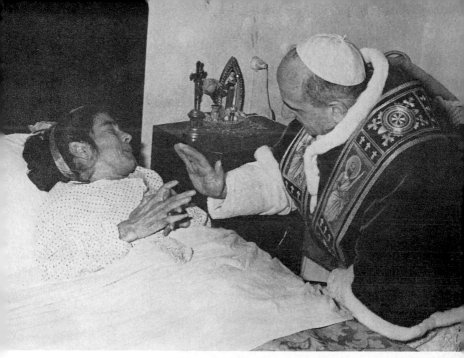

On October 13, 1963, Paul VI presided his first Beatification ceremony, that of John Nepomucene Neumann, C.SS.R., fourth Bishop of Philadelphia. This ceremony had previously been planned during the pontificate of Pope John XXIII but was postponed because of the grave illness and subsequent death of the Pontiff. Pope Paul VI decided to a numerous group of American pilgrims who had already set out for Rome for the Beatification.

THE
PILGRIM
POPE

"Behold, Lord Jesus, we have come like criminals returning to the scene of their crime ... We have come to strike our breasts, to ask pardon of You, to beg for Your mercy. (Paul VI). In the photos: The Holy Father kissing the ground on Calvary (above) and the Rock of the Primacy of Peter (below)

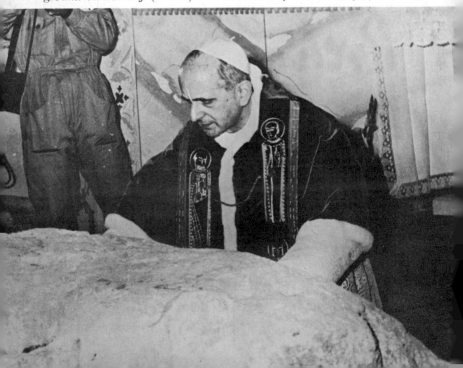

The Sovereign Pontiff, on his knees in the Cenacle. Here, on the night before His death, Christ had celebrated the Last Supper with His Apostles and had instituted the Holy Eucharist.

"From this land unique in the world for the grandeur of the events which took place within its boundaries, Our humble prayer rises to God for all men, believers and non-believers" (Paul VI). In the photos, from left to right: The portrait of the visiting Pope hung in the streets alongside that of King Hussein of Jordan; the Pope making his way along the Via Dolorosa; the Pope celebrates Mass at the Holy Sepulchre; Mass in the Grotto of the Annunciation.

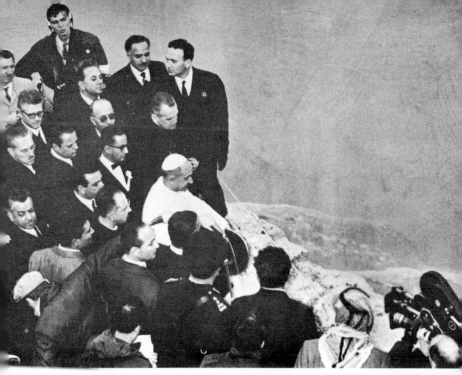

"We would want Our words express all Our emotion at eing with Our eyes and eading with Our feet this nd where lived for a time e Patriarchs, our Fathers in e Faith; this land where ere resounded for so many nturies the voice of the ophets, speaking in the me of the God of Abraham, ıac and Jacob; this land, tly and above all, which e presence of the Blessed sus has rendered blessed d sacred for Christians and, can be said, for the entrie man race." (Paul VI). In e photos: Paul VI on the nks of the Jordan where us was baptized by the cursor, John the Baptist, bove); and at the Lake of erias, which had witnessed er's call to be an Apostle l many of Christ's mir-es (photo at the side).

"It was fitting that in this spot, in this center forever sacred and
blessed, we pilgrims from Rome and Constantinople, should
meet and join in common prayer." (Paul VI to Athenagoras).

"May this meeting be the dawn of a luminous and blessed day, in which future generations will praise and glorify in charity, peace, and humility, the one Lord and Savior of the world." (Athenagoras to Paul VI).

The Pope did not miss up on any of the little details which make a guest's visit the more welcome. Thus, to the greetings and messages addressed to all rulers and peoples in the countries crossed by his jet en route to the Holy Land, he added gifts for his hosts. The photos show: medals commemorating the pilgrimage (above); the eighteenth-century clock given to King Hussein of Jordan (below, left); the artistic gift received from Patriarch Athenagoras, to whom Paul VI gave a golden chalice (below, center), and one of the nineteenth-century silver candlesticks, offered to His Excellency Salman Shazar, President of the State of Israel (below, right).

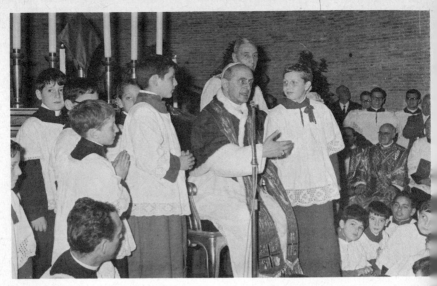

On one of his Sunday visits to the parishes of his diocese of Rome, Paul VI,
in the presence of the faithful assembled in the church, engaged in a catechism dialogue with the altar-boys whom he had gathered around him in
the sanctuary (above). One of the winningly human characteristics
of Paul VI, apparently timid in the presence of the great, but who
is expansive and cordial with children (below, right and left).

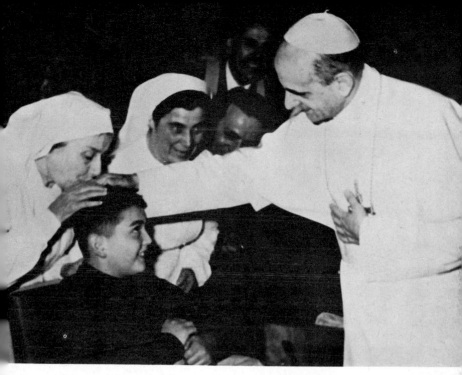

o more eloquent pictures (above and at
side) of a human and warm heart, the
rt of Paul VI, in the presence of the
fering and the innocence of children. It
uld be possible to make up an album, one
ich would be a visual poem, of photo-
phs showing his calm cordiality, the
erly warmth of the Archbishop of Milan
of the Shepherd of the Church with
dren and those suffering. It is signifi-
or, better still, deeply moving, to see
a man with the intelligence and moral
deur of Paul VI can so easily become
and simple with those who are little
simple. This could be Paul VI's person-
nd quiet realization of the condition
down by Christ when He said: "Unless
become as little children, you will not
r into the kingdom of heaven." At the
h of John XXIII, it might have seemed
the episodes of his kindly thoughtful-
could never be repeated in any other
. But Paul VI destroyed all such pre-
es, manifesting a most delicate sense
man feeling, perhaps less apparent and
gious than that of his predecessor, but,
that of Pope John, sincere and deep.

In 1960, His Holiness, Pope Paul VI, (then Cardinal Montini),
honored the Daughters of St. Paul with a visit to their Novitiate
in Boston U.S.A., accompanied by His Eminence, Richard
Cardinal Cushing. Having blessed a new press, he gave the
Community his blessing saying that he was doing so "in the
name of your holy Founder," whose apostolic founda-
tions he has always followed closely and warmly encouraged.

His Eminence, Richard Cardinal Cushing of Boston was one of the first Cardinals to be received in private audience by Paul VI after his election.

THE EIGHT YEARS AT MILAN

"... *my thoughts are not your thoughts, and my ways are not your ways (Isa. 55:8). These words of Isaias come to mind spontaneously as an introduction to this present chapter. Many, even among those who spend their lives interpreting the moves of the ecclesiastical world, had concluded that by turning down the Red Hat and accepting an appointment to Milan, the steps of Giovanni Battista Montini were moving away from a goal in which many saw the outlines of the Papacy. On the contrary, it happened that precisely where the most illustrious son of Concesio seemed to be straying from the road to the Throne of Peter, God was tracing out the straightest possible line towards a sublime destiny. Archbishop Montini's years in Milan were responsible for testing his strong personality in view of the loftiest mission a man can be summoned to carry out on earth. The eight years, six months and sixteen days spent in the administration of the largest diocese in the Church—from January 6, 1955, until June 21, 1963—were rich in experience and pastoral conquests and fruitful in their achievements. They were eight years which have inscribed the name of the future Pope in the most resplendent pages of a line of Bishops which includes Saint Ambrose, Saint Charles Borromeo, Andrea Ferrari, Achille Ratti, Eugenio Tosi, and Idlefonso Schuster. . . .*

It was natural that the highest recognition of Montini's accomplishments in the Secretariate of State should come from his direct superior, Pope Pius XII. In reality, no one could find a more flattering compliment than the one which His Holiness expressed on January 12, 1953, to the Sacred College in the second and last Consistory of his pontificate.

"There is another point," said the Pope on that occasion, "which We cannot pass over in silence. It was Our intention to add to the ranks of your Sacred College the two distinguished prelates who are in charge respectively of the offices of the Secretariate of State and whose names headed the list of Cardinals chosen by Us, and drawn up with Our own hand. Nevertheless, the above mentioned prelates, thus giving outstanding proof of virtue, begged Us so insistently to be dispensed from this lofty dignity that We thought it best to accept their repeated requests and their wishes. But in doing this We wished in some way to reward their virtue and in fact, as you know We have granted them a higher title, which more effectively and more fully attests to their generous activity."

Pius XII was referring to the new title he had just conferred on his two closest collaborators. They were no longer to be *minutanti*, nor even Under-Secretaries for Ordinary and Extraordinary Affairs, but Pro-Secretaries of State. For Montini this was his last official title in his long intense years of work in the direct service of the Holy See. Tardini, on the contrary, became Secretary of State of John XXIII some years later and received from the Pope the first confidence on his grandiose plan to convoke an Ecumenical Council.

"The work of Monsignor Montini," says *L'Osservatore Romano* for June 22, 1963, "first as Under-Secretary and then as Pro-Secretary of State, cannot be separated from that of the Pontiff whose intimate and esteemed collaborator he was, as also the interpreter and faithful executor of his directives, in a period of history ravaged by war and by its terrible consequences on the whole of the civilized world. The identity of purpose of these two men was always complete. This is to the credit of the future Paul VI, who thus throughout those many years had the good fortune not merely to co-ordinate and control in his own particular sector the ever-expanding activities of the Pope on behalf of peoples caught up in tremendous disasters, but also had the privilege of transmitting to each of the thousands upon thousands of suffering individuals the word of the Pope in its most faithful, most living, and most earnest timeliness. Thus today, as can be stated with well-weighed historical precision, no one knows more completely or more surely than Paul VI the secret sufferings of Pius XII and his unflinching determination to pursue justice and peace in the midst of that chaos of hate and blood."

On this point there is a very recent statement, so recent in fact that it goes back only to the days immediately preceding Cardinal Montini's election to the papal throne. It comes from the Cardinal himself and, although, indirectly, it sheds a light on his relationships with Pius XII during the war years. This testimony is taken from a letter which, just before the Conclave, the Cardinal Archbishop of Milan sent to the editor of the English weekly *The Tablet,* to deny the malevolent insinuations of the playwright Hochhuth in a theater production for which a scandal-mongering public assured greater success than was really justified by the play itself. The Cardinal wrote: "I had the good fortune to go to Pius XII and to serve him every day during his pontificate, beginning in 1937 when he was still Secretary of State, until 1954, that is to say, throughout the whole period of World War II. It is true that my duties in the Pope's service were not directly in the political field or in that of 'extraordinary affairs,' as they are known in the Roman Curia. But the kindliness of Pope Pius XII and the very nature of my duties as Under-Secretary of State gave me an opportunity to know the mind, even the soul, of this great Pontiff. The figure of Pius XII as portrayed by Hochhuth is false. It is not at all true, for example, that he was timid, either by natural temperament or because he was aware of being invested with a power and a mission. In this connection I could quote many details to prove how Pius XII, though in appearance lean and kindly, and with words which were always well chosen and moderate, hid, or rather revealed, a noble and virile character, ready to take stands calling for great strength and involving fearless risk."

This text shows that Cardinal Montini's language was becoming polemical. But the extract is so eloquent and significant that it will be in order to set before the reader other salient passages as well: "It is not true that he was cold and distant. On the contrary his was a most delicate and sensitive soul. He liked solitude because, precisely, the richness of his spirit and his extraordinary capacity for thought and work looked for opportunities to avoid useless distractions and needless recreations. But he was not a stranger to life, nor indifferent to persons or current events. Actually, he wanted to be kept briefed on everything and, even to the point of interior suffering, to share in the ordeal of the period of history of which he felt himself a part.

"It is not difficult to understand why Pius XII did not take a stand of violent opposition against Hitler in order to save millions of Jews from slaughter, provided one does not repeat Hochhuth's error, namely, judging the possibilities of an effective and responsible intervention during that tremendous period of war and Nazi domination in the light of what could be done in normal conditions, or in the gratuitous and hypothetical conditions invented by the imagination of a young playwright. Besides being useless, an attitude of condemnation and protest, which the Pope is blamed for not having adopted, would have been decidedly harmful. This is the nub of the whole question. The thesis of "The Deputy" is evidence of an insufficient psychological, political and historical grasp of reality, while attemping to turn it into a good play.

"Supposing that Pius XII had done what Hochhuth blames him for not doing, his move would have brought

on such reprisals and such disastrous consequences that
after the war Hochhuth himself, with a more precise historical, political and moral sense of values, could have
written another and much more realistic and interesting
play than the one he has so boldly but also so unfortunately
presented to the public, that is to say the drama of 'The
Deputy,' who because of political exhibitionism or lack of
psychological perception, would have unleashed on the
world evils bringing ruin to countless innocent victims. With
themes of this kind and with known historical personages
no one should play around with the creative fantasy of
dramatics, not sufficiently endowed with historical discern-
ment and, which God forbid, even human honesty. Otherwise, in the present case, there would really be a different
drama, namely that of someone trying to unload on a Pope
who was extremely aware of his duty and of the realities
of history and who was at the same time a faithful but im-
partial friend of the German people, the horrible crimes
of German Nazism."

Successor of Saint Ambrose in the Diocese of Milan

Life brings us into daily contact with individuals who
fill a post with admirable dignity, but who would be very
ill at ease in some other position. Others on the contrary
are fortunate enough, or perhaps unfortunate enough, to be
gifted with many talents and an ability to adapt to whatever
task is assigned to them. For many of them, this is the result
of an enviable natural gift or of an extraordinary spirit of
adjustment. For others it can be the result of Prussian
tenacity and extreme versatility.

Giovanni Battista Montini belongs to the ranks of
those who can be outstanding even in the most difficult

types of occupation. He showed this as a student, despite his weak health; as a professor and as an employee in the offices of the Vatican; as Ecclesiastical Assistant of the FUCI in the ten years he was associated with that organization, as a Church diplomat in the thirty some years he spent in the Secretariate of State. Nevertheless he had not had any broad-scale pastoral experience to round out those activities which can fall to a servant of the Church. Providence willed to fill this gap in really splendid fashion, guiding events with that higher wisdom which men are not always able to understand. In fact, at that time, in the "usually well-informed circles," not a few were wondering how Pius XII could ever have deprived himself of his closest collaborator, to send him to Milan to replace the late Cardinal Schuster. Certain individuals concluded that esteem for Monsignor Montini was waning at the Secretariate of State, and some bolder souls went so far as to speak of "exile in Milan." As always happens when men transform the figments of their imagination to facts, some newspapers wrote that the Pope was sending Montini to Milan for the precise purpose of preparing him for the papacy.

Montini received the official news of his appointment as Archbishop of Milan on November 3, 1954. In his letter of notification Pius XII laid aside the cold and rigid phraseology demanded by protocol, in order to express with great simplicity the sentiments then filling his heart: "You, O beloved son, have seemed to Us to be the person best suited for this task, because from almost daily association We are aware of your outstanding qualities, your natural talents, and your strength of character, as well as of your sincere piety linked with zeal for the salvation of souls. In the long years you have spent at Our side, devoting yourself to the business of the Church with a great spirit of dedication, not only have you deserved well of the Apostolic See, but you have also been able to acquire a vast experience of men and things, in such a way as to seem in all truth the person best prepared to take over the spiritual government of that metropolis."

Monsignor Montini was consecrated on December 12, 1954, in the Vatican Basilica. Pius XII had wanted to perform this consecration personally, but grave illness had confined him to bed and thus obliged him to have the ceremony performed by the Dean of the Sacred College, Cardinal Tisserant. When Archbishop Montini appeared at the side of the Cardinal Dean to receive from his hands the ring, the miter and the crosier, the Basilica, where applause is usually reserved only to the Sovereign Pontiff, echoed with the thunderous acclamations of the Milanese who had come down to the Eternal City to assist at the consecration of the most recent successor of Saint Ambrose and Saint Charles Borromeo.

Pius XII, who had followed the ceremony on television from his sickbed, added the final touch with a moving radio message in which he declared: "We have been spiritually present in this Patriarchal Basilica at an episcopal consecration which Our affection for the one consecrated really reserved to Ourselves, but which the adorable dispositions of Divine Providence did not permit Us to carry out. But it is now consoling for a father unable to impose his hands with the invocation of the Holy Spirit, to lift those hands up at this moment in blessing on his faithful collaborator, become today his brother in the episcopal order. Just as this blessing is filled to overflowing with the memories of long-standing service studded with joys and sorrows, thus also it shines with the light of Faith and with hope for the future of the new pastor, called to rule from the chair of Saint Ambrose such a large portion of the beloved people of Lombardy."

About one month earlier, when Montini had first learned that he had been chosen to succeed the deceased Cardinal Schuster, he had asked simply: "Are you sure, Holy Father, that I am equal to the task?" This dialogue took place at Castel Gandolfo, one evening when Pius XII had summoned him to his bedside, being already stricken with the first manifestations of that illness from which he recovered only by a miracle. The conversation had lasted about an hour. To this objection of his faithful collaborator Pius XII gave no answer. Perhaps he was more moved than the other was perturbed before the grave responsibilities about to fall upon his shoulders. Pius XII embraced him warmly. That gesture was more eloquent than any reply.

Saying good-bye to old friends

Notwithstanding many of the rumors circulating in the autumn of 1954, Monsignor Montini's appointment as Archbishop of Milan was a general surprise and filled his Roman friends with a presentiment of impending loss. He had countless friends in many sectors of the capital, especially in diplomatic circles, the ones with which he had been longest in contact.

On November 6th of that same year, just three days after the official announcement of the promotion of the Pro-Secretary of State to the diocese of Saint Ambrose, all the members of the Diplomatic Corps accredited to the Holy See assembled in one of the Vatican halls to take leave of Monsignor Montini. In the name of all those present, the farewell address was delivered by the dean of the corps, Wladimir d'Ormesson, Ambassador of the French government, now a member of the French Academy, who was linked with the new Archbishop by bonds of friendship which he often expressed openly. He lauded the spirit of charity and the sense of justice which had always distinguished the worthy prelate in the discharge of his delicate duties. But, more than his gifts as a diplomat, which were well known to all those present, Wladimir d'Ormesson stressed his more strictly priestly qualities: "What we respect and love in you is the fact that in the diplomat we have always sensed the presence of the priest."

The discourse of the French Ambassador was really eloquent, as befitted his friendship with the guest of honor and as was to be expected from his own marked artistic sensitivity. "Monsignor," he said, "in the service of a great Pope you have spent years of intense and splendid work, years which will become among the most important in the history of our poor human race."

Still more moving were the words of thanks spoken by the Archbishop-elect. He recalled the memory of the Popes he had served and of those diplomats with whom he had treated throughout his long years of service in the Vatican, mentioning by name those who had since died. He spoke of the consequences of World War II, which had forced the majority of the representatives of the Allied Powers to take refuge in Vatican City only to be succeeded later by those of the Axis during the Allied occupation of Rome. "Our personal memories are intermingled with those of events—and what events!—which must be retained not only by our own personal memory, but also by the impressive history of recent times, of which we ourselves have been the attentive, sometimes numb, and sometimes terrified witnesses. Some among you perhaps recall the almost dramatic death of Pius XI and the joyous advent of Pius XII. Then came the war. The war seen from the Vatican! Rather would I say the 'war lived by the Vatican.' Its annals will record that great numbers of our Diplomatic Corps had to be satisfied with taking modest but attractive quarters on Vatican territory. When liberation came to the city of Rome, those outside replaced those inside, in the same localities and under the same restrictions.

"How shall we ever forget," continued the new Archbishop of Milan, "how could we forget those contacts, more friendly and confidential than official, which came from such hospitality between the diplomats and the office in which I had the honor to serve? How could we forget those Christmas Masses, those assemblies of all the diplomats of belligerent and enemy nations who, around the Vicar of Christ, on that holy night so filled with human and divine mysteries, appeared to forget the raging conflict and to find it only natural that they should be there side by side in the cult of peace, brotherhood, and the love of Christian civilization?"

Montini's farewell discourse to the diplomats was long and marked with deep emotion. It reveals fully the sentiments with which the future Paul VI consecrated the best of his energies to the service of the Holy See for over thirty years: "To tell the truth, if we were to compare the activity of diplomats accredited to the Holy See with that of their colleagues accredited to civil governments, we would have to admit that the latter is at times more intense, more feverish, more exciting than the former. The Vatican lives in the atmosphere of calm so characteristic of spiritual places, and no one is aware of the struggles characterizing material interests. Yes, gentlemen, but it is precisely this relatively tranquil aspect of diplomatic life at the Vatican which sums up its genuine nature and deep value. It is calm and tranquil because it wants to be—because its supreme aim is to seek peace, to create peace!"

These clarifications may seem obvious to many, but not to those individuals, newspapers and parties which attribute to Church diplomacy intentions and aims frequently in conflict with its very nature. The testimony of the Pro-Secretary of State, as he took leave of the place he had occupied in Vatican diplomacy, has a special historical and apologetical value: "I should like, gentlemen, using the complete confidence with which your kindness has always honored me and of which I find confirmation in the moving and noble words I have just heard, I should ask of you a testimony which aims at nothing else than to render homage to the truth, which is so often distorted and denied when it concerns the Holy See and sometimes even the Holy Father himself. Is it not true that the diplomatic relations with the Holy See which honor the countries you represent have been marked on both sides by utmost frankness? Or again, has your mission ever encountered those unpleasant and myserious intrigues of which unscrupulous pam-

phleteers or ill-willed adversaries often accuse the Holy
See? Was there ever any disrespect for your feelings,
your customs, your laws, your nations? Did the questions
you discussed have any other purpose than religious and
civil liberty, justice and peace and, I would even say, the
spiritual and moral welfare of your respective great and
beloved countries?

"The reply to such questions is already contained in the
noble and wise words which I have just heard. This
answer opens our eyes once more to the scene which is so
ringing with the painful echoes of our contemporary world,
in order to inspire in it the hope that the powers of the
spirit, of which the Catholic Church disposes in such a
vast measure, will still have the upper hand over those of
violence and egoism. This reply touches my humble person
only in order to pay homage to the Sovereign Pontiff. For
this I thank you with all my heart."

A kiss for the land of Lombardy

The new pastor entered the diocese of Saint Ambrose
on January 6, 1955, the Feast of the Epiphany, commemorating the manifestation of Our Lord. He had left the Vatican three days earlier, after celebrating on the altar of
Saint Pius X in the Vatican Basilica one of the most moving
Masses of his entire life. The previous night, in the room
where he had lived for so many years he had written a
heartfelt letter to the Holy Father: "I cannot put my feelings into words at this moment of my physical departure
from this blessed residence. But with an effort to put some
order into my conflicting memories, impressions, thoughts,
and resolutions, I feel an absolute need to express to Your
Holiness my deepest filial gratitude for the favors, whose
number keeps me from counting them and whose greatness

prevents me from measuring them, favors conferred upon me by the fatherly, generous, unfailing and affable kindness of Your Holiness."

A vast crowd had defied the nasty weather to gather along the streets traversed by the cortege of automobiles accompanying the new Archbishop. It seemed as if the whole of Milan had wanted to join with the city authorities in welcoming him who came to them, in the words of his episcopal motto, "In the Name of the Lord."

The day of his entrance into the diocese had been preceded by an intense vigil of prayer in the sanctuary of the Madonna of Miracles, located practically on the boundary line of the diocese, after a week's retreat. Perhaps because of the new Archbishop's habit of preparing himself in prayer for all the important acts of his life, rumor has it that when the Cardinals assembled in Conclave had chosen him unanimously, he asked to spend an entire night in prayer before accepting the election.

The evening of January 6, 1955, brought to a close "a typically bad Milanese day, the kind when people stay home and read the paper, listen to the radio or the record player, or spend their time playing with the children." Nevertheless, the crowd applauded the Archbishop warmly as, from the Church of Sant'Eustorgio where the procession had formed, he started for the center of the city in an open automobile, with the Mayor, Commendatore Ferrari, sitting at his side. The crowd was applauding also because it had learned of a significant gesture of the Archbishop at the moment he set foot on Milanese territory and which had surprised and pleased everyone. Notwithstanding the almost constant snowy drizzle, just as soon as the Archbishop had crossed the Lambro River between Emilia and Lombardy, he had asked the driver to stop. Then he got out, knelt down and kissed the ground of Lombardy. This was a kiss of peace for all those sons whom "In the name of the Lord" he had agreed to feed and guide. It was the first sign of that love for his flock which the former Vatican diplomat had felt

burning in his heart from the very first moment of his
agreement to become pastor of such a vast and illustrious
diocese. The people who had gathered at the boundaries of
the diocese to be the first to hail their new Archbishop had
greeted this gesture of Archbishop Montini with thunderous applause and profound joy, and had sent the word
on to those awaiting him in the streets of the metropolis.

The Pope's gift

On the very day of his entrance into the Milan Archdiocese Archbishop Montini outlined partially the whole
program of his episcopate with a phrase which has become
famous: "I want to defend the working man. I want to act
in such a manner as to deserve the title of 'Bishop of the
Workers.'" On that first day of his episcopal ministry he
did not have the time to proclaim a very broad program.
His engagements were many and varied, as always happens
on similar occasions. But Pius XII had wanted in some way
to be physically near him on that occasion, via a radio message which well deserves to be recorded here:

"The contribution which Divine Providence asked Us
in providing the Archdiocese of Milan with its new pastor
calls for completion today through the good wishes coming
from Our heart for him who is going to this great city and
for the Catholic population of Lombardy which is rejoicing
as it welcomes him. On him we invoke from God, under the
auspices of the great Father of the Ambrosian Church, the
spirit of his admirable predecessor Saint Charles Borromeo.
Like Saint Charles, who was appointed to the metropolis
of Lombardy by a Pontiff whose valued collaborator he had
been in the government of the Church, thus also may your
new pastor, who is gifted with a practical knowledge of the
Church and a love which recoils before no sacrifice, set

for his flock the example, always old and always new, which the Pastor of Pastors and all souls with him are expecting from his activity and his life. May he be the glory of his children; may his children be his crown.

"To his children We say: 'In him who comes to you blessed in the name of the Lord, you have the pledge of Our affection and Our interest in you. As the faithful custodian of sound doctrine in his Archdiocese and in his awareness through long experience of the paths marked out today for the vast Christian family in the social order and the better world for which We hope with every fiber of Our soul, you must look upon his pastoral efforts with perfect unity of mind and heart, following his guidance with humble and wise docility. You must also help him to spread the kingdom of God in your souls and your institutions. This is demanded of you by the life of Faith, which is the life proper to the Christian.

"On this condition the grace of God which assists the pastor, will sanctify the flock, saving it from the ruins of pride and false prophets. The Ambrosian Church will carry on in peace its glorious traditions of apostolic and missionary zeal, efficient activity, and generous undertakings of every kind. Your common father will be able to boast of you as Saint Paul did of the Thessalonians: 'Being mindful before God our Father of your work of faith, and labor, and charity, and your enduring hope in Our Lord Jesus Christ.' (I Thess. 1:3)

"With these good wishes and these sentiments it is a joy for Us through Our Apostolic Benediction, to point out for the new pastor the path of an activity which We trust will be long and fruitful, and for the beloved family of Saint Ambrose to consecrate the happiness of a festive welcome with resolutions of unshakable faith in the Church and a sincere Christian life."

The workers called him "Our Bishop"

According to statistics, the Archdiocese of Milan covers a total area of some 3,125 square miles, and has 3,295,000 inhabitants, 912 parishes, and 3,602 secular and regular priests as also some 12,000 religious. Thus it is one of the largest dioceses of the entire Church and is undoubtedly the largest in Italy.

Cardinal Schuster's successor arrived in Milan with his own personal methods of action. After the first solemn acts of his installation, he took some time to feel his way carefully around the area which was to be the scene of his episcopal ministry. In fact one of the characteristics of his style is to measure his strength carefully and to have clear ideas on every situation which may confront him, in order then to move ahead with full knowledge of what he is doing. In a way, he acted no differently after his elevation to the papal throne, when he had to take in hand the reins of the entire Church. In this second case, if the expression can be used, the breaking-in period was certainly much shorter, because certain things had to be taken care of without delay, such as assuring the continuation of the Council. For the rest, one might say that he was perhaps less prepared in 1955 to be Archbishop of Milan than he was in 1963 to take over the government of the Universal Church. In 1955 he was beginning a ministry which, in the light of the duties which had until then absorbed his attention, could be called new, whereas the government of his vast Archdiocese could be considered as an excellent training ground for that of the entire Church.

Milan is a highly industrial city and thus very sensitive to all the problems and conflicts of the social order. The new Archbishop was well aware that in some areas of his archdiocese the workers would pay little attention to any pastor speaking to them of religion before social justice, and in language they could understand. This he knew and he was determined to act accordingly. In his first days

as Pope, in an audience for a group of chaplains and coun-
selors of the Italian Workers Catholic Action (ACLI),
Paul VI declared that, today more than ever, social speciali-
zation is essential in order to carry on dialogue with the
working classes without running the risk of driving them
away from the Church to certain forms of Catholic activity
which are now outmoded and which they detest. It is logical
to conclude that as he spoke these words the Pope was
thinking of the pastoral experience he had acquired in his
direct contacts with the working classes of Milan and the
surrounding areas.

Shortly after the public had been able to see the basic
policies of his pastoral "government," the new Archbishop
spent one full day of his second year at Milan with the
workers in the most important factory at Sesto San Giovanni, for the most part Communists. The workers had been
notified of the coming visit and had agreed that the Archbishop would get an extremely cold welcome and that no
worker would leave his place to kiss his ring. When the
Archbishop arrived, accompanied by the factory management, the workers kept their word. Not one of them left
his place, no one knelt down for the Archbishop's blessing
or made the Sign of the Cross or replied to the greeting of
their pastor. They were convinced that their problems and
their working conditions meant nothing for the Archbishop,
and they were going to show him in turn that his presence
in the factory meant absolutely nothing to them. Faced with
this hostile reception, Archbishop Montini was crushed and
could not hold back his tears, which were seen by the workers nearest to him. Like someone who has understood only
too well that he is not wanted, he was on the point of
leaving, when something happened which was not in the
original plans. The workers nearest the door, who had seen
the Archbishop in tears, suddenly began to applaud and
the applause was immediately taken up by all the others.
The prejudices which had blocked the dialogue between
the father and his sons had been whisked away in a

second. The Archbishop walked back, spent some time with
the workers and had the feeling that he had them closer
to him then than he could ever had hoped.

It is probable that on this very occasion Archbishop
Montini uttered some phrases which to some extent sum up
the general theme of his entire episcopal ministry: "I pray,"
he said, "and you must also pray for me, that the day may
come when the noise of your machines may become music
and the smoke from these chimneys may become incense,
rising like a hymn of praise to the Lord. . . . I have come in
order to know you better and to promise you that I will
pray for you to God.

"I begin here my dialogue with the people of Milan
and, because there should never be any secrets between
me and my children, I will confess to you that at this
moment I am seeing a dream come true which I have had
for many years, namely, to speak to real honest-to-goodness
workers. I would still be lacking in sincerity if at this deeply
moving moment I were to say nothing on a question which
is certainly in your mind and mine, namely the relationship
between the working classes and the Church. I hope that
my ministry here and elsewhere will enable me to dissipate
the misunderstanding which some individuals want to create
between the Church and the working classes, between the
Church and our age all intent on peace and technical
progress."

The workers of Milan certainly did not begin that very
day to say with a touch of pride "This is *our* Archbishop."
Many of them, however, while still remaining Communists,
began to be convinced that if the Church's representative
in the capital of Lombardy could speak in this manner,
then the Church is really interested in the social question
and in the problems of labor. Of the sincerity of his words,
there could not even be the slightest doubt.

The Friday "Round Tables"

More than any other diocese, the Archdiocese of Milan is made for top-notch men. With his dynamic personality, his openness to progress, his liking for rational organization, and a mind ever keen and tireless and ready for difficulty, Giovanni Battista Montini seemed made to measure for this diocese. Nor is it true that, as a diplomat by birth and education, he had to force himself to adapt to the mentality and ways of life in Milan. Milan is not Naples, and the Lombard temperament gives many common traits to the people of Milan and Brescia.

From 1955 to 1963 Milan was not merely a highly industrialized area or a city where clashes between labor and management hounded one's every step and could lead to an endless series of practical problems entailing serious worry for ecclesiastical authorities. Milan was then, as it still is today, an area affected by a strong migration movement, which annually brings in more than thirty thousand Italians from the south in search of work and better living conditions. The pastoral problems involved in migration are well known wherever it takes place. Provision has to be made for spiritual assistance for the new arrivals, charitable activities must be organized to help them get settled and to smooth over the rough spots in contacts between people of different religious culture and standards of living, who nevertheless must learn almost overnight how to live together in one big family.

From his very first day, the Archbishop threw himself generously into this new task. As far as zeal and tenacity in work are concerned we know that he had nothing "new" to learn. He continued to get up every morning at 5:30, to be most frugal in his meals and to allot no more than four or five hours a night for sleep. He continued to be orderly and methodical in all his work, to read eagerly the works of the best authors, both religious and lay, whether

Italian, French or English, and to follow with deep interest all the newest scientific discoveries then being announced with ever-increasing frequency. Anyone who reads his discourses or Pastoral Letters finds an impressive series of quotations from Christian and non-Christian thinkers, theologians and novelists—from Saint Paul to Albert Camus, from Saint Augustine to Bernanos, from Saint Ambrose to Jean Lacroix, from Saint Clement of Alexandria to Leprince-Riguet or to Fathers Lubac, Chenu, Yves Congar and others.

The following was a typical day for the Archbishop of Milan. At 6:30 A.M. he celebrated Holy Mass in his private chapel, then served the Mass of his secretary. Afterwards his morning prayer was continued with the reflective, almost choral, recitation of Matins, Lauds and Prime. After breakfast, during which he glanced through the local papers and some others, he began his office appointments, which usually lasted until 1:00 P.M. As a rule he preferred to have only a few appointments, but he liked to be able to allow his visitors, as far as possible, plenty of time to present their problems and to find a proper solution.

He then lunched with his two secretaries. This was followed by a brief rest, then he went to his chapel to recite Little Hours, with Vespers and Compline. At 4:00 P.M. he was back at his desk, where he remained until dinner time. After dinner and the recitation of the rosary, he usually spent some time with his private secretary going over correspondence. Then, when he was left alone, he continued work in his private office until the late hours of the night. Sometimes the light in his room was on until two or three in the morning, and this was an evident sign that the Archbishop was preparing a discourse or a Pastoral Letter, or was absorbed in some particularly important book which had been brought to his attention.

Frequently, while taking care of correspondence, he listened to symphonic records, showing a preference for Beethoven, Chopin and Bach. It had long been his custom to get up at the same time as the workers on the first shift. But, as can be seen from the above program, his work day kept pace with those of the second and the third shifts also.

On Friday evenings the Archbishop introduced the interesting practice of "working suppers," in which the supper part counted for very little. In reality, they could have been called "round tables," at which all the top officials of the archdiocese engaged in discussions of common interest, studying the progress of plans for the new pastoral campaign or other plans still under consideration.

The Archbishop "Technocrat"

On October 10, 1962, just before the opening of the Ecumenical Council, the Archbishop of Milan delivered an important discourse in which he stated: "There is about to open a solemn dialogue, lofty and new, between the Church and modern society." These words set forth a real program but they are also a kind of spiritual proclamation of the personality of Cardinal Montini as a churchman.

Archbishop Pignedoli, who lived with him for many years in Rome and in the Milan Chancery as Auxiliary Archbishop, is fond of saying that "Monsignor Montini is a man who finds himself completely at home in our century." He knows how to take hold with sound balance and to make his own, intimately his own, the conquests, the uncertainties and the demands of modern life. Referring to the innovations introduced into the Milan Chancery Office, someone described the Archbishop as a "technocrat." And no one can say that the term was completely wrong.

First of all, he got rid of the old furniture in the Chancery, which had a certain artistic value but was hardly functional. He sent off the old sofas and the ancient book-

cases to a museum, busying himself personally with order-
ing bookcases more according to his tastes and modern-
style furniture.

Archbishop Montini built many churches in the different zones of the metropolis most in need of them. Still
he never yielded to the temptation, which in some cases is
anything but merely hypothetical, to build monumental
churches. The possibility of the temptation was certainly
not lacking, because of the immense amount of such work
which needed to be done. No other diocese in the world
today has built as many churches as Milan in the eight years
it had Giovanni Battista Montini as its Archbishop. In his
first year in the diocese, twelve new churches were built.
They were followed in 1956 by ten more. In 1957, seven.
In 1958, twelve. In 1959, fourteen. In 1960, twelve. In 1961,
ten. In 1962, twenty. In the first five months of 1963, five.
The new parishes erected in those eight years totalled exactly one hundred, and the results of the Archbishop's work
can justly rival that of his great predecessor, Saint Charles
Borromeo.

New churches under construction or on the drawing
boards were one of the topics most frequently discussed
at the "round tables" or "working suppers," attended by all
the officials of the Archdiocese on Friday evenings. The
election of Cardinal Montini took place on Friday, June 21st,
the Feast of the Sacred Heart of Jesus. This momentous day
brought him a "working supper" of unheard-of proportions.
In the agenda found on his desk in the Milan Chancery,
the "round table" scheduled for Friday June 21st was to
discuss certain building projects aiming to provide churches
which would be spacious and functional, but devoid of
luxury and poor in ornamental decoration.

When, at the beginning of his pastoral ministry in
Milan, Archbishop Montini launched his campaign for new
churches, he said that he wanted to prepare a dwelling-
place for God among workmen who were without a roof
or a place to go. This was his aim because the scarcity of

churches pinched particularly in the outskirts of the city, in the areas occupied by the poorest of the poor. The drive to promote this imposing undertaking was opened with gifts received by the Archbishop for his episcopal consecration: a gold ring, a pectoral cross, a corporal ornament with four lapis lazuli and five diamonds.

The Milan Mission in 1957

Pius XII must have felt that Milan, the cross-roads of the far-sweeping European lines of communication, needed as its spiritual head a man solid and vigorous, calm in self-mastery, courteous and tactful, in a word, a man with a touch of the genius. To fill this unusual order, he had not hesitated to give up his Pro-Secretary. From the outset of his pastoral visits, Archbishop Montini had remarked that if religious practice were to become as intense as he wanted to make it, the existing churches would be unable to accommodate all the faithful. At the same time, he launched plans for closer contact with those whose lives were usually lived far from the Church and its representatives. This resulted in his decision to organize a mission, which was undoubtedly one of the most famous in history. The aim was to reach all families and all sectors of society, in order to insure for both the great and the small a mode of life inspired by the Gospel. Two Cardinals, Giuseppe Siri of Genoa and Giacomo Lercaro of Bologna, thirty Archbishops and Bishops, along with 1,300 priests, preached for three weeks in the churches, the *piazze* and the streets to a veritable multitude of the faithful. The organization was perfect and the participation of the faithful encouraging. According to statistics, more than a million of the faithful had been reached in some degree. The preachers took into account the needs of all professions and the modes of life of their listeners, presenting the Gospel message in a form which they regarded as best adapted to each one: the workers and management, lawyers and doctors, those in military service, artists, students and employees.

The first mention of this project came from the official announcement of the mission itself, dated September 24, 1957, and addressed "To the clergy and the faithful of the city of Milan, its magistrates and its citizens." The proclamation continued: "You are already aware that in the coming month of November there will be preached at Milan, in all the city parishes and wherever else it will be possible, an extraordinary city-wide mission. . . . It will last for three weeks. The first week, from November 5th to November 10th, will be for the hospitals and children; the second week, from the 10th to the 17th of the same month, especially for women; the third week, from the 17th to the 24th, especially for men. The central theme of this mission will be "God our Father," the first truth of Faith, the first Reality of the world and of life. The mission aims to honor God in His majesty and His goodness, that God who is so often offended by us today, misunderstood, denied, ignored, forgotten, not loved, badly served, and badly prayed to. This is the God who is the fountainhead of all being, the light of all thought, the law of all activity, the principle, the foundation, the end of all things, the God who is infinitely good.

"Consequently, the mission intends to recall to the conscience of every intelligent and right-minded person the necessity, the nature, the beauty of religion. It will aim also to present religion in its essential and authentic terms, such as, fortunately for us, Jesus Christ has revealed them to us and as the Catholic Church preserves and teaches them. This will be with the conviction that all human questions are unavoidably tied up with the religious question and that once we have provided for this question the luminous, vital and only true answer of Christianity, every other problem can find light and a solution. . . .

"Whoever thinks rightly of God, thinks rightly of himself. Whoever adores God, enters into order. The man who prays God, lives in hope. The man who loves God and through Him loves his neighbor, is sure of salvation. Consequently our city must have this moment of spiritual fullness, to re-enkindle the fire of its religion, to free ourselves once more from the intellectual and moral apathy to which we have gradually become accustomed, thinking that in this way we can get away from the inescapable reality of the problems of our destiny and, with no attention to principles and scruples of a higher order, can give ourselves more effectively to our feverish activities. . . .

"As you see, all these are great and human aims, so great and so human that the mission will certainly not succeed in achieving them completely. It can only expect to place them before the minds of whoever wishes to listen honestly. As heralds of the word of God, we shall have in our midst eight hundred priests, while five hundred others will accompany them as ministers of God's grace in the confessional. They will be preceded by several Cardinals and various Bishops and will be followed by numerous lay volunteers, each of whom will make his own proper contribution.

"It is our desire that their voice should reach every corner of our city, a voice which will be prudent and friendly, ringing and sincere, above all genuine and echoing with the marvelous proclamation: 'Remember that God is our Father. He cannot be ignored. He cannot be abandoned. He cannot be offended. He must be recognized, feared and loved! From this more than human relationship we must derive religion, which surpasses all human contacts. Let churches be opened, let cellars, houses, courtyards, schools, offices, barracks, factories, hospitals, hotels, institutions and hospices—let them all be swung open. Wherever men assemble, wherever they work, think or suffer, there should this blessed message reach. It will knock at every door, but will break down no door which opens of its own accord freely and cordially.'"

In this very announcement of the mission we hear the lament of the pastor over his city, so similar to that of the Redeemer over Jerusalem: "How often as we passed through the city, absorbed and tense in its endless and hurried activities, we have wondered with anxious hearts how to reach with a friendly word all these people who seem to be strangers to the vital treasure of our truth, and who are yet linked to us with bonds of civic friendliness and Christian brotherhood! How many times, gazing at the old and the new houses of this immense city, human beehives where our steps can never reach, we wondered if and how we could ever send through them the breath of the vivifying spirit of the Gospel! How many times our very position as a Bishop, which makes of all these citizens our children, weighed upon us as a heavy responsibility because it keeps us from approaching these people, instructing them, consoling them, and blessing them! At times, the texture of Christian society seems so inconsistent and un-community-minded, so little penetrated with faith and grace, that the city, instead of arousing admiration for its growing greatness, arouses rather sentiments of fear for the uncertainty of its salvation!"

Some time later, at the very peak of the mission, the Archbishop took up this theme on the radio. After explaining the difference between the mission then going on and other systems of preaching the Gospel he continued: "At Milan this time, the mission has very special characteristics. First of all, because of its proportions. It is not affecting one or several parishes, but the entire city, with its 126 actual parishes. Precisely because it must be considered as a whole, it demands that different classes of people which are difficult to classify among the faithful of the different parishes, should have special preachers. Thus different categories of persons have been invited to the mission, according to their specific individual professions, including, for example, university professors, bartenders, contractors, models, technical men and social assistants, doctors and lawyers, students and artists, etc.

"The city mission for adults is being held in 302 parish units and will call for 702 series of sermons, employing eighteen Bishops, thirty-three priests of the secular clergy, plus some three hundred belonging to religious orders and congregations. Other hundreds of priests are engaged in the mission for young people. Specialized preaching is being provided in thirty-five centers with a total of approximately forty-eight series, with the collaboration of two Cardinals—Cardinal Siri, Archbishop of Genoa, and Cardinal Lercaro, Archbishop of Bologna—three Bishops, twenty-five priests from the secular clergy and ten from religious institutes. The French colony and the German-speaking colony of Milan will likewise have courses of sermons in their own languages.

"According to the norms adopted for the mission, all or almost all the preachers have been brought in from outside Milan. Thus we have another new factor of importance, namely, that, numerically speaking, this is the biggest mission ever preached in the Catholic Church from the day of its foundation until now.

"Another special aspect of our city mission is the uniformity of the themes which all the preachers, each one according to his own aptitudes and gifts and the needs of his listeners, are bound to develop simultaneously. The central theme of this city mission is only one: God our Father. Thus it was our intention to link up this extraordinary spiritual meditation with the truth revealed by Jesus as a fundamental principle of His Gospel and basic fact of His whole religious system, namely, that our relationships with God do not lead us into a void, into the obscure, the terrible problem of the Divinity, but to the fullness of that life, goodness, providence, and love which Christ obtained for us and communicated to us. These relationships are such as to elevate human life to an ineffable dignity, that of sons of our Heavenly Father and of brothers with all our fellow men.

"This is a very simple outline, but it required careful study by the theological faculty of Milan, and it has been summed up and outlined in a Directory which was distributed months ago to all the preachers. . . . The organization of this mission was long and patient; it has been through various phases in these two years of constant work by a special committee, with His Excellency Archbishop Pignedoli, Auxiliary of Milan, as Chairman assisted by priests and deserving laymen. . . ."

At this point the Archbishop thought it well to clarify the genuine purpose of this great event, in order to reply to certain unfavorable, not to say tendentious, interpretations of the mission afforded by the usually well-informed sources: "Some might want to ask us what is the exact purpose of this religious manifestation, because some people have supposed that it had spectacular and purely devotional aims. Others have even insinuated that it might be only a front for propaganda anything but religious. No, the scope of the mission is essentially and exclusively religious. That is why we wanted to avoid surrounding it with a great deal of external show. That also is why we wanted to organize it during a quiet season and to throw it open to all men of good will. It was also agreed that the preaching of the mission would avoid any polemics which were not a simple and friendly presentation of Catholic doctrine. This is why our invitation was extended to everyone and why no one has been pressured into external, hasty or unwilling participation. It will be noticed that the mission was announced in some one hundred offices, factories, banks, stores, and other centers. Yes, but these announcements had been posted only where we had been invited to do so. It will also be noted that we avoided sending our preachers into the vast industrial, commercial, or administrative centers of our city, lest we incur even the shadow of a suspicion of carrying on polemical propaganda or forcing lessons on anyone.

"The mission bears the stamp of doctrinal seriousness, has been surrounded with cordiality and simplicity, has been made available to all, even to those far away, with full respect not only for legal requirements but also for personal liberty. All this has been done with the sole intention of re-thinking and, God grant, reviving the holy, noble, human, and Christian traditions of our country, with the certainty that from this inexhaustible patrimony of religious truth, the citizens of a living, intelligent and modern city like Milan can surely draw the spiritual strength needed for their civic progress and the grace of a new life for their eternal salvation."

Faraway brethren, pardon us!

Archbishop Montini addressed moving words to "those faraway," to those who wanted to ignore the mission or who openly derided it. As they are read now, these words are strongly reminiscent of the discourse with which Paul VI opened the Second Session of the Ecumenical Council and which echoes the self-same sentiments of pastoral sincerity and priestly charity: "The mission has only one main scope, namely, to echo the authentic voice of religion to the brethren who are far removed from us. Those far from us are those who do not come to church, those who no longer pray and who even no longer believe, as also those whose conscience has been saddened by the realization of sin or has been benumbed by an excess of earthly occupations. Lastly, they are those who show contempt for the Church and who blaspheme God, those who think they have reached a degree of social distinction and self-assurance because they never think of religion, heaven, or hell. How many of these there are! What voids we find in this community of brethren! What solitude this causes at times in the very house of God! How much suffering and how long the wait for one who loves those faraway as faraway sons!

"If one voice could reach you, faraway sons, it would be a plea for friendly pardon. Yes, we ask pardon of you,

before you ask pardon of God. In approaching one who has
been faraway, it is impossible not to feel a certain remorse.
Why has this brother of ours been faraway? Because we
have not loved him enough. We have not taken enough
care of him, we have not instructed him and led him into
the joys of our Faith. Because he judged our Faith from
those of us who preach it and represent it. It is perhaps
from our defects that he has come to look upon religion as a
bore and to despise and hate it. Because he has perhaps
heard more scoldings than admonitions and invitations,
because he has perhaps seen some petty interest at work in
our ministry, he has been scandalized.

"Those now faraway are often people who got a bad
impression of us, ministers of religion, and they have
dropped religion because for them it is identified with our
persons. They are oftentimes people who are more demanding than ill-intentioned. Sometimes their anti-clericalism
only hides an outraged respect for sacred things which they
feel have been disgraced in us.

"So, if such is the case, brethren who are faraway,
forgive us! If we have not understood you, if we have too
easily driven you away, if we have not taken an interest in
you, if we have not been the right kind of spiritual teachers
and physicians for your souls, if we have not succeeded in
speaking of God as we should, if we have been sarcastic
or have not taken you seriously, then today we ask your
pardon. But please listen to us.

"First of all, you do not know us. At least, you do not
know our ministry. We are not working for ourselves; we
are working for you. Our mission is for your welfare, your
salvation. Try to learn how to know us. Remember that we
too, at least as men, have 'a professional conscience.' This
obliges us to love you. If we are sometimes insistent, it is
only because you are so close to our hearts. We must seek
you out, we must care for you, we must make every effort
to see that you are not deprived of that gift of truth and
salvation which we hold out to you. We must love you.

"Are we treating you like enemies? No, never as personal enemies. Perhaps as enemies of God, of Christ and the Church, and thus as adversaries of our mission. Yes, such can be the case; in fact it is, because you oblige us to take such an unfortunate position. You force us to defend our mission, the truth of the Gospel, the holiness of the Church. But understand us this time. We are not hostile to you simply out of prejudice; we do not despise you; we have no desire to humiliate you; we do not want to exploit your much longed-for conversion. At least this time, we want you to know that we are not rejecting you, but that we are calling you. We do not want you, men like ourselves in need of pardon and salvation from God, to have to ask us: 'Why did you not invite us? Why were the doors closed in our face? Why did you not give us some understanding of our true destiny and our good lot?'

"This is why, at least this time, honestly, as friends, we invite you. Come to the mission and hear what we have to say. What shall we say? The usual things? Yes, but do you know what they are? Permit us to have some doubts about this, because if you knew what these things are, you would be enthusiastic about them.

"Are they the same old things? Say rather that they are eternal things, that is to say, always alive and always up-to-date. To whoever wants to recognize it, it is the task of modern progress to emphasize this unending vitality of the Gospel.

"Are these things difficult? Well, they are inspiring and they are indispensable. Any kind of knowledge is difficult. So if this is the true knowledge of God, no one should be surprised. But Christ has clothed His message, which is rich in meaning and mystery, with the royal mantle of simplicity. Everyone can hearken to it and get something out of it.

"Will we speak of useless things? No, but of things as useful as air and bread. Air and bread keep up the life of the body. But the soul needs to breathe truth, to feed on Christ, for He is the Way, the Truth and the Life.

"Will our talk be of things too serious and too binding? Perhaps, but they are not extras or things foreign to our conscience. Rather are they things which come into our conscience like light and strength.

"Why do you not listen to us? Why are you not inwardly free? Why do you stay in the clutches of a laziness which you cannot admit even to yourselves, or why are you held prisoners by some unclean passion, or paralyzed by wounded pride, or frightened by those who look at you and talk about you and laugh at you? If you are free, if you are honest, then you must be strong enough and independent enough to come and listen. Listen then, this is all we ask. Like serious and well-educated people, this is all we ask."

Lack of space prevents giving the entire message addressed by the Archbishop on the vigil of the mission to his "beloved sick." But some space must be given to the radio message with which Pius XII closed the extraordinary mission in Milan: "In this hour of religious fervor, enkindled and fanned by this extraordinary mission which you are preparing to seal with a common prayer to 'the Father of immense majesty,' may there come to you, beloved sons and daughters of Milan as a source of comfort and support in your holy resolutions, Our affectionate greetings. . . . Gathered as 'one heart and one soul' around your Archbishop and your parish priests, We seem to see your city at this moment—Milan, the vibrating heart of your national economy, the prestigious organizer of all types of activities in the fields of culture and art—We see you now gathered together in prayer. This suggests to Us the image of that 'City of God' which was described and hoped for by Saint Augustine: dedicated, of course, to working out its own proper destiny on earth, but in conformity with the supreme designs of the Almighty, in free subjection to His dominion, in a life of constant love of Him."

The Pope continued: "Elevating an earthly city to become a 'City of God,' is not this the final aim of the divine mission of the Church in the world? Such was also the scope of your extraordinary mission, that mission which has swept over your city like a saving wave of grace and with which you, the people of Milan, have corresponded with edifying docility. Intimate returns to God, generous progress in virtue, resolutions of sanctity, returns to the path of justice, secret miracles transforming cold or distracted hearts into living tabernacles of the Holy Spirit— all these things are hidden to the eyes of men, but they will remain forever written in the Book of Life.

"Within a few moments your hearts will break forth in a hymn of adoration and thanksgiving, the *Te Deum*.... The *Te Deum* will be to express your gratitude for the abundance of graces which have been showered upon you by God in these days of salvation. But it will not be, it must not be, the sign of the end, as though you have already completed the work which this extraordinary mission set out to accomplish. No earthly city is changed in just a few days into a 'city of God.' Milan must perfect what it has begun, deepen the knowledge it has begun to grasp, bring to harvest what it has sowed. The great mission must not be recorded in the annals of history as a splendid but ephemeral episode of religious fervor. Rather must it mark an historic date in the spiritual rebirth of an entire city, and remain as a proof of the pledge made by each one of you today before God and the Church."

"... *of the working man, yes, of the leftists, no! ...*"

As Pius XII stated in his radio message, elevating an earthly city to the dignity of a city of God, is the aim of the divine mission of the Church in the world. At that time, one of the Milanese newspapers wrote: "The Milan mission intended and certainly achieved a goal which was much more important, namely to reach those who are far from God, to open with them a calm and spontaneous dialogue, which would be the starting-point of lasting contact. It also intended to attract those who are not with the Church and in those who are already good Christians to stimulate a strong apostolic re-action, to commit them to seeking out, contacting, and intelligently winning over those living beyond the confines of Catholicism."

The results of the mission were very rich and, to thank God for this abundant harvest, the Archbishop, as the climax of the mission, had organized a pilgrimage to Lourdes on the first centenary of the apparitions of Our Lady, to lay at her feet the twofold promise to keep the faith of Catholic Milan strong and intact and to re-awaken its Christian traditions.

This promise was carried out through an impressive pilgrimage from June 26 to July 1, 1958, under the leadership of the Archbishop himself, accompanied by Archbishop Pignedoli, Bishop Luigi Pirelli and numerous civic officials of the Milan province. According to all accounts the pilgrimage was a moving spectacle. As he spoke to his children of the immense needs of the Archdiocese and entrusted them all to Our Lady of Lourdes, the Archbishop could not hold back his tears as he concluded: "My children, let us continue to pray, and certainly the Madonna will not be deaf to our prayers. We shall certainly not be left alone."

During the farewell dinner in honor of Archbishop Montini offered by the Diplomatic Corps accredited to the Holy See and his colleagues in the Secretariate of State, Monsignor Angelo Dell'Acqua, a Lombard himself and Montini's colleague for many years in the service of the Holy See, observed: "Certainly the Milanese will hail in you the Archbishop of the workingman." As a matter of fact the title of "Archbishop of the Workingman," first of all, and then of "Cardinal of the Workingman," was attributed to Montini by universal acclaim.

His concern for the laboring classes—a well-known French publication noted that Archbishop Montini was one of the few Italian Bishops to use this expression, while others preferred to speak of "the poor" or of "the lowly"— was unfailingly one of the essential characteristics of his personality as a shepherd of souls. "I am determined to defend the rights of the laboring man. With the grace of God, I will do my best to try to be the Archbishop of the laboring man."

In a discourse to a group of workingmen the Archbishop asked: "For whom do you put up with all your hardships? I know that you are enduring all this for your salary, and thus for your family and for your welfare. But in these years of social evolution you have understood that you are likewise suffering for others, that you are bearing a burden for the welfare of society, because not all would be able to do what you are doing. This is because you are doing all this for others, for your children if for no others, for your youngsters who are unable to work, You are doing it for the aged and the sick who are incapacitated. You are putting up with all this for others. . . . Do you not see, my children, that there is a certain oneness, I would almost say two parallel lines? Christ suffered for you; you are suffering for others. You have been modeled on Christ. Why should not these two parallel lines come together? Cannot this suffering be elevated so as to join with the sufferings which Jesus Christ underwent for us out of love, out of pure love?"

On January 29, 1955, just twenty-two days after his arrival in the archdiocese, Archbishop Montini pronounced his first discourse at Sesto San Giovanni, commonly called the "Italian Stalingrad," before a vast assembly of workers. The union directors passed out to the newspapers the text of the discourse, but only after they had deleted the following passage: "Religion is not an ally of capitalism, which is an oppressor of the people. The first ones to cut adrift from religion were not the laboring men, but the great boss-

es and the great economists of the last century, who
dreamed of founding a progress and a civilization without
God and without Christ. Let it no longer be said that
religion is the opium of the people and that it is involved
in a plot to quench all the energies of the people and to
smother its hopes of betterment. Religion is the light and
the glory of the people; it is its force."

It is certainly not an easy task to treat social questions
from the pulpit or in the press, even with a pastoral approach, without running the risk of being misinterpreted
by the excessively prudent or of being depicted by others
as symbols of outmoded realities. Archbishop Montini was
fortunate enough to rise above unfavorable criticism, of
which there had been plenty in his life from the very first
days of his pastoral ministry in the FUCI. Besides, he was
always too upright in his own life to run any danger of
being portrayed as an instrument or a symbol of realities
contradicting his inner convictions.

On one occasion, for example, while the workers were
listening to him, they became so enthusiastic over the
evangelical tone of his teaching and his evident sincerity
that one of them, with the best of intentions, shouted out:
'Long live the Archbishop of the Leftists!" Archbishop Montini stopped quietly, and declared with perfect calm: "The
Archbishop of the laboring man, yes; of the Leftists, no!"

It is evident that the social accent of his ministry was
not and could not be reduced merely to preaching the
Gospel and promoting solidarity with the working classes.
He was also able to turn his attention, with a warm fatherly
spirit, to management, inviting them to reconcile in the
harmony of Christian sociology the demands of the different
social classes.

·*The death of Pius XII*

It was only natural that, after so many years of intimate and faithful collaboration, Archbishop Montini should have felt deeply the death of Pope Pius XII. His sentiments are reflected with moving eloquence in his telegram to Monsignor Angelo Dell'Acqua, Under-Secretary of State, as soon as he received word that the Holy Father was in agony:

> *Sad news Holy Father's agony finds me in pastoral visitation in the remotest parish diocese Saint Ambrose, but my heart and that of the entire Church of Milan beat with filial anxiety at side most beloved and august patient while there pass through my mind countless memories of his great pontificate and my heart breaks into tears in prayer in sublime hope while remembering his fatherly goodness. Will Your Excellency please obtain for me and the diocese last Apostolic Benediction this incomparable Pontiff.*
> Signed: GIOVANNI BATTISTA MONTINI, ARCHBISHOP

Monsignor Dell'Acqua's reply was despatched the day after the death of the Holy Father:

> *Affectionate and filial homage Your Excellency brought consoling comfort august Pontiff in last hours precious earthly existence. I inform Your Excellency and entire beloved Ambrosian Archdiocese of the last Apostolic Benediction granted by incomparable Pastor of the Church.*
> Signed: MONSIGNOR DELL'ACQUA

Giovanni Battista Montini, the man who more than any other had lived close to the human greatness of Pius XII, and who with filial concern had followed the last phases of his illness, delivered an eloquent panegyric on October 12th, at the solemn Funeral Mass celebrated in the Duomo of Milan for the repose of the soul of the deceased Pontiff.

This discourse is a masterpiece of sacred eloquence, as it sets forth in a tone of sublime eulogy the wisdom and the teaching of the deceased Pontiff, his unique place as a world leader in the darkest days of World War II, and especially the deep spirituality which was the distinguishing mark of his approach to all problems. At times, the eulogy became almost a prayer itself, a dialogue with God, as if to remind the Eternal Father of how faithfully Pius XII had fulfilled his mission as High Priest and Vicar of Christ on earth. Extracts from this discourse would only detract from the nobility and eloquence, couched as it is in a language so directly personal and moving as really to defy translation. It may well stand as one of the most celebrated funeral orations of modern times, if not of all times.

Angelo Giuseppe Roncalli, friend of Montini

After the death of Pius XII, the press immediately set to work, with degrees of discretion and respect varying according to the usual attitudes of individual papers, to assess "Montini's prospects" as immediate successor to the deceased Pontiff. In fact, as far as public opinion was concerned, Archbishop Giovanni Battista Montini's election to the Chair of Peter was more than just probable; it was certain.

Amidst all this talk, the one who was perhaps least concerned was precisely the Archbishop of Milan. Deep in the heart of the largest archdiocese of the world he was spending, in recollection but without suspending his usual pastoral activities, the hours of mourning and suffering for the loss of the Pope whom, with greater right than anyone else, he could call his friend.

But the Cardinals' choice, which to so many seemed certain, did not fall on the Archbishop of Milan. His "prospects" remained simple possibilities. The usually well-informed sources, particularly in the period immediately before the Conclave, declared that "Montini's probabilities as a candidate would have become certainty if, instead of being just Archbishop, he were a Cardinal." But, as things were, it was most improbable that the Conclave would elect someone not among its members.

There had been some complaints, particularly among the clergy and the faithful of the Archdiocese of Milan, because Pius XII had not held a third Consistory to give the Red Hat to him who had once turned it down. Some feel that the collapse and the death of Pius XII came unexpectedly, since it seems hardly likely that, knowing as he did the merits and talents of his former Under-Secretary and Pro-Secretary of State, the Pope would not have intended to elevate him to the cardinalitial dignity.

Consequently, Montini was one of the *papabili,* without being in the Conclave. The newspapers referred to him as "the great absent one," at the very moment that once more, as always, he was seeking only to perform his duties as a pastor, inviting the faithful of the archdiocese to pray and to follow the very important event of the Conclave "invoking upon it in the richest possible measure the assistance of the Holy Spirit." This was called for also because, as he declared in the Pastoral Letter he issued for the Conclave, "the burden of powers and responsibilities laid on him, who is to represent Christ on earth and govern the entire Church, is such as to emphasize the extreme importance of the choice of the new Pope, especially if we stop to think of the present conditions of the world and the needs of Christianity itself." Then he continued immediately: "This is a critical moment whose happy outcome, humanly speaking, may depend largely on the choice of the person called to ascend the throne of Saint Peter."

In fact, the Cardinals assembled in Conclave were seeking a successor to the "Pastor Angelicus." On October 28, 1958, on the eleventh ballot, they agreeably surprised the world by electing an individual who had hardly

been talked about at all. The man they chose was called
Angelo Giuseppe Roncalli, and in memory of his father
he had chosen the name of John. He came from the Archdiocese of Venice, just like, some fifty years earlier,
Giuseppe Sarto, who had ascended the papal throne under
the name of Pius X. This, and not much more, was about
all the public at large knew about the new Pope. But his
"wonderful quips" soon made him better known to the
people and to nations, to those near and those far away,
to those on both sides of the Christian ideological frontier,
to the good and to those who perhaps until then had not
been so good, but who soon learned to become better,
whenever they heard "Pope John" mentioned.

People in general did not know who Angelo Giuseppe
Roncalli was when he was elected Pope. But Archbishop
Montini knew him well, and could even boast of being
his friend. If the election of Angelo Giuseppe Roncalli
to the papal throne brought amazement and surprise to
not a few, in the Archbishop of Milan amazement soon
gave way to deep rejoicing. Archbishop Montini was in
fact one of the first to express his sentiments of joy, in
an announcement addressed that same evening, October
28th, to the clergy and the faithful of the Archdiocese of
Milan. It began as follows: "The announcement that
Cardinal Angelo Giuseppe Roncalli, Patriarch of Venice,
has been elected Sovereign Pontiff under the name, which
will henceforth be for us most venerated and blessed, of
John XXIII, fills Milan with a lively and festive echo. The
exultation of the entire Church fills our spirit as sons of
our great Mother, the Church, and as brothers of the entire Catholic world. This union, this harmony of the soul
of the city of Ambrose with the world-wide family of
Christ, and this devoted loyalty to the Apostolic See, are
characteristic notes of the spiritual life of Milan, vibrating
in this hour of destiny with common and loyal happiness.
If the old saying 'Where Peter is, there is the Church,' as
voiced by our own Saint Ambrose and completed by one

of his recent successors as 'Where Peter is, there is the Church of Milan'—is rightly proclaimed with exultant spirit, then this is the hour when we make it our own, as a glorious indication of our history, a spontaneous cry from our souls, filial commitment of our hearts, and once again, we offer it to the newly elected Pontiff in most sincere and eloquent homage.

"To these considerations drawn from our common Catholic feelings and from the traditional piety of the Church of Milan, there are other particular and personal reasons which draw from the depths of our hearts inexpressible sentiments of emotion and joy. The Pope is a Lombard. . . . At Milan the Pope was a guest and a friend of our regretted and venerated Cardinal Schuster and, as Patriarch of Venice, he pronounced over the deceased Cardinal in our Duomo his memorable and affectionate funeral discourse. With that kindliness which is so much his own and that simplicity which is such a striking trait, the Pope had always wanted to maintain cordial and effective contacts with our diocese, making of the two names of Venice and Milan, an expression of spiritual and co-operative friendship.

"Consequently we want to call upon your hearts, beloved brothers and sons, to unite in mutual rejoicing and to express it in a hymn of thanksgiving to our Lord for having given to His Church a head who is *so wise, so kind, and so beloved*." These italics were not in the text issued by Archbishop Montini. They have been inserted as proof that the Archbishop of Milan already had a clear insight into the human qualities of the new Pope, who was for the general public, especially outside the Church, a real question mark.

Archbishop Montini's telegram to the new Pope was dispatched the very evening of the election:

> *To His Holiness John XXIII, Vatican City. Catholic Milan in exultation wishes to be first to express its joy for election your Holiness and to*

*offer to you its filial and most devoted homage love
and fidelity while assuring prayers Saints Ambrose
and Charles in order that with Saints Peter
and Paul they may sustain and comfort new Pope
whose apostolic blessing we humbly ask.*

MONTINI, ARCHBISHOP

The Holy Father replied as follows on October 31st:

*Message bringing us faithful echo vibrant joy
archdiocese Saint Ambrose Hour our elevation
Apostolic See with offer filial homage love and
devotion, finds in our fatherly soul full echo of
pleasure, gratitude, benevolence. Recalling bonds
of faith and tradition which unite in spiritual and
fruitful solidarity beloved Bergamo, Milan and
Venice, we recall affectionately pleasant memories
of cordial relationships and varied contacts offered
to us in that city, where we were often called by
the affection of dear friends, the pastoral ministry,
historical research on the life and activity of Saint
Charles Borromeo. Always mindful and deeply
grateful for valuable prayers to glorious Saints
Ambrose and Charles for our comfort and encouragement, we impart with effusion of heart to you,
most zealous and most worthy prelate, to the clergy, to the authorities, to all the faithful of this
beloved archdiocese the implored Apostolic Benediction as a pledge of divine favors.* JOHN XXIII

There is hardly any need to record any further comments of Giovanni Battista Montini on the new visible
head of the Church. Nevertheless this chapter would be
incomplete were it not to include at least some extracts
from the discourse of the Archbishop of Milan on November 1, 1958, just three days after the election of Angelo
Giuseppe Roncalli to the throne of Peter. The occasion
was the solemn *Te Deum* service in the Duomo of Milan.
These extracts are most significant because they show
how well Montini knew the new Pope at a time when the

most characteristic anecdotes of his human kindliness had not yet received that universal plebiscite of admiration which before long swept over the whole world.

After recalling the reasons for joy among the faithful, the Archbishop continued: "Anyone who knows anything at all about the new Pope personally will add further motives for satisfaction and hope in order to give to this ceremony a tone of open cordiality, knowing *how much quiet kindness, jovial simplicity, and human wisdom* is evident at even a first contact with this new Pontiff, in whom vast experience with serious affairs, coupled with a consummate humanistic and ecclesiastical culture, have not interfered with his simple story-telling conversation and his easy-going touch of delicate shrewdness reminiscent of Manzoni.

"Observations and impressions such as these will fill our minds with satisfaction, a satisfaction which we now wish to express in thanksgiving to Our Lord who has given us the grace to watch the advent of this new Pontiff under these happy auspices. His advent marks the perfect continuation of a thousand-year-old tradition which unfolds before our very eyes—tranquil, secure and regal—as one great Pope is followed by another who inspires sentiments of admiration, affection and hope, as also those of wisdom, kindliness and peace already shining bright at the dawn of this pontificate."

John XXIII's "First Cardinal"

The story is told that when, in January, 1953, Monsignor Montini had turned down the Red Hat offered him by Pius XII, one of his close friends told him: "They say, Your Excellency, that you missed the bus on your way to the top." The Pro-Secretary of State is supposed to have replied: "Perhaps I missed the bus, but perhaps also, in return, I got the coach for paradise."

Federico Alessandrini, a friend of Paul VI since his days as Assistant with the FUCI, gives the following explanation of this refusal, at least for Monsignor Domenico Tardini, the future Cardinal Secretary of State of John XXIII: "Monsignor Tardini did not want the Cardinalate because," as he explained, "this high dignity would have obliged him to stay on the job even when his strength might have failed, thus compromising his efficiency. By remaining as Under-Secretary, and later as Pro-Secretary of State for Extraordinary Affairs," he said, "it would be easier to disappear from the scene when the time came."

Montini and Tardini were too different both by temperament and education to have had the same reasons for asking to be excused from the high dignity of the Cardinalate. But they were also mutual friends—someone called them "twin brothers" because of their long association in high positions. Hence it is more than probable that their request to Pius XII to spare them the honors of the Purple came only after a lengthy exchange of viewpoints which convinced both of them that this request was necessary in order to enable them to serve the Church more effectively. Both Montini and Tardini shared a burning desire to serve the Church unselfishly and in the best possible manner.

In any case, on December 15, 1958, just a little more than a month after the election of the new Pope, the Cardinalate was imposed on both of them "with kindly firmness" by Pope John XXIII. In conferring on these two faithful servants of the Church the cardinalitial dignity, John XXIII accompanied his gesture with a distinction which had very special significance. The names of the two former Pro-Secretaries—Tardini had become Secretary of State—headed the list of the twenty-three new Cardinals.

That of Montini was first in the Order of Cardinal Priests, while that of Tardini was first in the Order of Cardinal Deacons.

Being the "first Cardinal" of a pontiff is not simply an honor, but it also entails a kind of moral pre-eminence over the other Cardinals designated by this same pontiff. It likewise involves the privilege of addressing to the Pope the discourse of thanks for the conferring of the cardinalitial dignity on the group and of celebrating the solemn Pontifical Mass in Saint Peter's on the anniversary of the Pope's coronation. In words attributed by an important weekly to Father Giulio Bevilacqua, of the Oratory of Brescia, John XXIII is supposed to have reminded his "first Cardinal" of the duties deriving from this distinction: "Now that I have made you Cardinal before all the others, you know what your duties are as 'first Cardinal.' You must come to Rome every year on the anniversary of my coronation and sing Mass for me. This is an obligation. I know very well that the anniversary of my coronation is November 4th and that November 4th is likewise the feast of Saint Charles Borromeo. But don't forget; I am counting on you!"

It was precisely by virtue of this combination privilege-duty of addressing thanks to the Holy Father that John XXIII's "first Cardinal" summed up in a warm expression of homage the gratitude and devotion of all his fellow Cardinals towards the Sovereign Pontiff: "Most Holy Father, the first sentiment welling up in my soul, and certainly in those of the most worthy prelates whom with me you have summoned to the Sacred College of Cardinals, and whom you now see all gathered around you, is one of admiration and gratitude for your fatherly kindness. This kindness is needed here. It is this kindness which here encourages us to accept this office which is so important in the Church of God.

"Already in these first weeks of your pontificate, most Holy Father, you have wanted to show your kindness in many, far-reaching ways, as though you wished to present yourself to the Church and to the world at once under that aspect which seems to be the best description of your August Person and your apostolic activity, namely that of kindliness, in which the Divine Master willed to give us such an unmistakable sign of His presence. The Church, as also the world, with eyes intent and ears opened to the appearance of the new Vicar of Christ, knew how to catch those parts of the evangelical image which in the gestures, the habits, and the very words of Your Holiness recall the figure and the message of the Good Shepherd. They felt themselves at once pervaded by a secret and soothing wave of happiness and confidence."

Cardinal Montini continued in his praise of the kindliness of Pope John, drawing attention to some of its more striking characteristics. He pointed out how this kindness was ever on the alert for opportunities to do good and was able to reconcile the exigencies of charity with modern demands for increased dispatch and efficiency in the government of the Church. There were words of praise for the wisdom of this kindness, growing out of long years of study and experience and prepared, though with simplicity and prudence, to make no concessions against the rights of truth and justice. Lastly, said His Eminence, the kindness of Pope John XXIII reflected virile strength, precisely because it was a reflection of Christ Himself.

But there is a still clearer evidence of the intimate reactions of Cardinal Montini in the face of his new responsibilities. It is found in his reply to the official notification of the conferring of the cardinalitial dignity by Monsignor Silvio Luino, Secret Chamberlain of the Secretariate of State: "In the most important and decisive moments of my poor life," the future Paul VI declared on that occasion, "I have always found joy in contemplating the ineffable and very human example of Mary most holy, as she pronounced those ever memorable words:

'Behold the handmaid of the Lord, be it done unto me according to thy word.' At this moment also, as though suggested by this sublime and maternal goodness, and with the consciousness of my littleness, I feel a similar expression rising to my lips as is fitting for a son and a servant: 'If this is the will of Him who is my Master, then so be it.'

"On another occasion I was permitted to decline this dignity and *for this favor*—italics ours—I am most grateful to Pope Pius XII of venerated memory. Now, however, other circumstances oblige me to accept it and for this further favor I am no less grateful to His Holiness John XXIII, happily reigning. I even desire to give open expression immediately to my gratitude. The conferring of the cardinalitial dignity on me, both for its own exalted value and for the manner in which it has been done, is a perfect reflection of the heart of this August Pontiff. As I accept with profound trepidation and humble joy the high office which he entrusts to me, I intend to honor his kindness, which has been motivated not by the merits of him who receives it but by the rich and generous soul of him who dispenses it. I must also add that another reason makes me happy over this event. It concerns, still more than my person, the diocese of Milan, the great and holy Church of Saint Ambrose, called once again by this gesture to take its place at the side of the supreme and holy Church of Rome."

These words, which were not the last to be pronounced on that occasion by Giovanni Battista Montini, to express his inner feelings for the honor done to his diocese and the new responsibilities entrusted to his person, indicated the reasons why it had not been possible this time to refuse the Red Hat. The new dignity culminated in his person a long and glorious tradition of pastors in the chair of Saint Ambrose: from Saint Charles Borromeo to Cardinals Tosi, Ratti, Ferrari, Schuster. . . .

Debtor to all

If until now Archbishop Montini had in any way or at any time spared himself in the discharge of his duties as pastor of the Archdiocese of Milan, the conferring of the Cardinal's dignity was for him a stimulus to a further and still more generous pastoral ministry. Although the successor of Ildefonso Cardinal Schuster really had no grounds for regrets, his elevation to the Sacred College gave him a new insight into the duties and responsibilities which four years earlier, at the prospect of his appointment as Archbishop of Milan, had made him ask fearfully of Pius XII: "But are you sure, Holy Father, that I am equal to the task?" In any case, even though this high dignity might provide some occasion for temptations to vanity, the new Cardinal had sought refuge in his own interpretation of these events: "The honor done to the See transcends that done to an individual."

Cardinal Montini returned to Milan, more thoroughly committed than ever before to the unselfish service of souls, and more keenly aware of his own duties and responsibilities. He made this clear in his discourse in the Duomo of Milan on December 12, 1958, during the Mass following the triumphal reception accorded him by thousands of the faithful: "As I return today to this Duomo, to this crossroads of the life of all Milan, and as, with deep fear and clear awareness of my unworthiness, but also with great simplicity and with great confidence, I ascend once more the chair of Saints Ambrose and Charles, I feel both the need and the duty to belong entirely to you. I am yours, to speak to you of Christ and to communicate to you His precepts and His graces. I am yours, to understand your life, your work, your aspirations, your destinies, and to put myself at your side, at your service. I am at your service, my fellow priests, to promote and to share with you the care and the problems of a faithful and renewed pastoral tradition. . . . I am yours, men of thought and action, to assist every enlightened and sound effort for growing progress in your culture and your prosperity. I am at your service, beloved workingmen, to support your lawful aspirations for greater security and better living conditions. Yes, I am a debtor to all men, to all I am indebted, in word, in example, in grace, in charity. Every class of persons is present in my heart as I celebrate this Holy Sacrifice: children, young people, Christian families, the poor, the suffering, again those who are faraway and, lastly, likewise our departed ones.... Of all of these I must ask something because I need all of them. Yes, my mission is truly great and is far beyond my strength. Please understand me! Help me!"

Milan's new Cardinal wore the purple so gracefully that perhaps it could be said of Montini as Cardinal what was later said of Montini as Paul VI: he seemed to have been born a Cardinal. But certainly the cardinalitial dignity did not really add to his gigantic moral stature. In any case, much more than himself, the Milanese, both clergy and faithful, rejoiced in the honor conferred on their pastor.

Four years had passed since January 6, 1955, when he had taken possession of the archdiocese, orphaned by the death of a great pastor. The same number of years were to pass before the definitive call which would thrust upon him an even greater responsibility, the greatest responsibility conceivable for any man, which would take him away from the children of Milan with whom he felt himself so closely united as to be regarded as a Milanese himself, even though he had been born in another province. He said this of himself speaking to a group of Sicilians arriving in Milan in search of work: "Can we be strangers, *we Milanese,* for you who have come from Sicily in search of a home, work, bread, and a new life? Our land is certainly not one bathed in sunshine like yours, but here there is work and we will not treat you like outsiders. You are our brethren and we shall prove it."

Four years had passed, and the initial impulse of love for his children in the Ambrosian diocese had never weakened under the wear and tear of time. Perhaps it might be said that this love was only becoming intensified and purified with the passing of time and that every day his charity was being enriched with unsuspected possibilities. "It seems to me that you have wanted to give such solemnity to my return among you," he said when he came back from Rome, "as to oblige me to greet the clergy, the authorities, the associations, the entire population, as though I were arriving in your midst for the first time. To this greeting I must add my thanks...."

These words are reminiscent of others pronounced exactly three years earlier on the first anniversary of his episcopal ministry in the Church of Milan. The passage in question comes from a sermon delivered in the Duomo on the Feast of the Epiphany, 1956: "Just a year ago, already a year, I ascended this pulpit for the first time, sent by the Vicar of Christ to succeed a most pious pastor— so learned and zealous, so justly mourned and admired— and to join a long line of Archbishops, some of whom have been marked by the titles of greatness and sanctity.

"Just how this happened, I still cannot understand, because not only in myself is there no merit, but also no particular qualifications for this fearful ministry. But so cordial and universal was your welcome, so many are the fruits of filial goodness and delicate deference given to me, so many affectionate and devoted meetings have been held, and in these last hours so many testimonies of affection and interest have been showered upon me, that I feel it my duty to all to make a public expression of my thanks with a renewed promise to dedicate to the pastoral service of this great and beloved spiritual family, which is the diocese of Saint Ambrose, my heart, my strength, the whole of my lowly life.

"I feel it also my duty to call attention to the kindness with which I have been received since my first arrival in Milan, to the special encouragement thus afforded me at once in my hesitant ministry, giving me a better understanding of an essential aspect of this ministry. It was made abundantly clear to me that on my arrival here a great dialogue was awaiting me, one far beyond my capacities, but also one that could no longer be avoided. I refer to the centuries-old and usual dialogue between the herald of the Gospel on the one hand and the world on the other. This dialogue has been given new aspects and has become much more demanding because of the insistent presence in Milan, not only of our wise and faithful audience, but also of a vast and indescribable public, in which are reflected the most significant forms of present-day modern life. Consequently, this is an unequal dialogue, between a weak voice and the rolling thunder of a feverish metropolis. But perhaps it is not a pointless dialogue if love cries out on the one side and if on the other there is still a human and kindly sense which listens and replies."

"Perhaps not a pointless dialogue if love cries out on the one side. . . ." No one could have the slightest doubt that it was love, the most impassioned love. . . . Even at that moment it could have been called a "Pauline" love of their souls which moved and inspired and sustained the soul of their zealous pastor.

The Cardinal's appointments

No biography of Giovanni Battista Montini could be complete without some remarks on his appointments. The reader might be tempted to think that there would be no difference at all between his appointments and those of any other Bishop or Cardinal Archbishop in his relations with his pastors and his faithful. Nevertheless, there was a marked contrast. There was above all the different approach to gauging the value and significance of dialogue with anyone, howsoever important or insignificant, learned or unlettered he might be. For Cardinal Montini there were no "little" problems and no "little" people. For him, everything and everyone was important. "Our Cardinal is a tremendous speaker," the Milanese said of him, "and you would think he is trying to make scholars out of all of us."

They were flattered at being able to say this. From his very first years in the Secretariate of State, this had always been his own personal method: receive everyone, speak to everyone, but especially and first of all, listen to everyone. At Milan, as Archbishop, and later as Cardinal, his system could not be different. Perhaps his warm hospitality, his availability to each and every one reached even higher degrees, precisely because of his attitude of "service," which he always recognized as being part and parcel of any position which entails helping others.

He had expressed these ideas himself on one occasion in his preface to a volume by one of his colleagues in the Secretariate of State, Monsignor Veuillot, now Coadjutor Archbishop of Paris. In the presentation of this book *Notre Sacerdoce,* he had written lines which have been included in anthologies on the priesthood as being among our clearest and most authentic documents: "The priesthood is a social service. It is for others. It is the organ of the Mystical Body destined to distribute grace and doctrine; it is the guide to salvation. Priesthood and egoism are contradictory terms. Priesthood and charity are synonomous." "The Cardinal has a heart of gold," declared the Milanese chauffeur of Cardinal Montini on the day when the latter was no longer Cardinal of Milan but the Pope of the Holy Church. "He received anyone who needed him and sent personal answers to letters from children."

A special place was reserved for appointments for pastors, for "his" priests. These appointments have become famous and can be well described by the following observations of one particular pastor: "Every meeting with him

was for us pastors a source of serenity and encouragement,
notwithstanding the difficulties and the diversity of our
problems. Even in his concrete vision of obstacles, he
evidenced strength greater than any human force, a
strength entirely hidden in the heart of God. ... He loved
his priests. How many times his voice echoed sadness as
he recalled some fellow priest who had proven unworthy of
his dignity. How often he repeated to his priests: 'Take
good care of young priests and help them; they need help
so badly!' "

It was a source of wonder for some people that even
in fields with which the Cardinal had no personal experience he could be so precise and so well informed, always
so practical in his advice. "Although he had never been
a pastor, he knew how to point out to us pastors the
basic virtues of the priest engaged in the care of souls:
patience, understanding, kindness, concern for those faraway. He enabled us to see and understand our parishes
for what each one really is, namely, a working Christian
community."

This should cause no surprise. He had said to one
pastor: "How lucky you are, to be able to hear confessions!"
The priesthood was for him a way of life. According to
Giulio Andreotti, from the very first years of his priestly
ministry among university students, no one looked upon
him "as a diplomat who said Mass," but everyone saw in
him "a priest who was particularly interested in diplomacy."

On the priesthood, on a priesthood totally "dedicated,"
he always had clear ideas, and he had showed this on
countless occasions. The priests of the Ambrosian archdiocese recall very well his annual Holy Thursday letters
on the priesthood. For his priests he reserved his most
penetrating words, his acts of greatest and most persua-
sive thoughtfulness. More than one Milanese pastor, and
these are men who are very practical and have their feet
solidly on the ground, was later amazed that during an

appointment with his Archbishop, he could become "senti-
mental," carried on by the thoughtful warm-heartedness
of his superior.

For the Archbishop, as is testified by many who were
close to him "no appointment could be rushed." It had
to take up important problems, and provide ways and
means to reach mutual understanding. His appointments
sometimes became lengthy, and a priest could no longer
come to Milan on personal business and then use his spare
time to drop in on the Archbishop. The fact that they had
to wait discouraged not a few priests from trying to see
him. This was brought to the attention of the Cardinal,
and he worked out a way to reserve one day a week for
his priests—without appointments!

Another means of personal contact which the Archbishop used on a wide scale was correspondence. These
letters—and many priests of the diocese now have some
in their possession—were written by hand, sometimes personally by the Archbishop. They were provoked by a host
of different circumstances: a name's day, an anniversary,
the need of a word of encouragement, a request for a favor,
sometimes the duty of giving a fatherly warning. "Nevertheless, they always went beyond the conventional phrases,
to become really and in princely fashion cordial and
friendly. . . . Even his letters of reprimand were couched
largely in terms of praise, in keeping with his personal
style which led him to stress and to emphasize the positive and to be brief and to the point in exhorting and
reprimanding. The addressees were able to understand
that the Cardinal was praising in them, not the talents
they already possessed but those he wanted to see in them.

Certain circumstances brought forth from the Archbishop his most heartfelt letters, when he was impelled
by the desire to lessen the suffering of others. In this connection there is an eloquent testimony from one who
received some of these letters: "There was a year when
I was seriously worried over the health of my wife, and

His Eminence came to know of it. It was between Christmas and New Year's. On Saint Sylvester's day . . . he sent for me to have the latest news. As he took leave of me and gave me his blessing, he remarked that he had written to me. In fact he had, and on my return home I found a moving and eloquent letter addressed to my wife, . . . a letter written in his own hand, a letter of blessing, comfort, and hope, and the hope which he thus nurtured flowered into the sweet and consoling riches of recovery. His letter is today a precious autograph."

Another incident is related by Luigi Santucci: ". . . About seven years ago I went through the saddest hour of my life when my mother passed away. There were the first painful weeks when I was completely lost, and when I reached the point where I could no longer find comfort in tears. All of a sudden, unexpectedly and almost mysteriously in its timeliness, I received a letter from the Archbishop, which had not been requested by myself or by anyone else. It was a long heartwarming letter, although he had not known my mother and knew me only slightly. He did not send me just general and noble words of comfort; he asked me humbly to take hold of myself in Christian hope and to do this for his sake. When, a few days later, I went to the Cardinal to stammer out my gratitude, he really tried to stop me, endeavoring to avoid any reference to thanks. Then the conversation switched to Pope John. He asked me all of a sudden, looking at me firmly with those light blue eyes which reflected both strength and child-like simplicity, if I would like to see the Pope. A few days later the Pope received me and with his words prolonged for me that unspeakable comfort which Cardinal Montini had preferred to hold in check in the lines of his most thoughtful letter. But in that same audience, my Archbishop, sitting alongside me and deftly turning the conversation to the subject of literature, more than once lifted up his hand and brought it to within

just a couple of inches from my hand, in a gesture eloquent with silent understanding which I shall never
forget."

The announcement of the Council

January 25, 1959, was a date which history has already
written in capital letters. It was the day chosen by Pope
John XXIII for a visit to the Basilica of Saint Paul's-
Outside-the-Walls, to observe the Feast of the Conversion
of the Apostle of the Nations and to proclaim to the world
that he was to convoke an Ecumenical Council. The
Archbishop of Milan was among the first to express his
satisfaction. On January 26th, the very day after the momentous announcement, *L'Italia*, the Milanese Catholic
daily, printed the text of the document in which His Eminence expressed his joy and his expectations as he looked
forward eagerly to this tremendous event.

Not a few persons saw very special significance in Montini's immediate favorable reaction, without waiting for the
impressions of his brother-Bishops. It may not be too far
from the truth to hazard the guess that Montini had already
been sounded out by Pope John on his plans. This thought
is suggested not only by his prompt favorable reaction
on the very next day, but also by the deep esteem which,
as a matter of common knowledge, Pope John had for
Cardinal Montini, an esteem which the latter reciprocated
most generously.

The following is the practically complete text of Cardinal Montini's announcement: "The announcement made
yesterday by His Holiness John XXIII, happily reigning,
of the imminent convocation of an Ecumenical Council, re-
sounds with such a deep and powerful voice in the Church
of God, in separated Christian communities, in the entire
world, that it would need no echo of our own to make

everyone, priests and faithful, men of thought and men of action, welcome and accept it with attention and emotion. An historical event of front-line importance is about to take place, not one of hatred or terror, as are the frighteningly great events of war; not one of earthly politics or of profane culture, with the fleeting greatness of so many human meetings; not one of scientific discoveries or temporal interests, with the dubious greatness of so many phases of our civic progress, but an event which is great with peace, truth, and spirit. It is great today and for tomorrow, great for peoples and human hearts, great for the entire Church and for the whole of humanity. This Council will be the greatest ever celebrated by the Church, in the assembly of its hierarchy in complete and peaceful unity. It will be also the greatest because of the universality of its dimensions, which really take in the entire geographical and civilized world. History is opening with immense and centuries-old visions before our eyes.

"Rome, the political capital of our country, will stand out as the spiritual capital of the world, such as it has been made and is still being made by its greatest apostles Peter and Paul. It will radiate everywhere the higher light illuminating straighter and surer paths, wherever men work for the union of peoples, social peace, the rehabilitation of the lowly, the progress of justice and freedom. We must understand immediately the hour of God. We must raise a cry of thanks to the Pope, who is thus opening up before the Church such an exalted path, and before the world such beneficial thoughts. . . . And we ourselves, lowly citizens of this earthly humanity and of this fleeting history, but sons of the Church of God and members of the Mystical Body of Christ, we must share in this solemn event, in the degree proper to each one, by rejoicing, hoping, praying. May prayer especially, which is the life-breath of the Church, animate our hearts and infuse into others the charism of our vocation as Catholics. May prayer, even now, make us watchful and eager with desire. Consequently, let prayer be our immediate reply to the Pope's announcement. May it be the humble, filial, fervent and choral antiphon of the Church of Ambrose."

This document was followed by many others. In fact it can be said that after Pope John's first announcement of this "historical event of front-line importance," The Archbishop of Milan spoke of it whenever he had the opportunity. Occasions for speaking on the Council were suggested by his zeal, either when he addressed the faithful of the archdiocese, or when he was invited to various localities to assist or to preside at conventions and other gatherings dealing with the apostolate and study.

His Pastoral Letter entitled *Thoughts on the Council,* written for the Lent of 1962, which had been termed one of the most important documents of the Italian episcopate on this theme, was more than significant. Because of its importance it was translated into many languages, even before its author ascended the Throne of Peter. But this passing reference needs to be completed by setting down in chronological order the other discourses of Cardinal Montini in regard to the Council: *The Papacy and the Church* (Milan, June 29, 1960); *Ecumenical Councils in the Life of the Church* (Passo della Mendola, August 16, 1960); *Unity and the Papacy in the Church* (Assisi, August 29, 1960); *The Ecumenical Council in the Life of the Church* (Milan, March 25, 1962); *The Ecumenical Council in the International Historical Picture* (Milan, April 27, 1962); *Councils in the Life of the Church* (Milan, University of the Sacred Heart, 1962); *Rome and the Council* (a most important lecture given at Rome at the Campidoglio, on October 10, 1962, to which reference will be made in the following chapter); *The Mystery of the Church in the Life of Saint Ambrose* (Milan, December 7, 1962); *Priests and the Ecumenical Council* (Varese, February 6, 1963).

As a partial explanation of Giovanni Battista Montini's preparation for discussing topics dealing with the Council, there is a quotation from one of his discourses: "I recall . . .

that Bishop Giacinto Gaggia, a prominent Bishop to whom I am indebted, among so many other benefits, for my priestly ordination, a man of broad culture and of intellectual gifts equalled by his strong will, was asked by me timidly, when I was as yet a very young priest, what line to follow in my studies, since I was then thinking of specializing in the life and history of the Church. He immediately replied: 'Read the history of the Councils. Take Hefele (eighteen forbidding volumes!) and study them. There you will find everything.' By this he meant that there I would find theology, philosophy, spirituality, politics, humanism and Christianity, errors, discussions, truth, abuses, laws virtues, and the holiness of the Church. The history of the Councils is an ecclesiastical encyclopedia. It shows the place of the Councils in the life of the Church; they pervade its entire existence, they sum it up, they clarify it, and they direct it."

"... one of the most outstanding figures of our times ..."

A well-known Italian weekly wrote of Cardinal Montini after his election as Pope: "Anyone who knows the missionary spirit of Paul VI, who as diplomat and as Archbishop made long journeys abroad and visited personally the heart of Africa, can foresee that he will widen the range of the travels begun by his predecessor."

The truth of the matter is that the prophecy came true sooner than anyone dreamed, so that no one is surprised now to hear it said that: "Just as Pope John traveled by train, Pope Paul will travel by plane." His pilgrimage to the Holy Land now belongs to history. Nevertheless, the significance of these new events in history in no way detracts from the two long trips undertaken by Paul VI while still Cardinal-Archbishop of Milan. Even at that time God was rounding out the pastoral experience of His future Vicar on earth through his visits to the Americas and to Africa.

On June 3, 1960, Cardinal Montini, accompanied by his secretary, Don Pasquale Macchi, set out on the first of fourteen hops to North and South America and return. The itinerary called for visits to Paris, New York, Notre Dame, Chicago, Boston, Philadelphia, Washington, Baltimore, New York a second time, Brasilia, San Paolo, Rio de Janeiro, Zurich, and finally back to Milan. At the urgent invitation of the Nuncio to France, Cardinal Montini spent some hours at the Nunciature in Paris before continuing on to New York. At 9:35 that night the jet carrying the Cardinal of Milan set down at New York, where Cardinal Spellman and the Apostolic Delegate, Archbishop Egidio Vagnozzi, were the first to wish him a cordial welcome to the United States.

After spending the night at Cardinal Spellman's residence and devoting most of the next day to a whirlwind tour of New York's main attractions—this was not his first visit to the city—Cardinal Montini left by private plane for Notre Dame, Indiana. At 6:35 in the evening his plane landed at Saint Joseph County Municipal Airport at South Bend, Indiana, where Father Theodore Hesburgh, C.S.C., President of the University of Notre Dame, welcomed him. In fact, the Cardinal's trip had been planned in conjunction with the University's invitation to celebrate solemn Pontifical Mass for the Commencement Exercises and to receive an honorary degree of Doctor of Laws along with the President of the United States.

On the morning of June 5th, Pentecost Sunday, His Eminence celebrated an outdoor Solemn Pontifical Mass on the University mall. In a brief discourse in English after the Mass, addressing the graduates, their friends and relatives, the six hundred faculty members and distinguished guests, Cardinal Montini declared: "I am firmly convinced that the basic need of the world today is the light and the life of truth."

At noon the President of the University hosted numerous local and state officials, as also notable personages from other fields, at a lunch honoring Dwight D. Eisenhower, President of the United States, and the Cardinal Archbishop of Milan. His Eminence had brought as his personal gift to President Eisenhower a bronze statuette representing an angel shattering the chains of a captive. The statuette is a reproduction of one of the artistic treasures of the Duomo of Milan and is mounted on a pedestal of Candoglia marble, the same as that used in the construction of the Duomo itself. President Eisenhower's sentiments of grati tude are eloquently expressed in the following letter of thanks to His Eminence:

THE WHITE HOUSE
Washington

June 10, 1960

Dear Cardinal Montini:

Before leaving for the Far East, I want to thank you for the meaningful figurine which you gave me at Notre Dame last Sunday. It could stand as a symbol of everything I am trying to accomplish on this trip—and in my lifetime.

The angel breaking the chains of oppression is a herald of freedom represents, I think, a challenge to the people of the Free World. We must be responsible to the hungry, naked and homeless— to all our neighbors in the underdeveloped nations of the world who are less fortunate than we. As the representative of my country abroad, I shall reaffirm our eagerness to fulfill this responsibility to the full.

With best wishes,

Sincerely,
Dwight D. Eisenhower

That same afternoon, the University of Notre Dame conferred honorary degrees on the President of the United States, Cardinal Montini, and several other distinguished individuals, among whom was the late Doctor Tom Dooley, world-famed for his selfless apostolate of medical mercy in the Far East. Immediately after the academic exercises President Eisenhower and Cardinal Montini took leave of each other, as the President had to return east immediately for a further appointment that evening. His Eminence, however, remained on the campus of the University for another full day, making detailed visits to various installations and centers of research. Father Hesburgh had seen to the organization of a special dinner to enable Cardinal Montini to meet and talk with the group of Italian-American professors on the University faculty. His Eminence also paid a rapid visit to the nearby Saint Mary's College, conducted by the Sisters of the Holy Cross.

After driving to Chicago on the evening of June 6th, the Cardinal of Milan was the over-night guest of Cardinal Meyer, Archbishop of Chicago. The following morning Cardinal Montini accompanied Cardinal Meyer on a tour of the various points of interest, especially the complex organization of the vast Chicago Chancery Office. His Eminence was particularly interested in the Columbus Clinic, founded years ago and directed for some time personally by the sainted Mother Cabrini.

From Chicago the Cardinal's itinerary took him to Boston, where he was greeted effusively by Richard Cardinal Cushing. With unflagging interest and tireless zeal the Archbishop of Milan visited several of the charitable institutions for which Cardinal Cushing is so justly famous, and found time for hasty calls at other nearby centers as well.

After Boston came Philadelphia, Washington, and Baltimore. In Philadelphia, Cardinal Montini went to call on Cardinal John F. O'Hara, who was then confined to the hospital by grave illness. In fact, just two months later Cardinal O'Hara died, to the great regret of Cardinal Montini who had always admired him greatly. During his visits to the shrines of American independence in Philadelphia, Cardinal Montini was visibly moved, especially as he stood beside the Liberty Bell. He seemed profoundly impressed as he recalled all the epoch-making history summed up in this bell, and appeared almost to regard it as a relic as he offered over it a special blessing.

In Washington the Cardinal of Milan was the guest of the Apostolic Delegate, Archbishop Egidio Vagnozzi. His first visit was to the National Shrine of the Immaculate Conception and to the Catholic University of America. The party then repaired to the Spanish Embassy where a large reception was marking the conferring of a high Spanish honor on Cardinal Spellman. With delicate thoughtfulness, Cardinal Montini had indicated his desire to attend this reception because of his long-standing friendship and admiration for the Archbishop of New York. That evening the Apostolic Delegation was the scene of another reception, which brought together important personages from the political, diplomatic, and religious circles of the national capital, in honor of the Cardinal of Milan.

The next morning His Eminence left for Baltimore, to which he wished to pay his respects as the primatial See of the United States, although a very tight schedule permitted only the briefest of visits. He then continued on to New York where, after a farewell dinner at six at the home of Cardinal Spellman, he emplaned at 9:00 P.M. for Brazil. After a first stop in the Bahamas and further calls at Trinidad and Belem, the Cardinal's plane landed in Brasilia at 1:00 P.M. the next day.

His reception by the Brazilian authorities could not have been more solemn. He was welcomed by honor guards while the military band played the Papal and Brazilian anthems. After the official reception, President Joscelin Kubitschek invited the Cardinal to a seat beside him for a helicopter flight over the new capital.

In an important discourse delivered before prominent national leaders, Montini had formulated hopes of "Christian prosperity for the whole of the Brazilian people." In reply the Brazilian President declared: "Your Eminence is one of the greatest figures of our time." This phrase, with almost a touch of the prophetic, was confirmed by the events subsequent to the famous "Thirteen Days in America" of Cardinal Montini. These thirteen days had begun on the morning of June 3, 1960 and closed at 9:00 A.M on the 16th of the same month, when an Alitalia jet on the Buenos Aires-Rome route made its second-last stop at the Milanese airport of Malpensa. It was the feast of Corpus Christi. The Archbishop celebrated Mass and then took a brief rest. A few hours later, he took part in the solemn Eucharistic procession as though the "Thirteen Days in America" had passed without leaving even a trace of fatigue in the strong constitution which had put up with so much during his hectic trip.

This trip to the United States was not the first for Cardinal Montini. Back in 1951 he had gone to the United States on an extremely delicate mission. At that time the President of the United States was Harry Truman, and the moment seemed right to realize the plan for diplomatic relations between that country and the Holy See. This was the purpose of the trip made by the then Under-Secretary of State, Monsignor Montini. President Truman appeared well disposed and had even indicated the choice of his personal representative to the Holy See in the person of General Mark Clark. But the unfavorable reaction in Protestant circles was so hostile that the President decided to drop the idea. This notwithstanding, the trip was not useless, since from that moment relations between the United States and the Catholic Church were more cordial than ever before, even though, officially, the general situation had not changed.

In the heart of Africa

On the day after Cardinal Montini's election as Pope, among the countless telegrams of congratulation pouring in to the Secretariate of State, there was one which stated: "Many of us have happy memories of Your Holiness' visit here last year." The message was from Mr. Humphrey Gibbs, Chief of State of Rhodesia, and reminded the new Pope of "an unforgettable experience," as he himself had called it, and which he regarded as one of the most thrilling experiences of his life.

On the eve of the Conclave from which Montini was to come out Pope, a French paper had written that the Cardinal of Milan was "the most intelligent of the Italian prelates, a man endowed with a dynamism which is the envy of all Rome." In fact, the illustrious prelate, whose ecumenical ideals were so far-reaching, did not limit his activities to the geographical confines of his own immense archdiocese. At Milan he had organized and promoted two eminently missionary projects, namely, providing spiritual assistance for Italian construction workmen in the Kariba area of Africa and the erection of an international college for foreign students. In view of its contribution to the human and pastoral formation of the Cardinal of Milan, it will be time well spent to present the highlights of the most important missionary episode in the life of the Archbishop of Milan during the period immediately preceding his elevation to the supreme pontificate.

Cardinal Montini's trip to Africa lasted longer than the "Thirteen Days in America" and was likewise more intense and demanded greater exertion. Accompanied by his faithful secretary, Don Pasquale Macchi, Cardinal Montini had left Milan on July 19, 1962 at 8:00 P.M. He returned on August 10th at 5:30 P.M., exactly twenty-two days later. The various phases of the journey, following the order of strict chronology, were first of all brief stops at Khartoum and Nairobi and then, after over-flying the snow-capped peak of Kilimanjaro, he arrived at Salisbury on July 20th, at 1:00 P.M. The Cardinal wanted to take a quick turn around the city and, after lunch and a short rest, he left at 3:30 by helicopter for Kariba, where an immense crowd was awaiting their illustrious visitor. From Kariba Cardinal Montini continued his journey to Kirundo, where his welcome was no less warm and "native." There he administered Confirmation to some fifty children and during Mass personally distributed Holy Communion to hundreds of the faithful, for the most part Africans.

From Kirundo the journey continued to Johannesburg, where he received a particularly warm and cordial welcome. It was July 24th. At the solemn evening Mass, celebrated by Bishop Boyle, Bishop of Johannesburg, there were present the Archbishops of Pretoria and Durban, besides Cardinal Montini in his scarlet robes. The next day, after a stop-over in Pretoria and a visit to the main religious and civilian attractions of the archdiocese, Cardinal Montini continued on to Lagos in Nigeria, with a stop at Leopoldville. Towards evening he landed at Ikega, about ten miles from Lagos. This city, which has a population of approximately 500,000, is the seat of the Apostolic Delegation for Central West Africa, whose incumbent at that time was Archbishop Sergio Pignedoli, one of the present Pontiff's very close friends and former colleagues in Rome and Milan and since transferred as Apostolic Delegate to Canada. In Lagos the Archbishop of Milan received from the religious and civil authorities the most solemn reception of his whole African trip. The morning after his arrival he was given a state reception by the President of the Federation of Nigeria, Mnaudi Azikiwe, who, although Protestant—out of 500,000 inhabitants there are 100,000 Protestants and 40,000 Catholics—had words of sincere praise for the Catholic missions and for the work accomplished by the missionaries. At the end of his talk he insisted on receiving the blessing of his illustrious guest.

In the following days, up to August 7th, Cardinal Montini continued his visits in the vicinity of Lagos, stopping at

Ibadan, where there are only 10,000 Catholics out of a population which is predominantly Moslem; Ilorin, which has 7,000 Catholics among 150,000 inhabitants; Akure, a diocese with 250,000 Protestants, 70,000 Moslems, 300,000 pagans, and 80,000 Catholics; Benin City, with 150,000 Catholics, and more than 60,000 catechumens; Owerri, with 400,000 Catholics, 80,000 catechumens and 305 seminarians. Lastly he went to Enugu where, on August 5th and 6th, he terminated his Nigerian visit, a visit which had been more than rewarding in human contacts and in meetings with flourishing local Christian communities.

On August 7th accompanied by the Apostolic Delegate, Archbishop Pignedoli, Cardinal Montini left by automobile for a visit to the young nation of Ghana. After traveling some sixty miles on country roads the group found its path blocked by a flood. The shortness of time forced them to return and then to continue the trip by plane, so as not to upset the pre-arranged schedule. Before arriving back in Lagos, whence it was to go by plane to Accra the group stopped in the shade of a little grove to eat lunch in the open. They soon saw between the trees the faces of several Africans who first looked very timid but then dropped all semblance of fear, came up to the Cardinal and his group and accepted their courteous invitation to join them in this unusual picnic.

The plane for Accra, Ghana, left at 5:30 P.M. on August 7th. The three following days, until his departure for Italy, were dedicated by Cardinal Montini to the capital of Ghana and to Akosonibo, where large groups of Italians are engaged in the construction of the Volta River dam. Then he returned to Lagos where he took a fraternal farewell of Archbishop Pignedoli in the residence of the Apostolic Delegate.

With his secretary, the Cardinal left for Italy at 2:00 A.M. on August 10th, arriving in Rome punctually at 7:00 A.M. Instead of continuing on to Milan, the Cardinal went to Castel Gandolfo where his good friend, John XXIII, was resting from the fatigue caused by the preparation for the Council. There the Cardinal had a long two-hour audience reporting to the Holy Father on his impressions of his African trip. Cardinal Montini could not have rounded out his missionary experience in any better way on the very eve of the Council. At 5:30 that same day, he reached Milan by plane.

"An extraordinary experience which made a deep impression on me"

Numerous prelates and priests, and a still larger number of journalists were awaiting His Eminence at the Milan airport. This reflected a tremendous universal interest in catching the impressions of the illustrious traveler. Cardinal Montini at once showed himself most affable, submitting with good grace to interviews and to questions. His first words as he came down from the plane were: "This has been an extraordinary experience, one which has made a deep impression on me. Perhaps because I was the first European Cardinal to visit their continent, perhaps for other reasons, my welcome was magnificent. I am speaking not merely of the Italians at Kariba and of the numerous others whom I met during my three weeks down there, but of the native populations. There we have a Christian community gifted with great faith, of which it gave proof on more than one occasion. My impressions and memories are those of deep faith, a lively desire for improvement, which give grounds for hope for the political and religious future of Africa and particularly of the nations which I visited. All this is dominated by the profound joy of a sense of the unity and universality of the Church. One comes away from such an experience with a soul filled and strengthened with lively hope."

Kariba and Akosonibo were the farthest points of the Cardinal's trip. Kariba is an important area of the Zambesi territory, where thousands of Italians have migrated, following construction companies under contract for a gigantic dam under the auspices of the local government. Akosonibo is not far from Accra and also is the center of a colony of Italian workers. Between Kariba in South Africa and Akosonibo in Ghana Cardinal Montini had covered a large part of the African continent.

These episodes and the need to provide adequate spiritual assistance for Italian families who had migrated to these areas in search of work were the reasons underlying the missionary projects of the Milanese archdiocese. In fact, it was the Archbishop himself who organized the recruitment of missionary priests and religious men and women, to assist the emigrants, thus erecting the missions of Zambesi and Upper Volta.

These circumstances helped to make of the Cardinal's trip a genuine pastoral visitation to the two missions. These main aims led to an extension of his original travel plans, in order to take in other African countries to have firsthand knowledge of the splendid flowering of life which characterizes these young African nations. In actual fact, this African "tour" provided Cardinal Montini with an opportunity to see the realities of Africa, and this on the very eve of his elevation to the papal throne. This emphasizes the spiritual significance of such a memorable experience.

Thus Cardinal Montini was able to see for himself that Africa is advancing with giant steps on the road to progress and civilization. At the same time, however, he was also able to sense the anxieties tormenting the new continent, the immense problems blocking it from effectively taking its place in the world community, problems which must be both faced and solved.

The visit convinced the Cardinal that the African continent is ready for the message of the Gospel, the preaching of which is hampered only by the scarcity of priests, religious and adequately prepared laymen. For this reason he returned with a clearly defined plan which he promptly announced in a TV appearance: "We cannot hide our desire to intensify our missionary cooperation, not only to have the joy of giving, but likewise to experience the other joy of receiving. The missions need our decisive cooperation, and they are even now in a position to show their gratitude through the witness of an intense spiritual life and Christian virtue, which we in turn, with equal gratitude and humility, must learn to appreciate."

When informing the faithful of his diocese of his experiences during his trip, the Cardinal stressed its apostolic and missionary character and then went into more detail: "We visited many missionary stations in South Africa and many also in central West Africa, coming away with excellent impressions. Still more, we must likewise say how edified we were by the religious spirit of the Catholic communities we visited. We could not refrain from comparing this spirit with the religious sentiments of our own people, which is of course deeply pious and faithful, but which in some degree has lost its grip on that intensity of faith, that totality of presence, that dignified comportment, that beauty of chant and that spontaneity of devotion which, with joy and amazement, we could admire in the sacred ceremonies, in Holy Mass and Holy Communion especially, in the flourishing African churches. . . . We have seen how the people there take their Faith seriously, since it is a fundamental premise for any correct idea of life. We have seen how the expression of religion—cult, prayer, devotion—is ardent and dignified in the lives of these new Christians. We have seen how youth especially is filling the missionary churches. We have heard full-voiced and moving chant from entire communities, singing in Latin our feast-day Masses."

THE HERITAGE OF POPE JOHN

After taking possession of the See of Milan Giovanni Battista Montini returned to Rome on several occasions. These were quick and brief trips, with no fuss or fanfare. But some visits could not pass unobserved. In October, 1958, Archbishop Montini was at Castle Gandolfo, in prayer before the body of Pius XII. At the beginning of June, 1963, he was once more in Rome, this time at the bedside of Pope John. But there was one other return which was to be definitive, and this was his journey to Rome for the Conclave convoked to elect a successor to John XXIII. The choice fell on the Archbishop of Milan, former Under-Secretary and then Pro-Secretary of State, who thus began a second and definitive residence in the Eternal City.

Intense preparation for the Council

The months of August and September, 1962, were marked by a crescendo of activity, provoked by the imminent opening of the Second Vatican Council. The Preparatory Commissions were straining to complete the final revision of the various schemas. Cardinals and Bishops thoughout the world were urgently inviting the faithful to prepare fervently for this great assembly of the Church. In many dioceses special religious services and devotions were organized, in keeping with the desires of the Pope, who used every occasion to urge all whom he received in audience to pray earnestly for the happy outcome of the Council.

About this time the names of some of the "Observers" began to be known. These Observers were representatives of non-Catholic Christian Churches, invited to assist at the Council meetings. The desire to have everything get under way at once created an atmosphere of intense expectation as the Council's opening day drew nearer.

Day by day new information came out on various points dealing with the Council. On September 6th, the Holy Father published his motu proprio *Appropinquante Concilio*, with the procedural rules giving the general principles on how to conduct the meetings, the persons to fill various offices, the appointment of the members of the Presidency Council—composed of ten Cardinals, later increased to twelve, chosen from among the most prominent members of the episcopate throughout the world—and the definitive list of the Presidents of the ten Commissions and of the Secretariate for Extraordinary Affairs.

In a collective Pastoral published on July 10, 1962, the Bishops of Lombardy organized a special Marian manifestation at the celebrated Sanctuary of Caravaggio, to be held on September 12th, the Feast of the Holy Name of Mary. Evidently Cardinal Montini was the moving spirit behind this project, whose success went beyond all expectations. More than three thousand religious and secular priests, with their respective Bishops and other prelates, along with civil and military authorities, walked in solemn procession and assisted at the Mass celebrated by Cardinal Montini. That evening the pilgrims assembled once more for a solemn Hour of Adoration. The Cardinal of Milan pronounced a discourse which had wide repercussions in the press and in other qualified circles. "The Council," he affirmed, "is a fact which must be studied not merely with the cameras of photographers or with the curiosity of tourists, but with the eye of Faith, and it must be accepted with the docility and the joy of charity. It is a fact which the clergy must assimilate and explain to the faithful in all its spiritual and other-worldly aspects, without which it would be only an imposing and strange pageant, dark and deprived of inner spiritual vitality."

Cardinal Montini invited all those present to pray and to implement obediently whatever directives the Council might adopt, recalling that the effectiveness of the Council depends not so much on what is said or written, as on the importance and the value attributed to it and the zeal with which its decisions are put into practice. In this connection he recalled the example of Saint Charles Borromeo, the man who had exerted such decisive influence on the implementation of the Council of Trent.

John XXIII sent Cardinal Montini an Autograph Letter in which he wrote: "The pilgrimage of prayer and penance undertaken by the Bishops and priests of Lombardy to the Sanctuary of Caravaggio moves Us deeply and is a consolation in Our apostolic service." The Pope stressed that, for the first time in history, Lombardy had witnessed a gathering of this kind as "an indication and a prelude to a more concrete and deeply felt spiritual unity which, on the vigil of a Council whose only aim is to give splendor and vigor to the unity of the Church, seems to anticipate its signs and give an encouraging preview of what it will accomplish. The Pope continued in a reminiscent tone, referring to his own various visits in quite different circumstances to "the blessed Sanctuary of Caravaggio," making it clear that he regretted not being able to be there on that September 12th with those taking part in this imposing gathering.

Some days later, on September 16th, Montini gave orders that throughout his diocese there should be a Solemn Novena to the Holy Spirit, and he once more urged the clergy, all Catholic associations, and the faithful to pray for an outpouring of the Holy Spirit on the Council, to meditate on His sanctifying mission in the Mystical Body of Christ, and on His indispensable and mysterious role in the government of the Church.

Lastly, the final solemn act of this preparatory period, even though in an indirect way, was the celebration of a "Minor Synod" at the end of that same month of September. With a master's touch Cardinal Montini took up a theme which was to be one of the main topics discussed in the First Session of the Council, namely poverty in the Church and, more concretely, among the clergy. The Cardinal Archbishop approached this theme by formulating the problem in the following terms: "We now take up the vast and delicate problem of our attitude as priests towards what, in our preaching and with the Gospel in our hands, we so frequently call 'the world.' What is the influence of 'the world' on the life of the clergy? Do we tend to conformism or to resistance? Have we clearly understood the dividing line between what is acceptable in modern life and what is not?"

The Cardinal then moved on to interesting points suggested by this theme, such as the search after money, the new concept of obedience now upsetting many minds, the evaluation of exclusively natural motives to the frequent detriment of those of a higher order. He then concluded with clear and trenchant directives: interior asceticism or the "priestly mentality" and external asceticism, in other words "stamping the priestly life with that simplicity, renunciation, and austerity, which must make it an evangelical life. . . . We ourselves must be courageous enough to adopt an attitude of unselfishness in our pastoral evaluation of the advantages of one position over another. Also, but on a lower level, this priestly mentality demands that we refrain from the habitual reading of profane and worldly books, that we mortify unnecessary curiosity about books and films of questionable morality (when no official duties demand otherwise), and avoid habitual smoking or the use of alcoholic beverages, giving up excursions or vacations organized for purposes of simple amusement and avoiding anything smacking of luxury in our houses."

Montini's realistic and open temperament always joined with a great breadth of view, is reflected in all these directives, which have no purpose of their own, but are part of something felt deep down in the heart, that is to say, the pastoral sense, the sincere conviction that the priest must be constantly serving the interests of the faithful. This idea is summed up in a specially significant passage: "Saint John Berchmans said of himself that his greatest penance was the common life. We should be able to say that our greatest penance is the pastoral life. Our principal asceticism must be fidelity to our daily pastoral work. In fact, it is pastoral life which obliges us to look after our children, our youth, our immigrants, our working men, our poor, our sick, those who are far away, and to provide for countless daily emergencies. It is pastoral life which consumes our days in the confessional, in taking care of baptisms, marriages, funerals, preaching, and sacred functions. This is an exhausting and ennobling penance, one which. among others, has been taught us by Saint Charles Borromeo, and which today more than ever before, must be the sanctifying center of our priestly life."

All these solemn acts wound up Milan's preparation for the Council. The Archbishop could now turn his attention more intently to the main themes which he was to treat personally in the great ecumenical assembly.

The great vigil of the greatest event of the century

As part of his own immediate preparation for the Council, Pope John XXIII went by train on an epoch-making pilgrimage to Loreto and to Assisi on October 4, 1962. After this journey the atmosphere of expectation grew still more tense in a week of at least relative calm. On October 7th, Feast of the Holy Rosary, at the conclusion of a solemn diocesan triduum in the Basilica of St. Mary Major, there was a penitential procession terminating at the Lateran Basilica. Taking part in this procession were nineteen Cardinals, the Latin Patriarch of Jerusalem, more than a hundred bishops, the Apostolic Nuncio in Italy, and a crowd estimated at about 150,000 people. The Holy Father was present at the ceremony and in the Lateran delivered a discourse in which he spoke frankly of difficulties which might arise in the Council, placing his confidence as always, and completely, in help from heaven: "Even though they may be complete," the Pope said, "human preparations will always reflect the limitations of our nature. But infallibly, to complete whatever is begun, there will be present He who brings light, radiates truth, gives a true sense of grace, proportion, and good judgment. He it is who gives unending life, the Supreme Organizer of the Holy Church— the Holy Spirit. These are consoling words, and in them We take Our stand, hope and work."

In the meantime, many of the Council Fathers were arriving in Rome and their numbers gave a new impression of the boundless universality and unusual activity of the Eternal City. Little by little, converging from all corners of the earth, the Council Fathers reached a record number. They were 2,627 coming from 116 countries, geographically distributed as follows: 332 from North America, 601 from Latin America, 250 from Africa, 95 from the Arab countries, 256 from Asia, 849 from western

Europe, 174 from the Communist bloc, 70 Australians.
Classified according to dignity, there were 85 Cardinals,
8 Patriarchs, 593 Archbishops, 2,131 bishops, 14 Abbots
Nullius, 67 Superiors General of religious orders. The total
number convoked was 2,850, but only 2,627 had been able
to come. The difference between the two figures naturally
spotlights the saddening fact of the "impeded Bishops," a
mild term used to express a harsh reality. There were many
vacant seats in the Council Hall, many of them intended
for Bishops from behind the Iron Curtain. Still, the empty
seats in the Council have their importance. All the Bishops
had been convoked individually by a personal letter from
the Pope sent out in April but published only at the end of
September, which began with the affectionate greeting
"Venerable and dear Brother." All of them would have
been most happy to come to Rome to see at close range
this most loving Father whose reputation for kindliness had
echoed to the farthest ends of the earth. Only a force greater than themselves, against their own will and at the cost
of harsh sacrifice, had kept this dream from coming true.
This was the significance of the empty seats.

A topic with grave consequences

In the very midst of the Council atmosphere, and
precisely on that intense vigil of October 10, 1962, Cardinal
Montini appeared on the Roman scene once more, this time
to deliver a lecture at the Campidoglio, one which had
world-wide repercussions. The event is described as follows
by a special correspondent of an important European daily:
"I could not actually get into the lecture delivered by
Cardinal Montini at the Campidoglio. But rarely have I
seen such a line of automobiles in front of a building or
such a vast public fighting to get in for a lecture! Sixteen
Cardinals, dozens of Bishops, diplomats and ministers

formed a multi-colored court which I could just make out from the door over a sea of heads. Fortunately a public address system had been installed and those on the outside could hear very well. It was an intriguing experience. The Cardinal of Milan, with his almost magnetic speaking style, who draws his hearers along irresistibly, talked on relations between Church and State, comparing the situation in Rome during the two Councils, Vatican I and Vatican II. In the First Vatican Council Rome was still part of the Papal States, and all Italy was rising up against the Pope, not as Pope, but as a sovereign who was allegedly opposing national unity. The First Vatican Council adjourned abruptly and is a symbol of the fall of the temporal power of the Popes: "The Pope was deprived, or rather relieved of his earthly possessions. Many persons felt that the Papacy would collapse with the crash of the territorial footstool on which it had rested its feet for centuries. But Providence had arranged things in different fashion, thus playing almost dramatically with events. The Papacy resumed with unusal vigor its function as a teacher of life and a witness of the Gospel, and thus reached such heights in the spiritual government of the Church and in moral influence over the world as had never been experienced before!"

With his usual breadth of view, Cardinal Montini spoke with perfect clarity and unquestioned competence of the Italian *Risorgimento*. To use the expression of the correspondent referred to above, he spoke "with elegance, without bitterness, without resentment, almost praising the men responsible for these events, not for the brutality with which they snatched away the possessions of the Church, but because through them the situation of the Church had been clarified and the Papacy stood out in a clearer light in history." This "conciliation" policy was the one followed by the Popes, beginning with Pius XI, who wanted at all costs to put an end to the painful situation of "the papal prisoner in the Vatican." Pius XII pursued the same policy and John XXIII brought it to its zenith, with his unpretentious travels into Italian territory and his last official visit to the Quirinal in the May of 1963. With good reason the street leading into Piazza San Pietro is called "Via della *Conciliazione.*"

- Montini referred to the Apostles Peter and Paul as founders of the Christian city upon the pagan city: "Marvelous and mysterious is the fact that the first Apostle of the Nations, the first promoter of Catholicity, Paul, came to Rome by divine command and there, himself a Roman citizen, preached the name of Christ both with his words and with his blood. . . . Thus these two lowly Apostles, the first, Peter, principally a symbol of the unity of the Church, and the second, Paul, the protagonist of its Catholicity, founded the Christian city upon the pagan city. Each of them had his own ideas but they agreed in harmony of concept, plans, and scopes, and together they were radically different in temperament and aims. Even in the midst of adversity, beginning with the arrival of the Caesars, they laid down the principle of twofold power of the State and of the Church, from which flows true civic order, the principle which postulates harmony between these two powers and at the same time their mutual liberation, that is to say the liberation of the State from sacerdotal functions which are not its own, and the freeing of the Church from temporal functions which are equally not its own.

"What was accomplished only on a small scale in the beginning, what was even in the thought and will of Christ, is today happily realized and so to speak proclaimed by the Ecumenical Council, an event grander and more symbolic than ever before of unity and catholicity, one which confers incomparable honor upon the city of Rome and what it represents and makes of it a most living reality, without thereby confusing their mutual relationships or lessening the liberty which they have mutually conferred on each other." According to the comment of an authoritative newspaper, this discourse of Cardinal Montini will go down in history as one of the most significant documents in the annals of the relationships between Church and State.

The thorny problem of the suppression of the temporal power of the Papacy, with the "case of conscience" which it entailed for citizens of the Italian nation, is now ancient history and material for the archives. In a twofold sense the Church is free and she rejoices openly over the seizure which relieved her of such a heavy burden. With this feeling of relief, she has absolutely no desire to reopen questions which have long since been settled by events. Church and State proceed, each along its own path, which must be one of collaboration, but without either of them trying to usurp functions and activities which are not its own. Montini took up this theme in still clearer and even more forceful terms in another important lecture delivered on April 27, 1963 as a prelude to the forthcoming visit of John XXIII to the Quirinal.

Autumn or spring

On the night of October 10th the Roman sky clouded over as if it also felt the need of unleashing a cloudburst to freshen up the atmosphere of tension which was lying heavy over the city and over the entire world.

Pope John XXIII was the calmest of all those concerned. He later explained to the press that he had not felt at all nervous, that he even had an excellent night's sleep and that he was not worried over what might happen, but was simply awaiting calmly the fulfillment of the will of God.

But with all his serenity, even Pope John got up at four o'clock on the morning of that historic October 11th. The skies were still pouring down rain. It was raining as it can only at Rome, with a slight drizzle alternating with terrific downpours. There were worries and anxiety that this miserable weather might jeopardize the success of the imposing and long-awaited procession of all the Council Fathers through Piazza San Pietro. But all of a sudden the skies cleared, making room for a bright shining sun. October 11th became a characteristic Roman autumn day, the kind that sheds the special hue of falling leaves over the whole atmosphere.

"A river of mitres!" All descriptions of the scene used this phrase, because in all the spectators this incomparable cortege had aroused the same impression. It crossed Piazza San Pietro through a vast sea of the faithful, moved by devout curiosity and standing on tiptoes. Two thousand and some Council Fathers, clothed in copes, chasubles, the exotic vestments of the Oriental Rites, jeweled crowns and mitres, slowly made their way through this many-colored multitude. It was almost like a Gulf Stream passing by and softening the climate, a white-robed Gulf Stream with its source in the Cenacle. Bringing up the rear was the Pope, Pope John, the Pope who had wanted this Council, who had dedicated his entire pontificate to making it a reality. As a "Bishop among Bishops" John XXIII walked down the Scala Regia like any other Council Father, then mounted the portable throne only to cross the Piazza, so that all the faithful might have a better view of him. When he reached the entrance to the Basilica, now serving as Council Hall, he entered on foot as a sign of respect for this august assembly. The Fathers did not know whether to applaud or to sing more lustily, to smile or to weep with emotion. The Pope was calmness itself. He himself said later: "I went into the Basilica very worried, almost frightened, but I came out radiant!"

The cortege advanced slowly, as though to reflect in its pace the prudence of the Church, the proverbial "feet of lead" marking her history for the almost two thousand years of her existence. The Council was to ignore haste. Among the Council Fathers were some venerable patriarchs with dragging steps, almost tired out with the weight of years and responsibility. Some Bishops could not resist the urge to pull out small cameras in order to have their own personal souvenirs of that incomparable scene. The vast majority walked very sedately meditating on the words of the *Ave Maris Stella* and the *Veni Creator,* penetrated with a sense of the uniqueness of the moment.

The liturgical ceremony was of the kind which only Saint Peter's Basilica can offer. John XXIII crossed the Hall with the step of a young man, a step almost seeming to take wings straight to a precise objective, and he surprised everyone with a discourse lasting thirty-five minutes, an Allocution which was a genuine achievement. It is true that up until that time he had followed the preparatory work of the Council, but he had never taken the initiative. But now, he took the reins decisively in hand and instead of pronouncing a kindly speech, as was his wont, he read a discourse which proved to be the pivotal point of the entire Council. It was a document reflecting optimism, vast sweeping ideas, a noble effort to achieve complete evangelization of the modern world. The discourse of John XXIII left a radiant halo in the annals of Christianity.

In the same way, the other discourse, this time ex tempore, which he addressed to the people on the night of that same October 11th, will remain forever in the hearts of those fortunate enough to hear him. That night the piazza was· like a fairy-land of tapers, chants, and the marching multitudes of thousands of people taking part in a torchlight procession in homage to the Pope of the Council. From the window of his study Pope John XXIII could see the entire Church united in sincere homage to the Vicar of Christ. The parish priests of Rome were there surrounded by their faithful, along with pilgrims from the entire world united with the Council Fathers. This time the Pope did not read, nor did he even pray. He simply spoke. His discourse, or rather his conversation, was an

outburst of the tenderness of his heart: "My children, my
very dear children! I hear your voices. Mine is only one
voice, but it sums up those of the entire world here represented. See how even the moon wanted to be present at
this spectacle! We are coming to the end of a day of peace.
Glory to God in the highest and peace on earth to men.
Repeat these words very often. . . .

"I am very happy to be here with you. My person does
not count at all. He who speaks to you is a brother who has
become your father only through the grace of God. Continue to love one another; lay aside everything which divides you. The important thing is to love one another. The
events of this morning were really magnificent. A spectacle such as not even the Basilica of Saint Peter, in all its
four hundred and fifty years of life, has ever beheld. I
bless you and I beg the Blessed Virgin to bless you with
me. You have carried out this procession in memory of the
Council of Ephesus. I have been at Ephesus and I saw it
with my own eyes. Of course, not at the time of the Council. . . . The spectacle unfolding before me now is magnificent. I assure you that it will never fade from my memory.
Now as you go back to your homes, you will find your children. Give them a hug and tell them that it is the hug of
the Pope. I want to give you still another blessing as I wish
you good night. . . . We are entering into a year which will
make it possible for us to meet very often. A year . . . very
well . . . the Council is now begun. We shall see when it will
finish. This time we shall be working up to Christmas. But
we certainly will not finish then. There are many things to
be discussed and in two months we cannot all get together
and agree on everything, can we? God will tell us. Very
well and now I give you my blessing. . . ."

It is easy to imagine the wild enthusiasm aroused in
the crowd by these simple words. A very serious writer, not
at all given to enthusiasm, stated on his return home that
night: "I am crazy, I am really crazy over the speech of
Pope John. No one could possibly speak any better!"

With his straightforward approach, his spontaneous gestures, his allusion to the moon, to the history of the Basilica and to his visit to Ephesus, John XXIII unleashed the enthusiasm of the assembled crowd. Parents embraced their children as they held them up in their arms; young men applauded wildly; the Bishops themselves, forgetful of their usual reserve, cried out, "Long live the Pope."

John XXIII came back to his window again: "Here I am again, because I want you to meet my collaborators. I am working here with them and I want you to give them a hand also and want them to have a chance to see this wonderful spectacle." Then, turning around to his room, he called out: "Come on, come on! Now here is my Secretary of State," he said as he presented Cardinal Amleto Giovanni Cicognani. "He is a great man, you know! Do you think that he was trained here at my side? No, he has traveled around half the world, even to America. He has traveled on all the continents. Very well, I want to give you a last blessing and then I must leave you, because it is getting late and I must wish you good night!"

Saint Peter's piazza thinned out little by little. Only the moon continued its work, creating jumping shadows around Bernini's colonnade and pushing them into all the hidden corners of this gigantic hemi-cycle. The two fountains filled the night air with their watery music, like the noise of a young brook awakening from its winter sleep. This expression is appropriate because that night everyone sensed an atmosphere of burgeoning spring. The Council was being born under the sign of renewal, the sign of the irrepressible vitality of the Church.

The hour of truth

October 13th marked the first General Congregation of the Council. The Council Hall began one of its usual days. In an atmosphere of solemnity, and likewise one of greater tranquillity than on the opening day, the 2,200 seats seemed to take life, with the seats in green assigned to the Bishops and those in red for the Cardinals. The public address system began to function, along with the internal telephone system.—As an interesting sidelight it might be mentioned that in the Council Hall there are approximately 250 miles of electric wiring.—Finally came the hour of truth. The Council was beginning.

The meeting opened with an inspiring prayer, traditional in such assemblies, and going back to the seventh century. It is attributed to Saint Isidore of Seville, who composed it to open the sessions of the celebrated Councils of Toledo.

According to the agenda of the Council, the first task was to elect the members of the various Council Commissions. Cardinal Montini has provided a brief account of the first Congregation: "The Council's work this week dealt, as everyone knows, with the designation of members for the various Commissions. It might be interesting to dwell on some of the facts involved in this preliminary work. The first is, that the Bishops are gradually beginning to know one another, as a result of their meetings in this great assembly and of their personal contacts. This mutual acquaintanceship is all the more necessary because each Council Father must indicate the names of sixteen Bishops for each of the ten Commissions, choosing them from lists presented by the various episcopates of the world. There are names and names, and how can anyone know them all or make a choice? The catholicity of the Church begins to be visible in its concrete dimensions, as also the practical difficulties of trying to have even a slight acquaintance with everyone. The Church is vast, the Church is composite, the Church is international and world-wide. But because it is united and is animated by a fraternal spirit, it opens up to each of its members a sincere fellowship which seems really to reveal rather than to create friendship among those who before were strangers and unknown one to the other. . . .

"On October 16th, the election of the 160 Council Fathers for the various Commissions put to the first test the complicated requirements of the Council regulations, and also tried the patience of the voters. The ten Council Commissions, corresponding to the ten Preparatory Commissions, had to be assured of a really ecumenical membership, that is to say, a membership made up of competent and selected persons from all over the world. Another interesting point which came to light was the practicality of the National Conferences of Bishops on a universal level. The presence of national groups was evident, but there was a marked difference from their first appearance in the Ecumenical Council of Constance. There, the various groups emphasized distinction, whereas here their aim was to coordinate the national episcopal bodies. There was the additional fact that language was often the basis for the formation of episcopal groups, thus giving them a broader and more different scope than one based strictly on national lines. . . .

"We must also note . . . that the first theme proposed for discussion by the Council will be the Sacred Liturgy. Although this was not quite expected and does not yet indicate what logical order the Council will follow, we welcome this schema with satisfaction, recognizing in it a magnificent witness to the primacy of the Sacred Liturgy, to that primacy which the worship of God in union with Christ must have in human life, especially in Catholic life. The prayer of the Church must take first place!"

The examination of the schema on the liturgy had not been expected in the opening days of the session. Some people thought that this discussion would be relatively easy, and would thus help to train the Council Fathers and prepare them for their subsequent work. But the discussion did not prove as easy as it had seemed at first sight. Cardinal Montini wrote in his *Letter from the Council,* which appeared in the Milanese Catholic daily *L'Italia*: "Although it had not been foreseen that this discussion would be first on the list, it was immediately evident that it was one of great interest, not only because of its practical importance but particularly because of the dignity of its content, that is to say, the prayer of the Church. It treats of our relationships with God, of the concrete expression of the spirit of religion. It discusses activities which touch upon Faith, feed our hope, and which express in words and gestures our sentiments of love. . . .

"This will certainly call for a lengthy examination, because it presents many different aspects of fundamental importance, which are now matters of common knowledge. What do we mean by the liturgy? The external rites of the official prayer of the Church? Or rather its doctrinal and sacramental content, that is to say, the mystery of truth and of the divine presence living in sacred ecclesiastical action? Is this prayer today faithful to itself, or in the course of the centuries has it been changed, become dull and overloaded? Why does the modern world not appreciate it and make it its own? Can it be modified? And how? Who would be empowered to introduce modifications? Questions such as these give rise immediately to certain criteria, which are easy to express and to understand, but difficult to apply. The first of these criteria is that of conservation. . . .

"The second is that of understandability. The liturgy is not a closed circuit; it is a sincere expression of both the divine and the human. It is a language. On the one hand it is a vehicle of divine teaching; it is the voice of one conversing with God. It is clear that the liturgy cannot abandon its teaching mission nor can it fail to make it possible for Faith and piety to express themselves with spontaneous intelligibility. In fact, the faithful must participate in the public prayer of the Church, which the precept of Sunday Mass has made obligatory. The faithful cannot, they must not, remain mute and passive. Material presence cannot supply for spiritual absence. This criterion has been achieved, especially after the celebrated encyclical of Pope Pius XII entitled *Mediator Dei*.

"But what are the limits of this participation and in what degree must the language of the liturgy be made understandable? Here there emerge two further criteria, both very delicate, namely that of the simplification and integration of the ceremonies, and that of the Latin language, which, by its fixed character and in its expressive capacity, serves to provide the Church with a better sense of unity and greater security in safeguarding its dogmatic truths. But we are already beginning to see how the Latin language can be kept in the parts of the liturgy which are strictly sacerdotal, and how we must make room in the teaching and prayerful part for popular languages, not only alongside of and outside the liturgical rite itself, but within its very context, conferring on these languages a certain sacred dignity.

"This is a difficult task, certainly, but the pastoral approach dominating the Council seems to demand a solution of this problem if we want our spiritual life to find in the prayer of the Church not a barrier but a channel of communication with God. It will be equally difficult to determine who is to introduce these eventual changes into the sacred liturgy. Up until now, as far as the Latin Rite is concerned, only the Holy See has had the power to legislate, and it will assuredly always remain the supreme authority in the liturgical field. But a plan is being discussed whereby certain faculties will be recognized subordinately to the National Episcopal Conferences in the various countries. All this explains why this theme is keeping the Council in lengthy discussion."

The Cardinal of Milan spoke only once in the discussion of the Schema on the Sacred Liturgy. This was in

the fourth General Congregation, when the chronicles of
the Council record a massive intervention of Cardinals—no
less than nine in one morning!—"some to defend the schema,
some to attack it," according to the clichés which abounded
in the official press communiqués of the first session. Keeping in mind what he had written previously, it is not
difficult to imagine which stand Cardinal Montini adopted
since, as far as liturgical questions are concerned, he was
always known for his progressive spirit, as well as for his
prudent adaptation of the liturgy to modern times.

On November 14th the two following statements were
approved by the Council: 1) The Second Vatican Ecumenical Council, having examined the Schema on the Sacred
Liturgy, approves the directive criteria which are intended,
with prudence and understanding, to render the various
parts of the liturgy more vital and informative for the
faithful, in keeping with the pastoral exigencies of our
times. 2) As soon as the reforms proposed in the Council
discussion have been examined and drawn up in proper
form by the Liturgical Commission they will be promptly
voted on in the General Congregation, in order that immediate steps may be taken for formulating the definitive text.

This approbation provoked the following commentary
by Cardinal Montini in his *Letter from the Council* of November 18th: "This first approval by the Council supposes
that the entire schema is to be amended and approved
article by article, and then submitted to the definitive
judgment of the Pope. It is to be expected that it will be
a long time before the reforms thus proposed can be put
into practice. Nevertheless this first declaration by the
Council is a happy augury and comes at the very outset
to confirm the main purpose of the Council, as also to
reward those who have labored long years in the liturgical
movement, not for motives of spiritual esthetics, learned
archeology, or devotional fantasy, but to bring the prayer
of the Church back to its essential values, its purest ex-

pressions, and its fullest pastoral effectiveness. Thus does the action of the Council get under way, summoning all the members of the Church, both clergy and laity, to a deeper, more authentic, and more strengthening conversation with God."

New meetings between John XXIII and Montini

In the full swing of the Council discussions two dates occurred which could not pass unobserved, namely October 28th and November 4th, which were respectively the anniversaries of the election and the coronation of the Pope. John XXIII's pontificate had already lasted four years and he had succeeded in effecting many changes through his kindness and understanding. This was recognized by the Council Fathers in their message of felicitations at the end of the General Congregation of October 27th: "On the vigil of the auspicious day on which the Catholic world commemorates the ascent of Your Holiness to the supreme pontificate, we the Council Fathers, assembled together, humbly but with deep fervor, elevate our prayers so that Almighty God, through the intercession of the Blessed Virgin Mary and her chaste spouse Saint Joseph, patron of the Ecumenical Council, may conserve you for long years, our most holy loving Father and Vicar of Christ, and may assist the work of the Council, so happily inaugurated, in such a way that it may become fruitful and may produce the results hoped for according to your desires. For this purpose may we be strengthened by your Apostolic Benediction which we implore with profound veneration, gathered around your Chair of Truth."

The Pope replied with a heartfelt message: "... You have offered Us most consoling comfort which has brought Us deep pleasure, giving Us joy in the depths of Our heart at being able, through a disposition of Divine Providence, to celebrate this anniversary surrounded by the splendor of your presence."

November 4th saw the solemn ceremony of the anniversary of the Pope's coronation in Saint Peter's. Cardinal Montini was once more charged by John XXIII to celebrate Pontifical Mass in the Ambrosian rite. The Pope pronounced an unusual homily, half in Latin and half in Italian, as if wishing to face up to the problems being discussed at that very moment on the adaptation of the liturgy to the people. This new gesture of deference and friendship for Montini on the part of John XXIII could have been inspired also by other circumstances. On November 4th the Church celebrates the feast of Saint Charles Borromeo, Archbishop of Milan in the period immediately following upon the Council of Trent. John XXIII always had a deep devotion to Saint Charles, to whom he consecrated his major historical work. He had wanted to be crowned on November 4th, and to the special litanies sung on that occasion in Saint Peter's, he had added the name of Saint Charles. He now wanted the Pontifical Mass on the anniversary of his coronation to be celebrated by Saint Charles' successor in the See of Milan.

Montini was the only Cardinal to have the distinction of being the Holy Father's personal guest in the Vatican during the Council. One would almost say that John XXIII wanted him close by, in order to be able to consult him. On the other hand, it is somewhat surprising that Cardinal Montini, who was so perfectly acquainted with the mind of the Pope, participated on only a relatively small scale in the Council discussions. He had addressed the Council only once during the discussion on the liturgy. Some might find it hard to explain such abstentionism in a man who was in a real position to teach, both because of his great personal experience and because of his unusual intellectual gifts, so universally recognized.

Why Montini did not speak

It is no secret that the Cardinal of Milan carried great moral weight among the Bishops and even among the other Cardinals. People had heard of the numerous visits of prelates who called on him in Milan either en route to Rome or on their way home. Even representatives of our separated brethren used to stop over in Milan on their way from Rome. It was rumored that the discourse pronounced by John XXIII at the opening of the Council was clearly inspired by Montini. Be this as it may, there is not the slightest doubt that Cardinal Montini was the first one to greet the convocation of the Council with enthusiasm and that he was always closely associated with the Pope's personal efforts in everything touching upon the Council.

His is the most important Pastoral Letter written on the Council in Italy and probably likewise abroad. It is dated February 22, 1962. The following are some passages of particular value and interest:

"Although only those charged in the Church of God with 'the service of authority' are entitled to sit in the Council meetings, still it is easy to understand why other members of the body of the faithful, namely priests, religious, and laity, do not appear there. Nevertheless the entire community of the faithful is present in the Council, because the Council expresses its Faith, discusses its interests, and assembles the pastors who are its guides, spokesmen and representatives. If the Council were regarded as a gathering of ecclesiastics separated from the rest of the Church, then no one could explain how it represents a synthesis of the Church. The priesthood is for the faithful. The greater the emphasis on the priestly character of an assembly, the more deeply felt is the moral presence of the Christian people. Thus the entire Church will be present in the Council, because there can be no conceiving of the Church or the episcopate without the rest of its members."

On the question of reform, Montini declared: ". . . Reform is ever going on in the Church; it is an effort aiming to bring together the divine ideal and the human reality. . . . Reform is part of the ordinary program of the Church. Reform is going on all the time. But when we speak of reform in relationship to an Ecumenical Council, we ordinarily think, on the one hand, of long-standing and widespread serious disorders, and on the other of some extraordinary measure. . . . But the characteristic of this Council, which is nonetheless tending towards noteworthy reform, derives from the fact that it was convoked more out of a desire for greater good than as a measure to eliminate downright evil. Thus it will be a Council of positive rather than punitive reforms, more a Council of exhortation than of anathemas. . . . This vigil of the Council is the moment for a universal examination of conscience, to which everyone feels he has been invited. Who is not aware of some need, some improvement, some perfectioning in Catholic life?"

On the subject of the nature of the Church there is a passage in the above mentioned letter which is very much like the Pope's discourse for the reopening of the Council on September 29, 1963: ". . . The discussion on the nature and the function of the episcopate in union with the Roman Papacy can lead to a new and spontaneous affirmation not only of the juridical but likewise of the living union of the Church around the Chair of Saint Peter, and without anything like recriminations, it can bring on a vaster and more organic internationalization of the central government of the Church. . . . It is likewise to be expected that in the Council the Catholic laity will have explicit and honorable recognition."

At this point the Pastoral Letter of February, 1962, continues: ". . . Two forms of Catholic life may be discussed, as we hope, for the adult vocation of the laity. First of all, its intense, virile, up-to-date spirituality developed in an ever more intimate and fortifying participation in the liturgical mysteries of the Christian community, and then, secondly, its vocation, now officially recognized, to collaboration in the hierarchical apostolate, so that the laity also may know how to give its own proper witness to Christ and to the Church in the world of today....

"... (The Church) will endeavor to make herself a sister and a mother of men. She will seek to be poor, simple, humble, and approachable in her language and in her practices.... For this purpose she will call upon the laity, her good and faithful lay Catholics, to become a channel between her supernatural and canonically organized sphere and the sociological and temporal sphere in which they are living, delegating as it were to their docile and effective collaboration the arduous and noble duty of 'the consecration of the world.'"

Regarding our "separated brethren" the Letter states: "... It is sufficient to bear in mind that this most difficult problem, one which is at the same time so important and urgent, is one of the chief aims of the Council. The Council, most probably, will not find a solution. Perhaps we have not deserved such a great miracle. But the Ecumenical Council will be in a position to prepare the way for the solution for which all of us yearn."

These extracts from the Pastoral Letter of the Cardinal of Milan show the perfect harmony of its essential points with those stressed by Pope John XXIII in his discourse to the Council on October 11, 1962. These selfsame points were repeated in more schematic, clearer, and more precise terms by Paul VI when the Council reopened on September 29, 1963. Thus it is clear that these ideas, so completely in harmony with those of the Pope, gave Cardinal Montini immense prestige in the Council Hall during the First Session of the Second Vatican Council. This prestige was subsequently augmented by his personal friendships and his contacts with Bishops throughout the world, during his years in the Secretariate of State and later in his journeys to America and Africa.

Perhaps Pope John was thinking
of his successor . . .

As early as February, 1962, Pope John XXIII, who had
offered his life for the happy outcome of the Council, was
certainly aware of the illness, with which he had been
stricken. With exemplary generosity, he not only did not
cut down on his work schedule but even intensified it and
speeded up his pre-Council activities, because he wanted at
the very least to get the Council started. God granted him
this grace.

It is always something of a problem to get work started
and to carry out plans which have only been outlined by
someone else. It is easy to understand, consequently,
John XXIII's intense interest in at least opening the Council
which he had willed and planned and which God had entrusted to him. No one can know if the preparatory work
for the Council would have continued if Pope John had
died before it opened. But no one should harbor any illu-
sions because of the apparent calm with which the Council
was inaugurated. The Second Vatican Council, of course,
did not have to battle against the difficulties which con-
fronted other Councils, as for instance the Council of Trent
or even the First Vatican Council. But certainly there was
opposition.

A book published at that time, entitled *A Plot Against
the Church,* under the evident pen name of Maurice Pinay,
contains grave and offensive insinuations against whole
blocs of Council Fathers: the ones from the North, the
Orientals, those from Communist countries, the ultra-mon-
tanes. Even the Pope personally, although he was not explicitly named, was placed in a very questionable light.
The book was "presented" to all the Council Fathers as
well as to the *periti.* Not a few of those favored with this
gift took steps to have it burned immediately.

Opposition such as this, hiding under the veil of anonymity, was not likely to cause any great trouble. But there were other hostile currents of greater importance. That is why John XXIII's move in convoking the Council was one which called for high courage. It is significant that the first announcement of the Council was made by the Pope himself, without warning, before a group of Cardinals, who were just as surprised as the simple faithful. Once the ice was broken, the idea began to take hold with relative ease and aroused universal enthusiasm. The idea of the Council was an inspiration, a breath of the Spirit on the heart of John XXIII. Its announcement was unexpected and almost offhanded and eventually gave rise to many stories. But once made, it could not be brushed aside or revoked.

Once the work on the Council was begun, John XXIII thought of nothing else but pushing it through to completion. With accents of tenderness he beseeched the Blessed Virgin to grant him the grace of concluding this colossal task. God preferred instead to accept the precious sacrifice of his life. The Pope was aware of the merciless ravages of the illness which was undermining his unusually robust constitution. It is logical to think that, as he dedicated every moment of his life to the Council, he was likewise secretly concerned as to who would be able to take over and carry it through to the end.

At this point the Archbishop of Milan comes upon the scene. John XXIII felt that Cardinal Montini was the man best qualified to follow him in the supreme pontificate. Another chapter of this book will relate a "prophecy" of the then Cardinal Roncalli in regard to Montini. On his deathbed he consoled those who were worried about the fate of the Council after the death of its great inspirer, assuring them that God had at hand good possibilities, as for example Cardinal Montini.

Hence it would not be surprising if John XXIII had advised or even asked the Archbishop of Milan to maintain an attitude of reserve in the First Session of the Council.

It is true that the Second Vatican Council carried on its work in an atmosphere of tranquillity, peace, and mutual charity. Nevertheless there would be no reason to cry scandal if, in particular circumstances, conflicting tendencies should clash openly on the Council floor. In situations like this, persons already "committed" encounter opposition from the other side. This is not intended to insinuate that the election of a Pope is influenced by considerations of interest or personal preferences, much less by ambition. The responsibility of choosing a new Shepherd for the Church is too grave and the dignity of the Sacred College of Cardinals is too great today to allow such considerations to sway their choice. Yet it is unquestionable that even in a Conclave God uses the freedom of the Cardinals, their points of view, their personal sizing up of individuals. If a candidate has proved to be a "moderate" in Council discussions, acting as a mediator between opposing tendencies and succeeding in softening even the slightest trends towards extremism, then undoubtedly he will win a high degree of confidence on both sides. This was probably the position of Cardinal Montini. To these considerations must be added his own personal prestige, which was clearly recognized in all quarters.

For these reasons, any Cardinal who, as he cast his vote, swore before God to elect *him whom he regards as most worthy*, could be perfectly at ease in choosing Montini. The brevity of the Conclave in which Paul VI was elected confirms these suppositions. Although many were claiming that the Conclave would drag out, because they expected the two open currents in the Sacred College to clash, nevertheless the Church was treated to a "lightning Conclave" as, in truth, not a few others had predicted. The "currents" agreed at once on the choice of the prudent man.

The pleasant "leisure" of a Council Father

Before the end of the debate on the liturgical schema, Cardinal Montini had one of his many private audiences with John XXIII on November 11, the feast of Saint Martin of Tours, after celebrating Mass in the Church of Saints Martin and Sylvester, his cardinalitial titular church. In one of his weekly letters to his diocese the Archbishop of Milan wrote: "It can be a motive for fruitful reflection to know that the long private audience to which His Holiness was kind enough to summon me on the evening of the 11th was an hour of edification, comfort and light, as he kept us in confident and affable conversation. . . . We are already well acquainted with the style of his incomparable kindness. His words flow simply and nobly, almost without interruption. Events stand out in the Pope's conversation in their ideal significance. His memories of the past, from which Milan is never missing, seem to become present and to be transformed into symbolic designs. The policies to be followed in thought and action unfold simply and directly, as though they could not be disturbed by the obstacles and the agitation of our era. Optimism, that is to say, good will and hope, becomes a duty and a joy. And the final blessing, which breaks the charm of this absorbing attentiveness, brings us back to the concrete, but no longer banal, reality of humdrum things, and takes leave of us with a generous measure of serenity and spiritual energy."

In the meantime, the work of the Council was going on. The "peaceful" schema on the liturgy was followed by the hotly disputed, and ultimately postponed, schema on the sources of revelation, that is to say, Sacred Scripture and Tradition.

The Archbishop of Milan informed his people of this discussion in a letter published in *L'Italia* on November 18th: "Everyone can understand how this theme is basic in the organization of our religion," began the Cardinal, after describing the new theme as "dogmatic" and "of basic importance," "and for this reason everyone will find it natural that the Council should discuss this matter with all proper gravity and solemnity. Only those acquainted with recent developments in theology, with the progress in biblical studies and the ardor of the controversies raging over these questions, whether inside or outside Catholic circles, can appreciate the concern, the hopes, the fear that this new topic brings into the Council meeting. A wave of questionmarks sweep over the mind. Was such a topic necessary? How can it be harmonized with the teaching of the Council of Trent and the First Vatican Council? Was not this whole question settled in our own times by the authoritative teaching of the encyclicals *Pascendi* of Saint Pius X and *Humani Generis* of Pius XII? Are not recent pontifical documents on biblical studies, plus the declarations of Leo XIII, sufficient to guide the speculative and practical attitude of Catholics in the field of Scripture?

"We refer to the discussion of these questions," continued the *Letter*, "in order that we may understand that the Council is entering into a most delicate and interesting field, and in order that no one will be surprised if this discussion brings out a great divergence of ideas, divergent opinions which become one not only in the minds of those who profess them, but likewise in the very complexity of the religious reality coming up for consideration.... Unity and catholicity, antiquity and modernity, permanence and development, interior values and public relations, search after the essential and concern for the particular, the vision of things in their roots and insight into the consequences flowing from them—all these constitute different perspectives in the judgment which can be formulated on a given religious problem, and they indicate how the discussion can be complex and heated because of the very love of the speakers for truth and because of the profound honesty which they want to reflect in their words."

The schema *De Fontibus Revelationis* occupied the attention of the Council for six General Congregations.

There was a total of 104 speeches, delivered by thirty-three Cardinals, Patriarch Maximus IV Saigh of Antioch, twenty-one Archbishops, forty-two Bishops and two Superiors General. On November 20th a proposal was put before the assembly for action at the following Congregation, to decide if the Council should continue its detailed examination of such a controversial schema. The vote was taken and, although its results were eloquent, they solved nothing. In fact there were twenty-one null votes, 822 in favor of continuing the discussion, and 1,368 for dropping it indefinitely. Nevertheless, notwithstanding this crushing "hostility" of the Council Fathers to the text, the rules required that the discussion should continue, because the balloting fell 105 votes short of the two-thirds majority (1,473) required to accept or reject a schema.

On that day John XXIII had gone to crown the image of Our Lady of Guadalupe in the Mexican College. He was scheduled to go there the day after, but on that Tuesday, November 20th, there was sun and the Pope wanted to enjoy it. Perhaps also he wanted to ponder a decision!

The next day an announcement by the General Secretary of the Council under orders from the Cardinal Secretary of State, informed the Fathers that the schema had been withdrawn from discussion by the Holy Father and had been turned over to a special Commission for thorough revision. According to the explicit wishes of His Holiness, this Commission was to be composed of Cardinals and members from the Theological Commission as well as from the Secretariate for Christian Unity.

John XXIII had once more intervened in the Council with prudence and tact. Once again, as had been the case with the voting for the Council Commissions at the very beginning, it was made clear that procedural rules were intended for the Council and not the Council for procedural rules.

Montini's second intervention

In the mind of the Holy Father John XXIII, Vatican II was to increase the spiritual riches of the Church, to be a new Pentecost. Consequently, the schema on the Church should have been the central theme of the entire Council. After the postponement of the schema on the Sources of Revelation, the Fathers took up two brief but important topics: the one on the Media of Social Communication and the other on the Unity of the Church. The discussion on both these subjects was completed in five Congregations. Some one hundred speakers opened new perspectives and new horizons on the importance of modern media of social communication and emphasized the strong movement towards unity which today is evident throughout the whole of Christianity. Nevertheless there was a certain uneasiness in the air as the central theme of the Council came closer. In fact several observations were made concerning the above mentioned schemas, with a suggestion that it might have been preferable to include them in the schema on the Church, particularly the one on unity, or at least treat of them after the discussion on the Church.

The great schema *De Ecclesia* came before the Council just six days before the end of Session I. The text was defended or attacked, according to the trends of the two groups which had become clearly marked in the Council. Cardinals Liénart, Ruffini, Bueno y Monreal, Koenig, Alfrink, Ritter, Siri, Spellman, McIntyre, Gracias, Léger, Doepfner, Frings, Godfrey, Suenens, Bea, Bacci, Lercaro, Lefèbvre, and other Council Fathers such as Bishops De Smet (Bruges), Elchinger (Auxiliary of Strasbourg), Van Cauveleart (Inongo, Congo), Musto (Aquino, Sora, and Pontecorvo), D'Souza (Bhopal, India) and others expressed themselves for or against the text, speaking their minds with utmost clarity, in the name of that liberty which was the outstanding characteristic of the Council.

In this array of illustrious personages attention must be called to the masterful discourse of Cardinal Montini, delivered on December 5th, in the 34th General Congregation. He expressed his congratulations for the homage paid by the Council to Saint Joseph and for the chapter on the Blessed Virgin. But he likewise expressed his ardent desire that the Council should direct its attention piously, solemnly, and explicitly to Our Lord Jesus Christ, because it is He who gives life to His Church. Without Him, we can do nothing, and the Church itself is nothing else but the instrument whereby Christ becomes present in the world. The Cardinal observed that the schema should have placed much more emphasis on this "mystery of the Church," and that the text on the episcopate could hardly satisfy anyone, since it was more juridical than theological. Lastly he mentioned that, in any case, the text should have been gone over by a mixed commission in order to be formulated in more satisfactory terms.

As a kind of supplement to this discourse in the Council, the Cardinal of Milan delivered a marvelous homily in Milan on the feast of Saint Ambrose, December 7th. He had left Rome without waiting for the solemn closing of the First Session, so as to be able to celebrate the feast of the patron of his archdiocese with his faithful. "The many thoughts and impressions which I bring back from the Second Ecumenical Council," he declared, "do not permit me on this celebration of the feast of Saint Ambrose to speak of any other subject than of this one, namely the mystery of the Church, which fills the soul of the Council, which is as it were obliged to seek out within itself the theme of its lofty considerations and which finds in Saint Ambrose one of its most ancient, most fruitful, and most loving defenders." The homily continued: "This great act of the life of the Church does not, as in the other Councils recorded in history, find any particular motive of urgency outside the very consciousness of Holy Church. We can well say that the Council is a moment of reflection of the Church upon itself.

"It would take too long to explain why this interior need has come to flower in the Church, precisely in an era characterized by external involvement in culture, activity, discoveries, and interests. Perhaps we would be unable to explain it without recognizing that, even more than the proximate causes which can be identified, an intimate and secret motion, like the one which gave birth to the Council in the mind of the Pope, a mild breathing of the Holy Spirit, is at the deep roots of this great event.

"This strikes us as being historically logical. As a matter of fact the theme of the Church was already on the agenda of the First Vatican Council, which disbanded after treating only the first part, the one dealing with the primacy and the infallibility of the Sovereign Pontiff. What had been interrupted needed to be completed. In the meantime, how many things have helped to awaken in the Church the need of a deeper and more precise knowledge of herself! The progress of Catholic thought, the teaching of the Popes—it is sufficient to recall the masterful encyclical of Pius XII on the Mystical Body in 1943— the development of Catholic movements, the spiritual experience of the faithful, the liturgical movement, the wave of missionary work, contact with the ecumenism of our separated brethren, the religious and anti-religious evolution of the contemporary world—a thousand and one considerations have spurred the Church on to look at herself in the light of her origins, to provide proof of her authenticity, to affirm her rights, to get a deeper knowledge of her essence, to answer, in a word, the twofold question which men put to her and which is put to her by her own conscience: What is the Church? What is the Church doing? In other words, what is the nature and what is the mission of the Church?

"The word *church* means a vocation, God's call to men. It means also the assembly of those who are called, of those who have answered their vocation, and it includes many other titles, titles filled with mysteries to signify the Christian community: house of God, column and foundation of truth, flock of Christ, kingdom of God, communion of saints, hierarchical society and community of grace, and particularly, following the lead of Saint Paul, spouse of Christ and Mystical Body of Christ.... We must deepen our study of our doctrine on the Church and make it a subject of meditation and an inspiration for action. The trends of present-day thought have perhaps influenced our ideas on the Church, leading us to look only at the human and earthly framework which is, like everything else in this world, limited and defective, while a widespread spirit of criticism and of short-sighted and vulgar anti-clericalism prevents us from recognizing the Spirit which gives life to the Church, the plan of God which in her is at rest and in her is also evolving, the illuminating and sanctifying riches of this Mother and Teacher, the immense good fortune of those who belong to her and are led by her to our supreme destiny....

"I would want each one of us," concluded the Archbishop of Milan, "to be able to repeat the words engraved as the only eulogy on the tomb of a great Bishop of the last century, Cardinal Mermillod: *Dilexit Ecclesiam,* that is to say, *He loved the Church,* just as Saint Paul said of Christ that He loved the Church and delivered Himself for her. Thus will be consummated in the mystery of the Church the mystery of our salvation."

The discourse was widely commented on in the press. Even a cursory reading uncovers perfect agreement between the thoughts thus expressed by Montini and the policies outlined in his Allocution for the reopening of the Vatican Council on September 29, 1963.

Montini looks at Session I

An undertaking as complex as an Ecumenical Council could never be completely perfect in all its details. Many of the Fathers mentioned the excessive amount of material on the agenda. At the beginning there were no less than seventy schemas. In two months of work the Council had not made a thorough examination of even one of them. This shows that, notwithstanding all the detailed preparation, the work of the Council was persevering and conscientious and the Fathers were open to any and all observations. But this very complexity of the work soon demonstrated the necessity of a more concentrated synthesis. The chief need was a guide line, an axis on which the whole Council could revolve, so as to forestall the danger of getting lost in minutiae, to the detriment of the essential.

Cardinals Montini, Lercaro, Suenens, Léger and Doepfner wanted this central point to be the schema *De Ecclesia*. Their proposal was accepted. On this general theme the Cardinal of Milan expressed his mind in his *Letter from the Council*, dated December 2, 1962, and published in his archdiocesan daily *L'Italia*. This letter is particularly important because it presents a panoramic study of the entire First Session of the Council. This time he was not satisfied with merely recounting events, but he expressed his own considered opinions on various problems and also proposed solutions:

"The imminent closing of the First Session of this great assembly naturally makes everyone ask just what has been accomplished. In reply, two main trends appear to dominate day-to-day conversations and the general comments of the press. The first is that the Council accomplished nothing of importance and the second, that the Council revealed disagreement in the ranks of the Bishops.

"This is true. This was to be expected and it is not evidence of failure. Rather does it point up a fact which can never be sufficiently appreciated for a world-wide Council of such vast proportions, namely, that the Council met under the standard of great liberty. First of all, liberty to make suggestions. These recommendations were bound into volumes, then examined and coordinated by the Preparatory Commissions. This in turn gave rise to other huge volumes containing very detailed and sweeping answers to all the various questions. This material is abundant and of great value, but at the same time heterogeneous and not all of equal importance. It would have called for courageous summarizing or synthesizing, if some outside disciplinary authority had controlled the logical and organic compilation of these magnificent volumes, and if one central dominating idea had directed and shaped this huge undertaking. This was not the case but this gap was due to respect for that criterion of liberty and spontaneity which gave birth to this Council, which was the focal point of its program and which fortunately had received wise and solemn directives from the Holy Father in the years preceding the Council, especially in his two discourses of September 11th and October 11th. . . .

"The speeches were very numerous and the discussions, as was only natural in the circumstances, were interminable. But they were always free. . . .

"This explains the second problem, if indeed we can use this word, namely the diversity of viewpoints which on some themes became collective diversity of tendencies and trends. It is common knowledge that this divergence reached its peak in the voting on the schema of a dogmatic constitution on the sources of revelation. . . .

"It is clear that the divergent judgments manifested in regard to this schema cannot be attributed to conflicting national feelings or to personality clashes, as certain individuals have tried to insinuate. They come rather from different evaluations of the doctrinal trends under discussion, or from different viewpoints on the opportuneness of a proposal or the manner of formulating it. These conflicts are due also to motives which are obvious in a discussion where the participants represent localities, schools of thought, experiences, and pastoral necessities which are naturally quite different but which are all guided by watchful and independent personal prudence. This is all to the honor of the Council, even though for the time being it is not satisfactory."

This objective appraisal of the First Session of Vatican II shows that Cardinal Montini was certainly not being influenced by unrealistic enthusiasm in his evaluation of the Council sessions. Honestly, he recognized the presence of defects, procedural and otherwise, in the workings of the Council, but he was also able to see beyond all this and to catch within his clear vision the over-all picture, which presents the Council as a whole and not as a series of individual events or sessions.

For reasons not easy to understand, this *Letter* of Cardinal Montini was interpreted as an attack on the Roman Curia. Such misunderstanding, or distortion, of clear language brought keen disappointment to the Cardinal, whose sole aim was to present facts as he saw them. In a letter written at this period he referred sadly to this unhappy experience with "an evidently unfriendly press."

With this same clear vision Cardinal Montini envisioned how the Second Session of the Council would profit from the defects of the First: "The Second Session will proceed much more efficiently, because plans are already under discussion to reduce the material to briefer schemas, to discuss in Council only topics of general interest and which are demanded by present-day pastoral necessities, and to postpone until after the Council, particularly in the reform of the Code of Canon Law, the full implementation of what will be decided.

"Thus, after a preliminary period the Council reaches the threshold of its main theme, that of the Church, and here it will suspend its work in order to resume it, God willing, next September, with equal effectiveness but better procedure.

"In the meantime, however, the Council can boast of having achieved not a few results which though intangible, are very evident: the union of minds and the exchange of ideas, the joyful and growing marvel of catholicity reflected from every part of the world. . . . This spiritual experience will certainly remain indelibly imprinted on those who have been fortunate enough to take part in the Council. It was an experience which was most of the time pleasant, at others forceful and telling, sometimes dramatic, and even at times reflective and sorrowful. This was the case, for instance, at the unexpected news of the illness of the Holy Father which cast over the Council a veil of spontaneous silence and filial sadness, while the atmosphere of the immense basilica seemed to echo the words of the Acts of the Apostles about Peter: 'But prayer was being made to God for him by the Church without ceasing.' "

This "intervention" of Montini outside the Council was a revelation. Cardinal Doepfner later stated that what the Cardinal of Milan had done during the last week of the First Session, both inside and outside the Council Hall, had a decisive influence on the subsequent trend of the Council discussions. A striking point in this *Letter* is the care with which the Cardinal speaks of "reform" within the Council, procedural reform. Everyone was asking just what Montini meant. They did not have to wait long for the answer. On December 6th it was announced that, on the basis of the vast experience acquired in the preparatory period and in the first two months of the Council, the Holy Father had issued special directives.

These directives can be summed up briefly as follows. In the interim period between the First and the Second Session, there would be a sweeping revision and improvement of the different schemas. This work would be done by the respective Commissions, assisted by mixed Sub-Commissions in order to insure more effective coordination. It was important not to forget that the scope of Vatican II was not to discuss isolated points of doctrine, but to make a great leap forward towards bringing doctrine into life and forming consciences in perfect harmony with, and fidelity to, authentic doctrine, as studied and expounded in keeping with the demands of scientific research and the literary requirements of modern thought.

The schemas were to concentrate on the key points, with special emphasis on the Universal Church, the faithful, and the whole of the human family, ignoring detailed discussions and leaving practical directives for the Commission for the reform of the Code of Canon Law, or for other post-conciliar commissions. A new Commission was to be organized for the coordination and over-all direction of all the work of the Council. It was to maintain contact with the various Commission presidents not only "on problems of competence, but on any point which might promote and assure the correlation of the various schemas with the aims of the Council."

This Coordinating Commission was made up of Cardinal Cicognani, as president, and of Cardinals Liénart, Spellman, Urbani, Confalonieri, Doepfner and Suenens. Provision was also made for summoning other experts in various fields, especially in the works of the apostolate. Just as soon as the schemas would be ready and approved in principle by the Pope, they were to be sent to the individual Bishops for examination and whatever observations the Council Fathers might deem advisable. Lastly, the Commissions would insert the necessary corrections, on the basis of the recommendations received, in such a way that the schemas might be presented to the General Congregations.

It is more than clear that these directives were perfectly in line with the ideas suggested by Montini in the *Letter* quoted above. This is a further indication of the close collaboration between John XXIII and Cardinal Montini during the months of the Council sessions. When the

Cardinal Archbishop of Milan spoke or wrote, the Council Fathers perhaps had the impression that they were listening to "an official voice" providing something of an authentic summary of the work that had been accomplished.

A story of universal mourning

Towards the end of November rumors got abroad that the Pope was ill. No one knew precisely what the trouble was, but only that audiences had been suspended. This news cast a pall of painful expectation over Rome, because everyone was aware of how prudent Vatican sources of information are when it comes to the health of the Pope. There is a proverb that "The Pope is always well unless he is dying." Even a slight reference to some illness of the Pope is enough to sow perplexity everywhere. Fortunately, a few days later, on November 30th, a new medical bulletin stated that the Pope was improving, that the treatment was producing good results, that he had been able to leave his bed and devote some time to problems connected with the government of the Church. The Council Fathers were the first to rejoice and greeted this announcement with hearty applause when Archbishop Felici so informed them at the beginning of the 31st General Congregation. The Pope, who was following the Council discussions on special closed circuit TV, was deeply moved as he witnessed this demonstration of affection for his person. On Sunday, December 2nd, he appeared at the window of his apartment for the usual recitation of the *Angelus*. Naturally, he would not miss addressing the faithful assembled down in the piazza, in greater numbers than on other Sundays, to see how the Pope was.

"Dear children," he said, "I wish you a Merry Christmas, even now. May this be a feast of kindness, happiness, and peace for all, for the entire world. Amen. Amen!" The

Pope was seen at the window of his study again on December 5th. But this time the faithful were not the only ones making the piazza live. The Council Fathers were also there as they had adjourned a bit earlier than usual in order to see the Pope. John XXIII made another short speech: "My children, Providence is accompanying us. As you see, every day there is a step forward, not on the path of relapse, but on that of improvement, bit by bit. First illness, then convalescence. The joy of this present meeting is a motive of consolation, a proof that strength and vigor are returning.

"Today's is a new spectacle: the Church fully represented. Here we have the episcopate, the priesthood, the Christian people. The whole family is here, the family of Christ. My children, let us bless the Lord for this joy and this unity. Let us endeavor to continue to help one another, as each one goes ahead on his own path. We are now in the novena of the Immaculate Conception. I do not want to take leave of you today without reminding you of this dear Mother of ours and without invoking her with you, as a powerful Mediatrix and one who brings heavenly life to everything we do.

"The Council is stopping temporarily, but we shall never forget the pleasant memory of this perfect mutual union, not only of representatives of the clergy and the people, but also of all the races of the world, because the entire world was redeemed by Our Lord Jesus Christ. To our Mother, then, we recommend the Church, our families, our lives, our health, because this health helps us to serve God well. There is a prayer which sums up all the various ideas I am setting before you. Venerable brethren in the episcopate, and all those who are here represented, true and very dear brothers in the social order, from the highest to those in the middle, down to the lowliest and the most humble, but all brethren, all belonging to one same family, I invite you all to recite this prayer together, this very beautiful prayer suggested by the Church: 'We fly

to thy patronage.' ... Dear Children, I give you my blessing.... The consolations of the Spirit, like the consolation
which is ours at this moment, are an element of unending
joy, of *strength* and of courage. Amen. Amen."

John XXIII was able to assist at the solemn closing of
the First Session in Saint Peter's on December 8th. Cardinal Montini was not present at this ceremony, because he
had wanted to be in Milan to be with his faithful for the
feast of the patron of the archdiocese, Saint Ambrose. "I
left Rome; I left the Council just before the end of the
First Session, which had lasted almost two months," the
Archbishop of Milan declared in his discourse in the Duomo,
"in order to be with you today and to celebrate with you
the feast of our great patron Saint Ambrose. Although I
would have wanted very much to assist at the climax of
the first phase of the great Ecumenical Council, it was
not hard to make the sacrifice when I thought of being
in your midst, brothers and most dear faithful."

"... from yesterday on, the entire world is a Council Hall"

"Yesterday was like a day for a first balancing of accounts," wrote Monsignor Spada in *Il Quotidiano* for December 9, 1962. "It was like the atmosphere of an assembly
hall, with everyone aware of living an appointment with
the greatest event of the century and even with the greatest in history....

"But, unfortunately, there was also in Saint Peter's
marked concern over the health of 'the Pope of the Council.'
Two months ago there were no grounds for worry. We had
become accustomed to the idea that, notwithstanding his
eighty-two years, Pope John XXIII could go through a
tiring four-hour ceremony without showing the slightest

trace of fatigue, without even a momentary weakening of
his strong, clear voice. But yesterday he came down to
Saint Peter's just a few days after an illness which had
alarmed the entire world. He was awaited with anxious
and worried whispering; even the applause in the basilica
was restrained and respectful, as if no one wanted to disturb him or to increase the emotion of the moment. Sometimes the hands disturb the genuine emotion of the soul,
and we are all deeply moved. The Holy Father seemed
a little more pale and his step a bit more hesitant, but his
smile was winning and calm as usual. He read his Allocution with his customary clear voice, without the touch of
fatigue which had been noticeable a few days earlier,
stressing as he was wont, the passages closest to his heart
with his rapid and spontaneous gestures.

"Only two or three times did he falter, pulling away
from the microphone, but he immediately resumed his
normal tone and volume. In the silence hanging over this
attentive and moved hall his discourse echoed with all the
solemnity proper to the vastest assembly of pastors of souls
on earth. The Holy Father's Allocution, rigorous in its construction, couched in a warm and noble style, was really
both a statement of policy and at the same time a check-
ing of results. . . .

"Before this assembly, the only one of its kind in history organized on such a vast scale, and which was now
ready to adjourn, before these thousands of Bishops for
whom planes were already waiting in the airport, before
this endless pentecostal Cenacle over which was soon to
be repeated the *'go forth into the whole earth,'* the Pope
was visibly moved. Now it was his turn to say the *'go
forth.'* Doing so with his inimitable kindness, he wished
all the Bishops a pleasant journey, *with a holy kiss.* He said
that he would follow them affectionately in their pastoral
ministry, just as he had done in their work in the Council.
Thus the Council was not dissolved, it had only widened
for a few moments the dimensions of the Council Hall. The

individual Council desks, now side by side and empty, would be separated by hundreds and thousands of miles. . . . In all truth, from yesterday on, the entire world became a Council Hall. Never before had a Pope had the grace of participating in a Council of such world-wide proportions. As was to be expected, John XXIII was doing so with all the unlimited perspectives of his pastoral soul, with the fullest possible confidence in God, and with that authentic and exultant love for the entire human family in every corner of the earth, which is clutching today at the heart of the whole world."

An H-Bomb in reverse

John XXIII, who had introduced himself as a new Joseph revealing himself to his brothers, embracing them and saying: "I am Joseph your brother," was like a patriarch laden with years, experience, and blessings, surrounded by his sons about to scatter to their various fields of activity. Never had the sickness of any Pope been watched over with such solemnity and such affection, even though at that time the Holy Father was only at the beginning of what was an incurable illness.

After all these meetings with their Father, a certain calm spread over Roman circles. People had confidence in the Pope's strong constitution. He had never been gravely ill and it was expected that his difficulties would pass without complications. In Lent he was seen again visiting the liturgical Stational Churches, making the rounds of the outlying parishes of Rome. He began to make detours on his way to or from his destination, in order to come into contact with as many of the faithful as possible. To all appearances, he continued his work as before.

During this period he gave to the world the marvelous encyclical *Pacem in Terris,* which really marks a timeless milestone on the road to world harmony, and which evoked a universal wave of approval, surpassed only by the later matchless lesson of his long agony. This encyclical aroused universal admiration, moving consciences to the point that the Pope himself exclaimed: "The world has awakened!" Yes, the encyclical *Pacem in Terris*, written by a man whose days were numbered, was destined to save millions of lives. It was described as "an H-bomb in reverse." Then came the conferring of the Balzan Peace Prize as a seal of universal approval on the papal document. Very simply, with his personal charm and his gift for simplifying everything, John XXIII accepted this award, provoking once again a wave of sympathy and universal admiration.

On the occasion of his visit to the Quirinal it was noticed that he was really tired. In order to remain seated without arousing suspicions, he quoted a text from the Gospel: "Jesus went up on the mountain, sat down and began to speak." The Pope added: "I shall do the same!" Good Pope John was most human, a Pope and a Father at the same time, who did everything to hide from his children the pain of seeing him wasting away. But illness continued to undermine his rugged constitution. The last time he appeared at the window of his apartment to give his blessing to the 15,000 people assembled in Piazza San Pietro, on May 23rd, Ascension Thursday, John XXIII seemed quite gaunt and gave signs of unspeakable suffering which it was impossible for him to hide. It was the beginning of the end.

This is not the place to chronicle the days of the agony of John XXIII, which lasted practically four full days, from May 31st to June 3rd, when he breathed his last at 7:49 in the evening. The gravity of his illness became evident during the last week of May. On Sunday, May 26th, the Pope was unable to recite the *Angelus* with the faithful. From that day on, he could no longer celebrate Mass and he had to be satisfied with assisting at the Masses celebrated in his private apartments and receiving Holy

Communion. On May 28th Cardinal Cicognani told him: "Most Holy Father, the whole world is praying for you." The Pope replied with a smile: "Since the whole world is praying for the sick Pope, it is only natural that We should have intentions for these prayers. If God wants the sacrifice of the life of the Pope, then let it serve to obtain abundant favors on the Ecumenical Council, on Holy Church and on the human race yearning for peace. If on the contrary God is pleased to prolong this pastoral service of Ours, then may it serve to sanctify the soul of the Pope and all those who labor and suffer with him, for the spread of the kingdom of Our Lord both in the old and in the new Christian communities and throughout the world."

On May 29th and 30th a slight improvement seemed to have banished the specter of the separation which all feared. John XXIII frequently received his Cardinal Secretary of State, to take up Church business. The Cardinal kept him informed of the world-wide crusade of prayer for the health of the Pope, and John XXIII showed his deep gratitude: "This is for me very comforting! When I see myself the object of so much kind attention I am deeply moved and perfectly at ease in my usual simplicity. I feel myself united as never before with the many persons who are suffering in hospitals or at home, with those who are suffering in any way. This interest in the Pope, who humbly represents Our Lord, aims to emphasize new fervor in prayer, thought, and resolutions for peace, the clear and unmistaken impression that what counts in life is always the sense of the Gospel, that is to say, meekness, kindness, charity. I want everyone to be assured of my deep gratitude, so that just as they want to be close to me, they may learn now to revive the impulse of fraternal and mutual love.... I bless them and I encourage them."

Messages were pouring in from the entire world. from those near and from those faraway, from those within the Church and from those outside the Church, because John XXIII had said of himself: "The Pope is not only the head of the Church, he is likewise the father of the entire human race." Pope John's illness was followed with love and respect from all over the world. Affectionate telegrams poured in on the Vatican: "Holy Father, please stay well!" Another: "insofar as an atheist is capable of prayer, I am praying for your health." Such messages are evidence of the immense attraction of a holy life even for those apparently farthest removed from things spiritual and religious. Buddhists, Moslems, Jews, Shintoists, and Christians of all persuasions were united around the sickbed of the Pope. The heart of the world seemed to be beating in unison with the fearless heart of John XXIII, which was fighting off the attacks of his illness with amazing vigor. On May 31st, the crisis became more acute during the night. Intervals of lucidity were followed by periods of unconsciousness. He received the Holy Sacraments and the Anointing of the Sick.

Every word uttered by John XXIII during these days was marked with a sweet unction, a perfect resignation to the Divine Will, and an enviable serenity: "I rejoiced in the things that were said to me, we shall go into the house of the Lord." Again: "I have followed death step by step. Now I am on my way to the end, as a victim to the altar: for the Church, for the Council, for peace." He asked his private secretary: "My boy, why are you crying? You were perfectly right to tell me that my condition is very serious. You certainly did not give me any bad news." Again: "I am suffering in pain, but with love." And: "With death begins a new life: I am the resurrection and the life." To those around him he said almost playfully: "Do not worry about me. My bags are packed, and I am ready, most ready, to go." To Monsignor Capovilla, his private secretary, he insisted thoughtfully: "When it's all over, don't forget to go and spend some time with your mother."

The whole world was keeping vigil on tiptoes. With its interplay of organ music and news bulletins in all languages every fifteen minutes, the Vatican Radio seemed like the echo of that most precious existence balanced on the edge, a prey to all the winds. At any hour of the night the radio could be heard with its selection from Bach, followed by the words: "He is still living. God grant that he may live." John XXIII awoke from his coma to repeat: "*Ut unum sint!* That they may be one." He looked at those around him, showed that he appreciated their attention, and consoled them: "Take heart, this is no time for tears, but rather a moment of glory and joy!"

In one of his conscious moments he recognized his brothers from Sotto il Monte: Saverio, Alfredo, Giuseppe and his sister Assunta. Cardinal Montini had accompanied them from Milan. The friend and intimate collaborator of John XXIII had performed his act of delicate kindness. When the Pope regained consciousness at 2:50 A.M. on June 1st, he was able to see his family around him, recognized them, blessed them, and greeted them most tenderly.

Montini left for Milan shortly after, very quietly, as always. It was enough for him to have brought the dying Pontiff the great joy of his presence. On his arrival in Milan on that same night of June 1st, he organized an impressive Eucharistic vigil at the Vigorelli stadium. Thirty thousand men and youths of Catholic Action took part in this Eucharistic service, assembled in prayer to plead for the health of the Pope. On June 2nd Cardinal Montini delivered in the Duomo of Milan a moving sermon on the dying Pope.

His last words

John XXIII was wasting away gradually. He made efforts to follow the Masses celebrated in his room, and joined in the prayers being said by those around him. He asked pardon of them and of all those whom he might

ever have offended. He mentioned his first Secretary of
State, Cardinal Tardini, all the members of the Sacred
College, missionaries, all the dioceses of the world and especially his own Bergamo, the problems of Latin America,
all men, his children. The Cardinals and the prelates of the
Curia all filed by his bedside. A Mass was being celebrated
in Piazza San Pietro by Cardinal Traglia, the Assistant to
the Cardinal-Vicar of Rome. Hundreds of thousands of
people were assembled inside Bernini's colonnade. It was
a recollected, silent, devout mass of people, throbbing with
hope. Everyone was expecting a miracle. But the miracle
was already there, in the piazza. The miracle was being
worked across the face of the earth with its eyes glued to
TV, since this Mass was being televised on the European
network "Eurovision." The miracle was in the whole world
reaching out to this generous heart which, as though by
miracle, still continued to beat, the big heart of John XXIII:
"May they all be one! . . . Hail, Mary, hope of the world!"
These were perhaps the last words heard from the lips of
the dying Pope. But even when his voice was stilled, there
were still his gestures. He acknowledged the request for a
special blessing for the sick and for children, those children
whom John XXIII liked to caress, for the poor, and for
those in prison. Whenever gestures became impossible,
there was always his heart, alone, struggling against his
illness, but still loving.

In the piazza the Mass was finished. Finished also
was the Mass of the pastor. It was 7:50 P.M. when Vatican
Radio broadcast the sad news: "The Sovereign Pontiff,
the Pope of kindness, died piously and calmly at 7:49,
today, June 3, 1963." It was Pentecost Monday. The Church
was in mourning and men of good will the world over
mourned with her.

At Milan, with tears in his eyes, moved as never before,
but in a spirit of Christian resignation and with the determination to carry on, Cardinal Montini declared to his
faithful in the official communiqué issued on the very day

of Pope John's death: "It is the Pope of the Council who is dead.... A great Pope, a Pope with a simple and open heart, with a good and kindly soul, a Pope who has left on the Church and on the world the mark of a friendly and happy life.... We shall have to remember this pontificate as a great phenomenon of interior Catholic rebirth and of a new capacity for dialogue and common salvation."

A *"compromising"* eulogy

The Church has very minute legislation on the details of everything to be done on the death of a Pope. Crossing Piazza San Pietro, John XXIII completed his last apostolic journey, through a countless multitude of the faithful. His mortal remains lay in state in the basilica for two days and two nights, during which more than a million persons filed by the body of the "kindly Pope." He lay on the very spot where a few months earlier he had inaugurated the Council. The Council Hall now seemed sad and empty. There were even some who asked if it would ever be used again....

The burial ceremony took place the evening of Thursday, June 6th, according to the prescriptions laid down by John XXIII himself. From June 7th until the 17th the Chapter of Canons of Saint Peter's celebrated the *novemdiali*, or nine days of Requiem Masses. At the last of these Masses almost all the members of the Sacred College were present. On June 17th, at the final solemn funeral service, there were present in the basilica, eighty-five special Diplomatic Missions, representing States or international organizations, and delegations from other Churches. This is not the place to set down, even in summary fashion, the innumerable messages of sympathy, all of which were eloquent in their admiration for the deceased Pontiff. A single example might be the very significant radio statement by

Doctor Fisher, former Anglican Primate and Archbishop of Canterbury: "What was begun by John XXIII cannot remain paralyzed by his death. God will carry it on, even intensifying this new orientation."

It was Cardinal Montini who pronounced the finest eulogy of Pope John at the solemn funeral service celebrated in the Duomo of Milan on June 7th. On that occasion he declared: "Pope John has turned our path in a direction which it will be the part of wisdom not merely to recall but likewise to follow. No one will ever forget the proof which, in a certain measure he incarnated in the very human spontaneity of his own holy life, namely, the proof of a deep-rooted and essential capacity of the Christian religion to provide ever-new spiritual resources for the modern world.... Can we ever wander from paths so masterfully traced out by Pope John, even for the future?"

It is a matter of common knowledge that everything the Cardinals do during the vacancy of the Holy See takes on exceptional significance. For a few days they are the chief protagonists in news stories and predictions of things to come. This happens whenever a Pope dies. But it was particularly true this time because the world at large knew more about things touching the Vatican. The Council had attracted world-wide attention. The world was already aware of the various trends revealed in the Council and also knew pretty well how the individual Cardinals had lined up on the various issues at stake. Such knowledge helped to complicate further the already complex maze of predictions in which journalists, and many non-journalists, like to indulge at such times. On the other hand, this also points up the interest aroused by matters concerning the Church. Names are considered and weighed in the balance. The everlasting question of "Italian" or "non-Italian" comes up for discussion. Montini's name always figured among the favorites. The public recalled his stand in the Council and attention was called to the natural reserve which always characterized him.

In the midst of all this agitation, which generally never plays a decisive role in influencing the Cardinals, since they are in a better position than anyone else to understand how journalists and others indulge their fantasies in such circumstances, there echoed the funeral discourse of Cardinal Montini for John XXIII. After this funeral sermon, no one could speak of Montini's "neutrality." Hence people immediately seized upon the word which seemed most appropriate for the occasion, stating that Montini had "compromised" himself. They reached this conclusion because the Cardinal had made it clear in his eulogy that the Council had to continue, that discussion could not stop either on problems already on the agenda or on others falling within the complex program of the Council. It should be noted immediately that, according to Canon Law, a Council is automatically suspended on the death of a Pope, and it depends on his successor to decide whether it shall be resumed, because it is the exclusive prerogative of the Pope to convoke or to continue an Ecumenical Council.

No one was forgetting that John XXIII had organized a Council which, historically, was completely new, a Council in which the supreme law was the holy liberty of all the individual members, the one restriction placed upon the Fathers being that they should "not condemn." This orientation was in some sense revolutionary or, if one prefers, it was a stroke of genius. Just as some individuals always see corruption in anything new, thus it is not surprising that there should have been reactions of this kind even inside the Council. This does not mean that a Council, a Conclave, or the very life of the Church is merely a game of theories or trends. Over and above all, there is always the assistance of the Holy Spirit. But at the same time it is no secret that God knows how to use men even more skillfully than men could ever imagine. History in general, and also the history of the Church, is woven by men, but it is God who holds the threads.

People were already shouting "Long live the Pope!"

Thus, in the judgment of the day-to-day "specialists," Montini was now "compromised." But it is not clear why there should be any talk of "compromise." The Cardinal of Milan had always been an enthusiastic supporter of the Council. He greeted its first announcement with greater jubilation than anyone else, and kept his eyes on its work and on how things were shaping up as time went on. Lastly, in the First Session he played a role which many described as decisive. Consequently no one could say that Montini had in any way shifted position. It is only natural that he followed a consistent and clearly defined line. His eulogy of June 7th was widely commented on and in not a few hearts re-enkindled a flame of hope. The name of the Archbishop of Milan headed all the lists of the *papabili*, so much so that when Montini passed by, some groups of the faithful already began to shout: "Long live the Pope!"

Any visit, any public appearance, any particular attitude brought on a wave of comments and conjectures. When, during the funeral services for John XXIII and later, during the Mass of the Holy Spirit, mobile TV cameras caught the face of one or other of the Cardinals, everyone tried to read in those facial expressions so strangely recollected, at times almost appearing absent, a name, an indication, perhaps some tendency. It is easy to understand why Montini was more than prudent, because he had always been extremely reserved, never drawing attention to himself as he moved around the Vatican, as it was then said, almost on tiptoes! For this reason he decided to leave Rome in order to spend what proved to be his last free hours quietly, and withdrew to Castel Gandolfo. From his years in Vatican circles he had many friends and he was now a house guest of Doctor Bonomelli, the superintendent of the papal villas. There, unexpectedly, he received a visit from Cardinal Spellman. For Montini there was no peace. Events were rushing on decisively.

Diary of the Conclave

During the Conclave one of the authors of this volume was keeping a diary at the request of a foreign newspaper. The following account comes largely from those pages.

June 16th: At Rome, where the death of a Pope and the election of his successor are events which recur roughly twice every generation, a popular proverb, on the surface irreverent but at the same time expressing a deep truth, states that "When a Pope dies, we make another." Things could hardly be otherwise. The Church just could not remain without a Pope, just as a house cannot stand without a foundation. The Pope, as Peter, is the foundation of the Church. And the Church cannot fall. This was declared by Our Lord, whom the passage of centuries cannot prove false: "The gates of hell shall not prevail against My Church, which I shall build upon the rock of the papacy." The mourning of the Church at the death of every Pope is very brief. Hardly a month passes from the first funeral of a deceased pontiff and the festive jubilation for the election of his successor.

June 17th: Today is the last day of official mourning for John XXIII. The mourning of hearts will continue for a long time yet, while the light of Faith invites us to rejoice for the victory over evil and sadness as represented in the triumphant death of the Pope, who was "good" in a very special way. This morning in Saint Peter's Basilica there was the last of the *novemdiali* for the deceased Pope. Celebrant of the Mass was Cardinal Eugene Tisserant, the Dean of the Sacred College. Seventy-two Cardinals were present. Ten of the actual members of the Sacred College were missing. Present also were the official delegations of eighty-three States and international organizations, the same number as had taken part in the opening of the Second Vatican Council on October 11th.

June 18th: Today is the vigil of the opening of the Conclave. It is a day for a halt. It is a day for predictions. There is insistent talk about Montini as the leader of one "trend" which would be identified with assuring the continuation of the Roncalli policies, and of Cardinal Siri, Archbishop of Genoa, as spokesman for another tendency. There is also talk of Cardinals Lercaro and Confalonieri among the Italians, of Cardinals Suenens, Koenig, Agagianian and Larraona among the non-Italians.

June 19th: At 5:00 P.M. the Conclave opened with the solemn invocation of the Holy Spirit and the singing of the *Veni Creator Spiritus*. Eighty Cardinals were present. Absent was the Primate of Hungary, Cardinal Joseph Mindszenty, a "prisoner" in the United States Embassy in Budapest. He could not come even for the Conclave which elected John XXIII in 1958. Absent also was the Cardinal Archbishop of Quito, Ecuador, Cardinal de La Torre, who is gravely ill. The *All out!* was proclaimed by Archbishop Enrico Dante, Papal Prefect of Ceremonies and Secretary of the Congregation of Rites, at 5:10 P.M. Because of illness three Cardinals, namely Micara, Vicar of Rome, Chiarlo, Cardinal of the Curia, and Concha, Archbishop of Bogotà, were unable to take part in the preliminary ceremonies but went directly to the Sistine Chapel from their cells.

June 20th: This was the first day of voting and the first *fumata*. It was a foregone conclusion that the first smoke would be black. The more audacious predicted forty probable votes for the Cardinal of Milan on the first ballot. But forty votes are not enough; fourteen more are needed in order to obtain the two-thirds plus one, required by the latest dispositions of John XXIII, who was not satisfied with just two-thirds, as had been the rule previously. One of the morning papers declared that the election would probably take place before the second *fumata*, which consequently should be white. Because of this "certainty" the number of those in Saint Peter's Piazza that evening was greater than in the morning. Another reason was that at six in the evening, when the second *fumata* was expected, the temperature was more bearable. That evening, notwithstanding the precautions allegedly taken, there was the same confusion as had marked the first *fumata* of the Conclave which elected John XXIII. On that occasion, the very first puff coming out of the chimney above the Sistine Chapel seemed white. The same thing happened this evening, at least partially. At the beginning, the smoke seemed white, but it immediately became black. Everybody regarded this as altogether normal since, because there are eighty Cardinals taking part in the election, it is obvious that the election of a new successor of Peter might be more difficult and trying than in previous elections.

June 21st: Last night, the guests in the house where I am living in Rome played a special game. Someone had pinned on the wall a page from one of the newspapers with the portraits of the eighty-two Cardinals of the Church. Then followed a kind of referendum to see which of the candidates would prove to be the most popular. The choice lined up as follows: first, Montini, by a great majority, followed by Lercaro, Urbani, Suenens, Koenig, and Confalonieri.

It is now 10:00 A.M. In a quarter of an hour I shall be going to Saint Peter's for the *fumata* which with increasing probability will be white. But I do not want to go out without first setting down my impressions of an article I have just read in a publication which is certainly not Catholic and much less "committed" to anything reflecting the Catholic viewpoint. The article says: "It is dangerous to make any predictions on the public activities of any new Pope, if we take into consideration only where he came from and the main lines of his thinking. The first social encyclical came from a Pope who belonged to the aristocracy, and a lowly son of the people, Saint Pius X, who had been heralded as 'the lowliest pastor in the world' was one of the most energetic defenders of authority. A

new Pope is never just an ex-Cardinal. In the complex
mystery of his election, a thousand and one things combine
to make of him almost always a new man. He is a man to
be discovered in his entirety, an enigma clothed in white.
... Men from fifty to ninety years old are called to cast
their votes in the Sistine Chapel. They must look each other
in the face, and choose the one among them who is the
best prepared and best disposed to do whatever, as
Saint Bernard says, is demanded by the times."

11:22 A.M. the same day. The *fumata* was white. Un-
questionably white from the very beginning. The moments
after the first evident signs of a new election are moments
of dramatic tension and anxious expectation, while everyone waits for Cardinal Ottaviani to appear on the loggia of
the Vatican Basilica to announce the great and joyful news
of the election of the Pope. The interval between our certainty that we should rejoice and our curiosity to know
exactly for what name we should exult, was more propor-
tionately long.

We had to wait until Cardinal Ottaviani announced
the baptismal name of the new Pope, stating that it was
"... the Most Eminent and Most Reverend Lord, Cardinal
of the Holy Roman Church, Giovanni Battista—" Everyone
knew the rest. All the faithful assembled in the piazza
knew that this was the name of the Pope whom almost
everyone was expecting, and which was that of the former
Cardinal Archbishop of Milan, Giovanni Battista Montini. . . .

By what name do you wish to be known?

In the endless moments between the traditional white
fumata announcing the election of the successor of
John XXIII and the appearance of Cardinal Ottaviani on
the loggia to proclaim the "*Annunitio vobis gaudium
magnum*," the Italian radio announcer who had been nar-

rating the events of the morning indulged in predictions on the possible names the new Pope might choose. For him, the new Pope might be John XXIV, continuing the long series of the predecessors of John XXIII. He might also take the name of Benedict XVI, Pius XIII, Leo XIV, Gregory, Stephen, or choose any of the other names used over twenty centuries by the 262 Popes known to history. Only two names were left off the list of possibilities. These were *Peter,* out of respect for the first poniff of the Church and, according to the judgment of the announcer, it was improbable that the new Pope would choose the name *Sixtus* for reasons of philology or euphony. In fact as the last Pope by this name had been Sixtus V, it was regarded as most improbable that any new Pope would want to have the name of Sixtus VI, or, as would be even still more curious in Italian, *Sisto Sesto.* But before long the world knew that Cardinal Montini had chosen the name of Paul VI. His choice was prompted by special admiration for, and devotion to, the Apostle of the Gentiles. The new Pope let it be understood clearly that his choice of the name of Paul was more closely tied in with Saint Paul than with the other Popes who had borne the same name.

While the people applauded, Paul VI continued to greet them

No sooner had the news of the white *fumata* reached all the corners of the city via radio, than the crowds began to swarm in on Saint Peter's. The Bernini colonnades began to take on their special crowded festive air. A merciless noonday sun was beating down, making the wait all the more trying. It was a typical Roman dog day. Uncontrolled applause swept across the piazza as the double doors of the central loggia over the entrance to the Basilica were opened for the arrival of Cardinal Ottaviani. Every word aroused in the vast piazza echoes, memories, and images. The name of Montini was drowned out by enthusiastic acclamations. Immediately there was silence to hear the name, the new name. It was also welcomed enthusiastically, because no one can fail to catch the hidden echoes aroused by the name of Paul in all Christian hearts: ecumenism, the open-door policy, evangelization, holy liberty, generosity. All these great realities go flashing through the mind at the mere mention of the name of the great Apostle.

But there was no time to think of all these things. On the loggia there appeared the papal cross, the side loggias filled with beaming Cardinals, quietly jostling each other to get a place. Then there arrived the papal cortege and, at the end, the slim white clothed figure, his face very pale, of the new Pope.

He greeted the immense throng with gestures reminiscent of Pius XII. The piazza was transformed into a huge ovation, with cheers, applause, tears, smiles, deep emotions, and a blazing sun. Yes, the pontificate of Paul VI was born under the sign of the sun. The zenith of the pontificate of John XXIII had been marked by the gentle sign of the silvery moon which, punctual as though by appointment, had come to illuminate the historic night of October 11, 1962, at the end of the day which had witnessed the opening of the Council. On that occasion even John XXIII gazed up and wanted the moon to have its share in the solemn Council celebrations, in a world-embracing desire to reach all men. Paul VI came to the Church under the sign of the sun. His coming was to mark an epoch of renewed fervor, missionary zeal, ecumenical achievements, and luminous activity over the entire world.

All of us were applauding. Paul VI continued to greet the people. Perhaps he was the least happy of all. The piazza was telling him certainly many things which we cannot imagine. The Cardinals too were applauding and smiling. Some of them were even in a joking mood. The

Vatican band struck up the Papal March, and the Italian armed forces presented arms to the new Pope. As the climax of this historic moment, Paul VI imparted his first papal blessing *Urbi et Orbi,* to the city of Rome and the entire world. His words were pronounced with effort, haltingly, as though he were feeling the immense significance of the rite he was performing. But for us those gestures brought a feeling of comfort, knowing that we were once more being protected and guided by a father loved of God. We felt the comfort which comes from the continued presence of Christ on earth.

As we left the piazza, newspapers were already on sale, in extra editions, with the first photograph of the Cardinal Montini who had become Paul VI. These papers were evidently made up of articles already previously prepared, and showed an ignorance of many details, as for example the name of the new Pope. Still the papers were soon sold out, because everyone was anxious to know something, no matter how small, some detail, some editorial remark, a date, a conjecture which no one had paid attention to before. The piazza emptied and entered into a long sun-bathed siesta. It had well deserved this rest, after the hectic days it had lived.

We went away asking a question which still haunts us: What will the new Pope do? What line will he follow? Will he continue the Council? We know that to speak of a "line" in connection with a pontificate is not altogether proper. Nevertheless the expression has been confirmed by usage and is now common currency. Consequently, what line will Paul VI follow?

He himself gave the answer the day after his election, in his discourse to the Cardinals assembled in the Sistine Chapel, and to the entire world which was eagerly hanging on his words and waiting for an indication of the policies of his pontificate. These policies were proclaimed again in even more solemn form in his Allocution opening Session II of the Council, with which this volume opened.

THE ECHO OF THE ELECTION

The following pages make no claim to presenting all the world press commentary on the election of Cardinal Montini as Pope Paul VI. This would take volumes. An attempt has been made to provide a sampling of authoritative opinion from various quarters and different countries, in order that these passages may reflect the warmth with which the announcement of this election was welcomed throughout the world.

GIACOMO CARDINAL LERCARO,
Archbishop of Bologna

"Pastoral concern even to the point of suffering"

Everyone was very pleasantly surprised by the speed of this Conclave. On the other hand this rapidity was only natural. Pope John had died with one supreme hope in his heart and on his lips—that "they might be one." His dying concern was the unity of the faithful in Christ.

It was known, and the Council had helped to emphasize this point, that the Cardinals had their own personal viewpoints. Since they are prominent individuals, accustomed for the most part to being in positions of command, they naturally tend to state their individual ideas with deep sincerity. But the love of the Church dominates their souls and directs their actions and, particularly, the Holy Spirit invoked by Our Lord guides them. Thus, at noon on June 21st, eighteen days after the death of John XXIII, from the loggia of the Basilica, Paul VI gave his blessing to Rome and to the world. He was the elect of God. We do not even need the life of faith to understand the reason for this election. It is sufficient to have just ordinary powers of perception to discover why God, through unusual and sometimes contradictory circumstances, prepared him for the great task he was to take up at the moment fixed by Providence. . . .

Anyone who knows Paul VI recognizes that his profound culture has never deadened in his soul that sense of pastoral concern which he feels even to the point of suffering. Those who know him are aware that he chooses his words carefully like a diplomat; at the same time that he is a man of cordiality, and that the ardor of his spirit is reflected in his eyes and in his incisive and ardent speech. It is known also that he is bold in his plans and at the same time careful and ready to listen.

But above all, those who know him are sure that he is a man of God, a stranger to all self-interest, ambition, and earthly sentiments. He is profoundly good with a vast and understanding kindness built on dedication and anxious concern, even though it is serene and recollected. The world has already sensed this and the filial confidence which it felt for John, it today reposes in Paul. The dimensions of the Church in the world are expanding almost visibly. The Basilica to which Paul V gave its imposing facade is no longer big enough. The immense Piazza of Saint Peter's, surrounded by the colonnade of Bernini, is a temple for the coronation of Paul VI.

> Extracts from a discourse of the Cardinal Archbishop of Bologna at a special service celebrated in his cathedral on the day of the coronation of Paul VI.

Franziskus Cardinal Koenig,
Archbishop of Vienna

"He understands all the problems of our times"

I am most happy that Cardinal Montini has become Pope. I am also happy to have been right when I said that the Conclave would be brief. Lastly, I am more than satisfied that the election of the Pope has had such favorable echoes throughout the world.

... I am most pleased to have been elevated to the Sacred College along with Archbishop Montini, in the first Consistory held by Pope John XXIII. All this has built up a particular bond of closeness between the Holy Father and myself. He was the first of the twenty-three Cardinals created by John XXIII at the beginning of his pontificate. It was Cardinal Montini who on that occasion addressed the speech of thanks to the Holy Father in the name of all the new Cardinals.

I had more than one opportunity to speak with Monsignor Montini, when he was still Under-Secretary of State. Later I had many contacts with him when he was Archbishop of Milan. I have always esteemed him highly, not only for his outstanding and valuable human qualities, but also for his well-known experience in ecclesiastical affairs and for his understanding of the problems of modern times. . . .

... His first message contains the essential points of the program of his pontificate. In my opinion, this first message is stupendous, and I hope that it has had good repercussions throughout the world. I would like to stress certain points which I noted particularly. Above all we find in this discourse a clear indication that the new Pope intends to continue the great undertakings of his predecessor. . . . Secondly, there is in this message a definite reminder of the last encyclical of John XXIII, *Pacem in Terris.*

This, to my way of thinking, shows without doubt that Paul VI sees in this encyclical the dominant task of the Church, that is, on the national and especially the international plane, to serve the cause of justice and peace in the world. . . .

Certainly, in the choice of a name, whether of John XXIII or of Paul VI, we can see a policy. No historical consideration motivated this selection, but rather an ideal. Personally, I see in this choice a reminder of Sacred Scripture, of the universal figure of Saint Paul, who at the gates of Damascus felt himself completely swept away by the grace of God: "By the grace of God I am what I am." Besides, in the choice of this name, I see a reminder of Christianity's task to unite the peoples of the world. In fact, Saint Paul was the first one to reach out beyond the people of Israel and to make contact with the Greeks and the Romans—the ecumenical movement of his times!—preaching to them Jesus Christ, as the unifying sign of the entire human race. Thus also the new Pope, through his choice of a name, wishes to point out that he beholds in Christianity the mission of uniting the peoples of the world and conserving peace.

From an interview appearing in *L'Osservatore Romano,* June 29, 1963.

RICHARD CARDINAL CUSHING
Archbishop of Boston

"Paul VI has
the determined character of Pius XI,
the superior intelligence of Pius XII,
the warm heart of John XXIII"

Pope Paul VI was the choice of the Holy Spirit as the successor of the beloved John XXIII. It is true that His Holiness was elected by the College of Cardinals but our votes represented the will of God.

A letter from the Sisters of Saint Joan of Arc who staff the residence of the Cardinal Archbishop of Boston reveals my thoughts. These Sisters, dedicated to the sanctification of the clergy, wrote as follows to me on June 25, 1963:

"We congratulate the Cardinals of the recent Conclave on the selection of the extraordinary and lovable Pontiff, Pope Paul VI. We had the honor of having him as our guest in 1960. We remember him as a humble, scholarly, kindly and totally dedicated prince of the Church. Please tell His Holiness that he will always be in our prayers. Before you departed for the Conclave you foretold that one who had visited this house would be the next Pope. Your prophecy came true. As we listed the names of prominent visitors we all concluded it would be Cardinal Montini. Never a day will pass without our prayerful mementoes for Pope Paul VI."

These are the words taken from a letter I received from the Sisters who staff my residence, our Chancery Office and a rectory for priests assigned to special apostolic works in the Archdiocese of Boston. They express my own thoughts and those of countless people of all faiths in the United States.

If I would comment on them to greater extent I would add that by every human measure, we have in the person of the new Pontiff all the qualities of character, mind and soul that can lead the Church through the troublesome days in which we live and bring to new greatness the appeal of the Gospel of Christ among the children of men.

There is a sense in which, under the guidance of the Spirit of God, the whole life of Pope Paul has been a preparation for his present office. His scholarly career as a youthful priest gives him an understanding of those values which only a profound Christian learning can provide and on which the Church must always depend for Christian understanding and defending the Church against errors of changing times.

The many years of diplomatic service of the Vatican have added world-wide vision which comprehends the special problems of all nations and recognizes their common unity in the single human family.

In recent years the pastoral and apostolic work of Pope Paul VI in the world's largest diocese has brought the new Pope into personal contact with people in a manner of a true shepherd who understands the lives and labors of his people and makes it his task to find spiritual remedies for the anxieties of men in contemporary times.

Moreover the personal character of Pope Paul VI is one that meets the demands of the challenge of the days that are before us. A mind keen and well-informed blends with a spirit that is warm and interested in things human; a truly noble personality is touched with a directness and simplicity that is at once attractive and disarming. In Pope Paul VI, the Christian world has both a blessing and an inspiration.

I unhesitatingly say that Pope Paul VI combines so many of the qualities of those great popes of recent times as to be their successor and their product. One sees in him the determined character of Pius XI, the superior intelligence of Pius XII, the warm heart of John XXIII ... and with all of these qualities of his own individual person which add new dimensions to the man and the office. Providence has blessed us, and the universal Church rejoices.

In a world of constant changes, of new solutions to age-old problems and of modern innovations what can we expect from the successor of Pope John XXIII? In the light of his background and especially of his work as the Cardinal Archbishop of the Archdiocese of Milan, the largest archdiocese in the world, we can anticipate that His Holiness will make all things new. The program of Pope John XXIII will be continued and extended. The Ecumenical Council will be resumed. The principles behind a new social order spelled out by his predecessors will be reiterated. The progressive policies of recent years will be pursued and expanded. The innate beauty and glory of the Church for the consolation and salvation of mankind will be presented in virile and understandable language. The laity as indispensable aids of the clergy will be made aware of their apostolic mission in the structure of the Church as witnesses of Christ in their respective fields of activity. Those outside the fold of the Catholic Church will understand that we recognize their conscientious religious convictions while at the same time we hold fast to the truths revealed by God and interpreted by the teaching authority of his Church.

In brief we can expect our new Pontiff, the Vicar of Christ on this earth, to show all mankind the Way, the Truth and the Life.

Complete text from *L'Osservatore Romano,* June 27, 1963.

JULIUS CARDINAL DOEPFNER,
Archbishop of Munich

"The election has brought widespread rejoicing"

After the death of Pope John, which also in Germany was deeply mourned, there was among German Catholics as well as among the Christian Evangelicals, great concern over who might be elected as his successor, to carry on, and in the same spirit, the work which Pope John had launched with such promise.

Now Pope Paul VI has been elected after a Conclave which was shorter than anyone expected. The joy over the election of Cardinal Giovanni Battista Montini, Archbishop of Milan, was spontaneous and widespread, because everyone recognized in him an ardent guardian of the heritage of Pope John.

His choice qualities of soul, his inborn religious spirit, his rich Curial experience, and his fruitful ministry in a vast and difficult diocese stand out as an imposing prelude to the mission of the successor of Peter throughout the entire world.

From certain personal conversations and working contacts with Cardinal Montini, as a member of the Secretariate for Extraordinary Affairs, I know what his hopes are for the Council, which was the main theme of his great pastorals and which can contribute to the dynamic renewal of the Church. In Germany, the fact that the Cardinals reached agreement so rapidly was considered as a sign of how the Church is clearly convinced of the necessity of vigorous continuity of action.

I have also encountered pleased reactions over the name chosen by the new Pope. The name of the Apostle of the Nations has been understood as a program, in its inexpressible but clear outlines: his ardent love for Christ, his apostolic zeal which the narrow limits of his country forced him to diffuse and spread throughout the entire world, his resolute defense against errors which can interfere with traditional doctrine, the courage needed for adaptation to the necessities of the day, his preoccupation for the unity of the Church and at the same time for the multiplicity of its members and for the vitality of its individual communities.

For these reasons, at the beginning of this pontificate, German Catholics are filled with confident expectation. They know that the great hopes awakened by Pope John are certainly safe in the hands of his successor. In addition to this, our people knows from its own experience the grave dangers threatening the Church and humanity from any system which would root out faith in God and weaken the strength of the Church itself through all possible means.

Consequently the Church must be attentive and ready, but at the same time clear and resolute in recognizing and carrying out its own mission. We trust that Paul, in this field strewn with risks and responsibilities, will be a sure guide, in the strength of the Holy Spirit, and we ask this grace for him with our most fervent prayers.

In this way the Catholics of Germany, in unfailing fidelity, are united to the Holy See and present their good wishes to Paul VI with filial affection.

From *L'Osservatore Romano*, June 29, 1963.

THE GRAND RABBI OF FRANCE

The election of Cardinal Montini took place under most hopeful auspices, and is welcomed with fervor and hope. I unite my fervent good wishes to those coming to him from all sides. I formulate the hope, and I am sure that in doing so I am not alone, that he will continue and carry on to completion the great work so magnificently begun by Pope John XXIII.

Quoted from *La Stampa*, Torino, June 22, 1963.

WLADIMIR D'ORMESSON,
Diplomat and Member of the French Academy

The Conclave has elected the successor of the great Pope John XXIII, and now another great Pope becomes the 263rd link in the sacred chain. Henceforth Cardinal Montini will be governing the Catholic, Apostolic and Roman Church under the name of Paul VI! Ah, God be praised! ... Ah, how happy I am!

The election was rapid, belying all predictions. When I was at Rome a few days ago I heard people saying: "The Conclave will be difficult." It seemed to me on the contrary that no Conclave could be easier.... Whatever might be the qualifications of the Cardinals whose names were mentioned, the personality of Montini always dominated. All the qualities, all the gifts required to exercise supreme authority in the Church—he has them all! A rightist? A leftist? A traditionalist? A progressivist? Only God knows what nonsense has been uttered in efforts to make such classifications. But Cardinal Montini rises above all such small talk and all such miseries! The truth is that he unites everything which must be united. And, above all, he is a priest!

He is a priest whose soul is on fire with faith and evangelical love. This man gifted with such perfect self-control, whose prudence and wisdom are exemplary, is, under a somewhat cold exterior, a man of fire. It is enough to listen to him, to look at him, when he is defending principles close to his heart, to see the flash of the secret flame which animates him.

I am not writing these words simply at random. Circumstances were such that Monsignor Montini was Under-Secretary at the Secretariate of State when I arrived in Rome in May, 1940, to spend inside Vatican City the frightful summer of that year. I found him still in the same position when I came back eight years later, in the September of 1948. After making him Pro-Secretary of State in 1953, Pius XII promoted him, in 1954, to the Archepiscopal See of Milan. During these long years I saw Monsignor Montini every Thursday, and often enough more frequently than that. This means that I had the privilege of coming close to him and knowing him well. For the loftiness of his spirit and the breadth of his vision are equalled only by the exquisite delicacy of his heart. I should like to point out particularly that in the difficult days of the summer of 1950, Monsignor Montini, whom I saw during this crucial period almost daily, was not merely most helpful in our discussions. He was a friend, and in very special circumstances. This is something I can never forget.

Nor shall I ever forget the consecration of Monsignor Montini, before his departure for the archbishopric of Milan. It was on December 12, 1954 in Saint Peter's Basilica. Pope Pius XII was already gravely ill. Undoubtedly he would have consecrated personally his most faithful collaborator. But he was confined to bed and his physicians had forbidden him to move. It was Cardinal Tisserant, Dean of the Sacred College, who acted as consecrating Bishop. Saint Peter's was filled. At one point in the ceremony, in a moment of absolute silence, a weak voice was suddenly heard. It seemed to come from the heavens. From his sickbed, by radio, Pius XII was addressing a few words "to his well-beloved son who was becoming his brother in the episcopate."

I have always felt that on that day Pius XII had sealed the destiny of Monsignor Montini....

At the hour when the eyes of the entire world are turned towards Rome, when the moral authority of the papacy has been elevated by Pope John XXIII to a degree never attained before, when the peoples of the world are in need of a supreme judge, when men, even though not Christians, instinctively feel the necessary supremacy of spiritual values, lastly, at the hour when the Council, providentially assembled by John XXIII, is to carry on its work to find the right balance between what is absolutely necessary to maintain and what is absolutely necessary to change, the Sacred College, assembled in Conclave, has not only given to the Catholic, Apostolic and Roman Church, but to all men of good faith and good will, the Pope they were expecting.

From *Le Figaro*, Paris, June 22, 1963.

La Civiltà Cattolica:

It is not without a special design of providence that the man destined by God to such an arduous and vast task has been prepared for it by an ensemble of experiences with very special qualifications: thirty-four years of priestly life, intense with piety and study, spent in the city of Rome in varied apostolic activities particularly among university students, but especially in the direct service of the Holy See and for a long time even in most intimate collaboration with the activities of a great Pope. Then the incomparable experience of immediate contact with the most characteristic expressions of modern life in the pastoral guidance of the vast and complex Archdiocese of Milan, and contact with problems of every kind. . . . In this varied experience . . . there are fused a deep piety and a lively sense of the liturgy, a vast culture centered on the theology of the Church and fed on the Word of God, and at the same time sensitive to the currents of present-day thought. There is his direct knowledge of the central government of the Church, his immediate vision of the problems of missionary life, immigration, and the social order. . . . How could anyone imagine a better or more complete preparation for the tasks of the "pontifical service" in this present day?

Rome, July 6, 1963, page 12.

INFORMATIONS CATHOLIQUES INTERNATIONALES:
". . . a pure, burning and unfailing Faith"

Some people are saying that Paul VI will be a leftist Pope. Others are claiming that he has been a rightist Bishop. These words are deprived of all significance when there is question of a priest of this caliber. What has always been most impressive in him, every time we had the privilege to be in contact with him, was his independence and his exact knowledge of the situation of the Church in the twentieth century. It is this which basically is important and what attracted us to him. . . .

We must add that the outstanding intelligence with which Paul VI appears to be endowed has always been used in the service of faith in Christ. He has a pure, burning, ardent, and unfailing faith. It is a faith in which he ardently wants to help others to share. And this, without doubt, this apostolic fire is what the new Pope has brought with him. He wants to take the Gospel to the world. . . .

Paul VI will start from the very heart of the Church to achieve the goal of evangelization which he sets for himself. He will be an organizer. He will take decisions. He will negotiate. He will give concrete form to many things which his immediate predecessors had only been able to indicate or to outline.

Paris, July 1, 1963.

JEAN GUITTON,
Lay Auditor at Vatican Council II:
". . . *Paul VI reminds me of Saint Paul*"

Paul VI is a friend of men. According to the words of Terence, nothing of what is human can be foreign to him. When a truth has been known and set down, Paul VI is concerned with knowing how the man of today will assimilate it, how it can feed his daily life. From this viewpoint, Paul VI feels that the transmission and the spread of religious truth are part of the task of the laity also. For this reason he summoned some laymen as auditors in the Council, some by personal title, and others as representatives of Catholic organizations.

Whenever he met up with serious difficulties, John XXIII rose above them with an act of supernatural faith. Like the eagle, whose blue-green eyes he reflects, Paul VI soars above difficulty, penetrates it, feels it, sees it, I would even say that he suffers it, and seeks out a solution with really profound efforts. Paul VI likes to go deeply into problems, to mark out a solution from the inside. If I were to sum up my thoughts of these two Popes I would say: John XXIII reminds me rather of Saint John, while Paul VI reminds me of Saint Paul. In his latter years the Apostle John never tired of repeating: My children love one another. Saint Paul burned with a desire to travel the entire world in order to make Christ known.

> From an interview in *Famiglia Cristiana*, December 15, 1963.

LA PRESSE:

We have a new Pope with a name which commands respect, a man of gigantic stature, who will continue the policy of the great Popes of our age. . . . Even a summary analysis of the career of Cardinal Montini provides full justification for the joy and the hopes aroused by his election to the papal throne.

Montreal, June 22, 1963.

LA CROIX:

"The Pope our times need"

We wrote on the eve of the Conclave that the Church could not find for itself any Pope except one who would be great in spirit and in heart. Who else, better than Cardinal Montini, verifies this definition? His greatness, in fact, seems so evident to public opinion that, immediately after the death of John XXIII, this public opinion had already made Cardinal Montini the deceased Pope's successor. Indifferent both to favor and to disfavor, the Cardinals of the Conclave have given the Church the kind of Pope called for by our times.

Paris, June 22, 1963.

CHARACTERISTIC GLIMPSES

If Giovanni Battista Montini had followed immediately after Pope Pius XII, instead of after Pope John XXIII, there would be no need for a chapter of "stories" in his biography. This does not mean that the life of Eugenio Pacelli was completely devoid of anecdotes. But in any case it was "Good Pope Roncalli," or "Good Pope John," as the French baptized him, who restored to the field of "papal stories" that vigor and authenticity which it had received from Pope John's great predecessor in Venice and in Rome, Saint Pius X. Stories on Montini are as different from those on John, or rather perhaps we should say those on Roncalli, as their personalities are different. But even here there is an element which brings them close together to the point of making them alike in spirit. This element is the common denominator of an exquisite charity: disarming and simple was the charity of Angelo Roncalli, more reserved and retiring is that of his successor. It is this exquisite charity which characterizes the incidents in the life of Giovanni Battista Montini, as it characterized also those of the life of his immediate predecessor.

It would be to no point to seek out in the life of Paul VI the countless anecdotes filled with exuberant human feeling which are so abundant in the life of his predecessor. Everyone knows that Pope John was more unique than rare, and that he holds something of a record. Nevertheless the biography of Paul VI is not complete without its little pleasant incidents, although such episodes are doubtless less frequent and more sober than those recounted on Pope John.

The life of Giovanni Battista Montini did not lend itself frequently to stories, either because of his education, or the circumstances in which he had to carry on his work. Nevertheless in the kindliness of his look, with its touch of sadness, there is a tenderness which makes him very much like Pope John, in his remarks and in his heartfelt good humor.

A prophecy of John XXIII on Montini

It has already been said that Montini's name headed the list of Cardinals created by Pope John XXIII a month after his ascent to the papal throne. This is a significant point, if we bear in mind that elevated with him at the same time were Monsignor Tardini, who had become Pope John's Secretary of State, and Monsignor Urbani, who had taken over the heritage of Roncalli in the government of the Patriarchate of Venice.

John XXIII was linked with the Archbishop of Milan through particular bonds of affection and esteem, and he made no secret of his sentiments. He gave proof of this in many circumstances in which he either had, or actually sought out, occasions to meet with him, first as Under-Secretary of State, then as Pro-Secretary, and then later as Archbishop and Cardinal at Milan, Venice and Rome.

In the book entitled *John XXIII*, composed of seven talks given by his faithful secretary Monsignor Loras Capovilla, we have the chronology of some of these meetings. There is for example, the meeting in 1956, on the occasion of the Centenary of Saint Lawrence Giustiniani, when Cardinal Roncalli invited his friend Montini to preach in the cathedral at Venice, and had him as guest in his patriarchal palace. In the March of 1958, Roncalli was the guest of Archbishop Montini for some days at Milan.

Roncalli's esteem for Montini was such that John XXIII always regarded him as his successor on the Chair of Peter. During his illness, in the March of 1963, a certain individual was complaining confidentially with the Pope about the difficulties which would arise in choosing a successor, should he happen to die. John XXIII replied: "Providence has most worthy priests all ready to take my place. The first of all of them is Montini."

Cardinal Roncalli and Archbishop Montini had met in a celebrated Marian sanctuary on the occasion of a solemn celebration in honor of the Madonna. As the Patriarch of Venice was always deferring to the Archbishop of Milan, someone asked him why he was doing so. His only reply was: "One day you will see him Pope." Why "*you* will see him" and not "*we* shall see him?" Because Cardinal Roncalli would have disappeared from the scene before Montini became Pope. This could be interpreted as though the Patriarch of Venice already had some presentiment of his own elevation to the Chair of Peter and, if this is supposed, it is clear that he would not have been able to "see" his successor. Or it may be that he was simply thinking of the end of his life before Montini should wear the tiara. In any case, this is a "prophetic" phrase which was heard and attested by numerous persons.

The old lady's suitcase

A young man employed in one of the Vatican waiting-rooms, was amazed some years back, in a street not far from Saint Peter's colonnade, to see the Pro-Secretary for Ordinary Affairs, Monsignor Montini, carrying two heavy canvas suitcases, alongside an elderly lady very modestly dressed. "This is the right moment to get a word with him," the young man thought right away. "I'll go up to him, take the valises, which certainly belong to some relative of His Excellency who, for want of a better method, has himself taken the trouble to carry them. This will give me the chance to tell him what I want. And all this, while I am doing him a favor!" As the young man approached, Monsignor Montini told the elderly lady to turn everything over to him because, as he knew him well, he could guarantee that everything would be all right. Then Monsignor Montini greeted the lady, and stepped out towards the Portone di Bronzo.

The young man thought that he would later on have his chance to talk with Monsignor Montini. He recounted that he had made the long ascent to S. Onofrio, perspiring heavily, because the valises were heavy, but feeling quite rewarded at the thought that this would give him an opportunity to talk to the Monsignor later on. But once he had put down the suitcases before one of the doors in that heavily populated street, the good man was amazed to be asked who that very kind priest had been. "But what," said the young man, "you mean to say you don't know him? That is Monsignor Montini, one of the really big shots in the Vatican."

"I have seen him today for the first time," was the old lady's answer.

"But how is it that he was carrying your valises?"

"He came out of the door of a building where I had stopped to catch my breath, and seeing me struggling with the valises, he offered to carry them for me. Well, you can still find many good souls and true Christians. But I never thought that I would stumble upon such an important personage. May God bless him."

"Too many barques of Peter"

On one occasion *L'Osservatore Romano* was planning an article on the charity of Pius XII. The task of drawing up the article was entrusted to one of the young staff members. Before sending it on to the press room, the budding journalist had it read by Monsignor Montini, who was then Under-Secretary of State. The latter, noting the excessive rhetoric and evident bombast of the text, said to the writer: "Oh, there are too many 'barques of Peter,' and too many 'fishers of men' in these pages!... The people prefer to know right off what the article is about

without having to practice so much patience in reading!"
He asked the writer to kindly sit down at the typewriter,
and then he dictated an article which took no more than
half a column of the newspaper. But it said everything
that had to be said.

A *country peasant's gift*

Shortly after his ordination to the priesthood, young
Montini began his pastoral ministry in the populous section of Brescia known as Verolanuova. He was so sickly
and thin that he seemed like a chronic invalid. Hence it
was not to be wondered at when an old man of Verolanuova, seeing the young priest pass in front of his house,
went straight to the chicken coop, brought back a handful
of fresh eggs and handed them over with these simple
words: "Take them, Don Battista; they'll do you good."

Montini did not know where to put them, but understanding that any hesitation would have offended the good
man, he took off his hat, held it out to the peasant with
his nicest smile and said: "May God reward you." Then
he continued on his way, the eggs in his hat, happy at
having given some satisfaction to a generous soul.

Ludovico's *suitcase*

On that cold day when he went from Rome to Milan
to take possession of the Chair of Saint Ambrose, Archbishop
Montini had a woolen shawl over his knees in the train.
Completely incognito, there was among the passengers
in the same compartment a special newspaper correspondent, taking note of even the slightest gestures of the

famous ex-Pro-Secretary of State. His archiepiscopal cassock bordered with silk and his gold cross gave him an atmosphere of harmonious elegance. The cross had been a gift from Pope Pius XII. His baggage consisted of one valise, from the handle of which hung a little card bearing the name of its owner: *Dr. Ludovico Montini.* This was the Archbishop's brother. This detail did not escape the attention of the journalist and he concluded that the valise had been borrowed, because Montini, the former Pro-Secretary, probably did not have one of his own.

The papal audience for Don Giorgio and Donna Giuditta

Pius XII had not been Pope for a year when one day he saw a request for an audience signed by a couple from Lombardy whose names seemed somewhat familiar. The couple was Don Giorgio and Donna Giuditta Montini.

"Could I know with greater precision who these people are?" he asked the Maestro di Camera who had presented the list to him. "Your Holiness," responded the Monsignor, "if my information is exact, they are the parents of Your Holiness' Under-Secretary of State."

Pius XII granted the audience, directing that the Montinis should have priority over all other visitors. The couple bought their ticket for Rome, uncertain whether their biggest joy would be to spend some days with their son from the Secretariate of State, or the privilege of being received in private audience by the Holy Father.

Giovanni Battista Montini introduced his elderly parents into the presence of the Holy Father. In his more than fifteen years in the direct service of the Vicar of Christ, he had never experienced any emotion like that which seized him as he opened the door of the Pope's office for his parents. His emotion quickly changed to deep embarrassment when Pius XII said to his parents: "I congratulate you most sincerely. You have given to the Church of God a man who possesses all the virtues in an eminent degree."

Don Giorgio and Donna Giuditta were already well-convinced of this, but they kept a record of those words as the most precious treasure of those days of immense happiness.

Christmas with a fallen priest

One Christmas evening, there were perhaps a few knowing smiles at the sight of a priest making his way along the street in one of the notorious quarters of the city of Rome. The individual was more than just a simple priest. It was Monsignor Montini, on his way to visit an old seminary schoolmate, who had long been tormented by doubts and had ended up by abandoning the priesthood. He was living alone, abandoned by everyone, and he would very likely have spent that Christmas night much more sadly than any other night, with only his doubts and his remorse as companions. When he saw at his door the classmate whom he had always admired for his faith and his charity, and who had reached such heights of priestly dignity, the poor apostate could only gasp. But his friend's affectionate hand and his discreet charity brought him comfort, while the light of that Christmas took on a new meaning because of this pleasant and unexpected visit.

Thanks for congratulations from Khrushchev

Nikita Khrushchev sent a telegram of congratulation to Paul VI on the day after his election. The newspapers immediately published the text. It stated textually: "I ask you to accept my congratulations and my best wishes for the success of your activities in favor of peace and of peaceful cooperation among peoples, to which John XXIII had dedicated so much effort. Nikita Khrushchev."

No one was surprised that Paul VI should reply to the telegram of the Soviet Prime Minister. His reply in the official translation stated: "I return my lively and sincere sentiments of gratitude for the congratulations and good wishes which have reached me from Your Excellency and while your message arouses in Our mind the features of the Russian people and the remembrance of its human and Christian history, we ask God that, in prosperity and in the good order of civil life, it may contribute effectively to the true progress of humanity and to just peace in the world."

This was the official translation of the reply of the Holy Father to Khrushchev's telegram, as published by the Press Office of the Holy See. The apparent divergence of the version published in Russian by the state agency *Tass*, is not very great, but in reality, the Russian agency substantially changed the text, transforming an article into a possessive adjective. The Holy Father had said: ". . . in prosperity and in the good order of civil life," but *Tass* had translated the text ". . . in its prosperity and in the good order of its civil life . . . ," thus giving the impression that Paul VI was formulating a positive judgment on the social system prevailing in the Union of Soviet Socialist Republics.

After the assassination of President Kennedy

Within hours after receiving word of the assassination of President John F. Kennedy, Pope Paul VI sent the following message to the people of the United States via ABC-TV:

"We are deeply shocked by the sad and tragic news of the killing of the President of the United States of America, John Fitzgerald Kennedy, and the serious wounding of Governor Connally; and We are profoundly saddened by so dastardly a crime, by the mourning which afflicts a great and civilized country in its head, by the suffering which strikes at Mrs. Kennedy, the children and her family.

"With all Our heart, We deplore this unhappy event. We express the heartfelt wish that the death of this great Statesman may not damage the cause of the American people, but rather reinforce its moral and civil sentiments, and strengthen its feeling of nobility and concord; and We pray to God that the sacrifice of John Kennedy may be made to favor the cause he promoted and to help defend the freedom of peoples and peace in the world.

"He was the first Catholic President of the United States: We recall Our pleasure in receiving his visit and in having discerned in him great wisdom and high resolution for the good of humanity. Tomorrow, We shall offer the Holy Sacrifice of the Mass that God may grant him eternal rest, that He may comfort and console all those who weep for him on his death, and in order that not hatred, but Christian love, should reign among all mankind."

Milanese like the Milanese

On a night in 1960 there arrived at the Archbishop's house in Milan a prelate from the Vatican, a friend and former colleague of Montini. The newly arrived prelate expressed some surprise at seeing his old friend still at table, buried under a heap of papers, and engaging in animated discussion with his table companions. "But," asked the visitor, "you're still working at this hour and you are still at table?" Cardinal Montini replied with a smile: "Evidently I have gotten into the habits of the Milanese industrialists. I have lost all my Roman habits. Just imagine, here no one goes to rest after a meal!"

"The Pope? It's Uncle Giovanni!"

On June 21st, the day of the papal election, the family of Cardinal Montini's brother was gathered around the TV in their home. When the Pope appeared on the loggia of Saint Peter's Basilica to give his first Apostolic Blessing to the city of Rome and to the entire world, the Cardinal's sister-in-law said to her little Elisabetta: "Look at the Pope, how fine he looks!" The little girl squinted her eyes at the TV screen, took a better look at the face of the man in white and then cried out: "What do you mean, the Pope? That's Uncle Giovanni, Uncle Giovanni! The Pope is fatter than that!"

Frightened children

On the occasion of one of Cardinal Montini's pastoral visitations in Milan, he was listening to the traditional little entertainment presented by the children of the parish. One of the little girls, completely carried away by the solemnity of the occasion, ended up by confusing the terminations of her words and spoke of the Archbishop's zeal for "the shost leep," when she was thinking of "lost sheep," and instead of speaking of *Gesù Bambino*, she ended up by saying *Gesino*

Bambù. Throughout the whole of the little speech, Cardinal Montini sat there, inwardly amused, but making no out-ward sign at all of surprise or displeasure.

The Archbishop gives out candy at the window

On another occasion the Cardinal Archbishop was visit-ing a parish in the outskirts of Milan. First there was the examination in catechism, then Confirmation. It had not taken the Archbishop long to win the sympathy of the chil-dren, so much so that at the end of the ceremony, he ac-cepted the invitation to pose for a picture with the newly confirmed children and their godparents. Then the pastor told the children to be about their business and took the Cardinal into the parlor of his rectory. The children stayed outside, but were so unhappy that the boldest among them worked their way up the walls of the parish house and tried to climb on to the iron grating outside the window in order to get a better look at His Eminence. The Archbishop no-ticed what was happening and opened the window himself, to the delight and applause of the little rascals down below. As was only natural, the curiosity of the children was not concerned only with the Cardinal Archbishop, but also with a dish of candy which the pastor had put out for the visiting authorities. The Archbishop understood the looks in their eyes and amid the enthusiastic shouts of the children, began to toss candy to them through the window. When the pas-tor saw what was happening he wanted to put a stop to this little scene, so he said to the Cardinal Archbishop: "Your Eminence, I think that this window is letting in a draft, which might be bad for someone who has been per-spiring." He tried to close the window, but the Archbishop stopped him until the last of the caramels on the table were in the hands of the children waiting and shouting outside.

The Pope's good memory

One of the most striking things about Pope Paul VI is his unusual ability, even after many years, to recall long quotations from speeches, the names of persons, facts, and even details of secondary importance. Ludovico Alessandrini, of the editorial staff of *L'Osservatore Romano*, and an old acquaintance of the Pope, wanted to present his respects as soon as he heard of his election as Pontiff. Paul VI received him with an embrace and asked him how his daughters were, mentioning each one of them by name, although it had been eight years since he had seen them.

How about the Control Room?

Father Stefanizzi, S.J., technical director of Vatican Radio, was on his way into the Sistine Chapel after the Holy Father had read his first message to the world, when he heard someone call him: "Father Stefanizzi, has that work in the Control Room been taken care of?" The reference was to 1954, when the new Pope had been Pro-Secretary of State and was living in the Vatican. At that time there had been plans for several technical improvements at Vatican Radio and the Pope had not forgotten this, although in the meantime he had spent eight years in Milan.

Feast-day greetings from the Pope

Don Luigi Sala can boast of having a great friend, because in his years in the Chancery Office at Milan, close to Archbishop Montini, their friendship was always grow-

ing stronger. The Archbishop was made Pope on the very
day on which Don Luigi Sala celebrates his name's day,
because the election took place on June 21st, the feast of
Saint Aloysius (Luigi) Gonzaga. The Archbishop had never
missed presenting his good wishes, but on that day this
seemed to be out of the question.

Towards nine that evening Don Luigi was summoned
to answer a phone call from Vatican City. To the question
"Who is asking for him" the answer was: "Tell him that
Don Macchi wants him"—Don Macchi was the new Pope's
private secretary. "Yes, Don Pasquale, here I am" said
Don Luigi as he lifted the receiver to his ear. But in
the meantime Don Macchi had handed the phone to someone else.... "Oh, Your Holiness ... !" And the voice came
from the other end: "Yes ... I wanted to wish you a happy
feast-day. Today is the feast of San Luigi. And you thought
that I had forgotten!"

The future Pope came down the gangplank

It was in the September of 1932, just before Monsignor
Montini's resignation as central assistant of the FUCI. At
Cagliari, in Sardinia, the FUCI had held the Congress
which eventually led to the organization of the Catholic
Graduates Movement. Anyone present as the congress dele-
gates were getting ready to return from the port of Olbia
to the mainland at Civitavecchia, would have seen a large
number of young people, boys and girls, standing on the
pier and unable to board the ship. They were being told
that the ship was filled up and that no further accom-
modations were possible. Monsignor Montini was already
on the ship but as soon as he saw the situation he came
down the gangplank, after having seen to it that his

Fucine were taken care of. He wanted to be with his young men who had to spend the night sleeping in a train, while waiting for the departure of the next day's ship.

The gesture was significant. The young university students were deeply moved when they say the future Paul VI come down the gangplank of the small ship in order to be with them at a time when they were being treated unjustly. It was commonly felt that the "No space available" sign which had been run up on the ship was simply part of the boycott program organized by Fascism against the movement directed by Montini and Righetti.

He never thought he would become Pope

Antonio Mopelli was Archbishop Montini's chauffeur and valet at Milan. When, on the day after the election of Paul VI, many journalists were going to all possible sources for general information and tidbits on the new Pope, someone thought of going directly to Antonio. It was June 21, 1963 and in his memory he still had many recollections. Antonio recalled very well, for example, that five days earlier, at the airport where the Cardinal was taking the plane for Rome and the Conclave, His Eminence had replied to his good wishes for a safe journey and a quick return: "Oh, I'll be back! I'll be back!"

"Certainly, he wasn't expecting anything like *that*," repeated Mopelli. "He certainly was not expecting to become Pope—of that I am sure."

The price of a donkey

Antonio continued his reminiscences. "His last assignment to me was to find out how much a donkey would cost. He had received a letter from a peasant in the mountains whose donkey had died, making it impossible for the poor man to do his work. I told him the price and he signed the check."

As seen by his chauffeur

Antonio Mopelli spoke of the various episodes of his years of service with the Archbishop. During his seven years and a half at Milan, the Archbishop had no other chauffeur. "He liked to go fast," said Antonio, "even at very high speeds. If he was in a hurry he would ask: 'Antonio, are you asleep?' Last Sunday I took his bag to the Linate Airport; it was very light; he was sure he was coming back.

"I know his habits, I have served him at table. He eats little, just a bit of soup or rice, with a slice of meat, a glass and a half of wine. The Sisters prepared dessert only when we had guests. He sleeps hardly at all, only four hours every night. In his bedroom he has a little moveable table, and in the morning, when I put his room in order, I usually found six or seven letters already written."

I couldn't sleep without knowing how your mother is

On one occasion Don Pasquale Macchi, the Archbishop's private secretary, was much concerned over the serious illness of his mother. He had gone home to spend some time with her and returned to the Archbishop's residence after midnight. What was his surprise to find the Cardinal still waiting up for him. The Cardinal's reply to his secretary's surprise was: "I couldn't go to sleep without knowing how your mother is!"

Don't prepare anything; I'll be back!

A priest in Milan recounts that the Cardinal made this remark several times before leaving for the Conclave. As a matter of fact he had already drawn up the list of appointments for the following days and had arranged his agenda. Professor Giuseppe Lazzati, editor of *L'Italia*, in an editorial dated June 22, 1963, wrote: "He took leave of us Sunday evening at the airport with his usual affability. He seemed to want to repeat what he had told us several times the previous Saturday in our discussion of various problems: 'Next week, after the Conclave, we will take up this matter also!' "

A priest and a soldier as hitchhikers

On his arrival in Rome for the Conclave, Cardinal Montini was on his way in from the Fiumicino Airport. He ordered his driver to stop along the highway, to pick up two hitchhikers, a cleric and a soldier. It was already late at night. Montini was wearing a simple cassock, and the little priest and his soldier-companion both Neapolitans, did not recognize him. He took them to the entrance of the Autostrada for Naples, and then put ten thousand lire ($17.00) into the hands of the priest saying: "Just in case you don't find a lift. . . ." The priest was deeply moved.

"Monsignor," he asked, "what is your name?" "It makes no difference what my name is. I am only a poor man who needs the help of prayer."

The "black sheep" as well as the others...

Archbishop Montini's two secretaries, Don Pasquale Macchi and Don Bruno Bossi, were kept in Rome by Cardinal Montini after his election as Pope. Before becoming secretary to his Archbishop, Don Bruno had been chaplain of the "Beccaria" the Milanese prison for minors. About a month after the Conclave, a group of these "bad boys," as they were commonly called, happened to be in Rome and remembered that they had a good friend who had become Pope. They telephoned to Don Bruno asking if they might see him.

If the request had had to go through "channels," it would not have been an easy matter. But Don Bruno was a shortcut and the Holy Father gladly granted this audience to his old friends from the Beccaria. The littlest of their number, in shirt sleeves, read a short speech of homage to the Pope. He got all mixed up, smiling nervously as he looked sideways at the gestures of the Pope who was trying to encourage him. In the end, he broke down and cried. Paul VI gave him a "special" medal. Then to make the occasion complete, because he was happy to see them and to thank them for the visit he told them: "Today you will eat in the Vatican." He had arranged a *pranzone*, a big dinner, at the Hospice of Santa Marta. The Pope wanted the dinner to be perfect in every detail, with cake, *spumante* and even cigarettes for the older boys. The Sisters in the kitchen had done themselves proud because the Holy Father had warned them: "Don't make me make a bad impression!"

A *bouquet of snowdrops for the Holy Father*

Two Lombard children, brothers named Fulvio and Giorgio, on a trip out to Monte Nese had picked a beautiful bouquet of snowdrops. On their way home they wondered what they would do with their flowers. All of a sudden they got the idea that they should send them to the Holy Father. The flowers reached Pope Paul VI safely. Deeply moved by this gesture, since Paul VI appreciates deeply all the simple gestures of little children, he answered the two children with great affection, sending them a handwritten letter which reads: "To dear Fulvio and Giorgio Pelliccioli, We express thanks for their flowers. We exhort them to be always good and We send to them and to all their dear ones Our fatherly benediction." The signature was in Latin, with the usual initials, *Paulus PP VI.* But little Giorgio and Fulvio found out immediately that this was the signature of the Holy Father, because they found out that *Paulus PP VI* meant Pope Paul VI.

A *delicate and sensitive heart*

Those close to Cardinal Montini at Milan knew that every Friday in Lent he went out absolutely incognito, accompanied only by his secretary, and dressed as a simple priest, to visit the sick poor in the outskirts of the city. He used to send everybody out of the room, urge them not to tell anybody about the visit and, after embracing the patient, he remained on his knees sometimes for an hour, praying and doing little services for him.

Once, as he was traveling by automobile, he witnessed a serious accident, in which a head-on collision between two cars had killed a young man instantly. The Archbishop had his driver stop immediately and after doing what he

could in the circumstances, he remained on his knees praying beside the body of the young victim, until the authorities came to remove the body. He was so impressed
by this experience that the recollection of it saddened him
for several days afterwards.

Encouragement and inspiration for
a bedridden priest

During his visit to the University of Notre Dame in
1960, Cardinal Montini was lodged in the VIP guest quarters
in the University Infirmary. On the same floor, as a patient
in a body cast, was a priest with whom Monsignor Montini
had had occasion to deal years earlier in Rome in connection with a project close to the heart of Pope Pius XII.
Several times during his short stay at Notre Dame, His
Eminence took time out to visit the priest. He came in
after the solemn Pontifical Mass on Commencement Day,
to say that he had remembered him and his intentions in
a very special way in the Holy Sacrifice that morning. In
his farewell visit the Cardinal gave the patient one of
the silver medals struck for his appointment to Milan.

When the priest asked His Eminence for his blessing
and a prayer for a speedy return to Rome, the Cardinal
blessed him warmly, and embraced him saying: "I shall
surely pray that you get back to Rome soon, but do not
forget that even here in bed you can still be working for
the Church!"

The priest, now back in Rome, will never forget
these encouraging and inspiring words, which could only
have been prompted by a spiritual man's deep understanding of the interlocking mysteries of suffering and grace.

(Translators note: I was the priest.)

DAUGHTERS OF ST. PAUL

IN MASSACHUSETTS
50 St. Paul's Ave.
Jamaica Plain
Boston, Mass. 02130
172 Tremont St.
Boston, Mass. 02111
381 Dorchester St.
So. Boston, Mass. 02127
325 Main St.
Fitchburg, Mass.

IN NEW YORK
78 Fort Place
Staten Island, N.Y. 10301
625 East 187th St.
Bronx, N.Y.
39 Erie St.
Buffalo, N.Y. 14202

IN CONNECTICUT
202 Fairfield Ave.
Bridgeport, Conn. 06603

IN OHIO
141 West Rayon Ave.
Youngstown, Ohio 44503
Daughters of St. Paul
Cleveland, Ohio

IN TEXAS
114 East Main Plaza
San Antonio, Texas 78205

IN CALIFORNIA
1570 Fifth Ave.
San Diego, Calif. 92101
Daughters of St. Paul
Oakland, California

IN LOUISIANA
86 Bolton Ave.
Alexandria, La. 71303

IN FLORIDA
2700 Biscayne Blvd.
Miami, Florida 33137

IN CANADA
8885 Blvd. Lacordaire
St. Leonard Deport-Maurice
Montreal, Canada
1063 St. Clair Ave. West
Toronto, Canada

IN ENGLAND
29 Beauchamp Place
London, S.W. 3, England

IN AFRICA
Box 4392
Kampala, Uganda

IN INDIA
Water Field Road Extension
Plot No. 143
Bandra, India

IN THE PHILIPPINE ISLANDS
No. 326 Lipa City
Philippine Islands

IN AUSTRALIA
58 Abbotsford Rd.
Homebush N.S.W., Australia